P9-DWB-508

The Embattled Vote in America

The Embattled Vote
in America

From the Founding to the Present

ALLAN J. LICHTMAN

Harvard University Press

Cambridge, Massachusetts
London, England
2018

Library of Congress Cataloging-in-Publication Data
Names: Lichtman, Allan J., author.
Title: The embattled vote in America : from the founding to the present /
Allan J. Lichtman.
Description: Cambridge, Massachusetts : Harvard University Press, 2018. |
Includes bibliographical references and index.
Identifiers: LCCN 2018006882 | ISBN 9780674972360 (alk. paper)
Subjects: LCSH: Suffrage—United States—History.
Classification: LCC JK1846 .L53 2018 | DDC 324.6/20973—dc23
LC record available at https://lccn.loc.gov/2018006882

To my extraordinary family: Karyn, Sam and Kara, Steven, and Ronnie

CONTENTS

PREFACE

My interest in voting rights is both academic and practical. As a first-year graduate student at Harvard University in 1967, I wrote my seminar research paper on the U.S. Justice Department's enforcement of the Civil Rights Act of 1957, which Congress had enacted to protect black voting rights in the South. For reasons that I still cannot fathom today, John Doar, the assistant attorney general in charge of the Civil Rights Division, gave this twenty-year-old student unfettered access to the records and staff of the division's Voting Rights Section. I could poke through any files that I found of interest, except for personnel records, and interview the section's attorneys without restriction.

I found to my discouragement that nearly a decade of enforcement by these dedicated, competent, and hard-working lawyers had led to minimal progress toward enfranchising black people in states like Mississippi and Alabama. A weak law, protracted litigation, political meddling, and resistance by local officials and some southern judges crippled enforcement efforts. I was excited, however, by the prospects of renewed progress under the recently enacted Voting Rights Act of 1965.

At the time, of course, I had not an inkling that some fifteen years later, in 1983, I would contribute to progress on voting rights by serving as an expert witness in enforcing the 1965 act. I began work for the same Voting Section that I had studied as a student but eventually branched out into working for civil rights groups, private plaintiffs, and independent redistricting commissions. When justified, I also testified on behalf of state and local defendants in voting rights litigation.

In the 1980s, I mostly worked on challenges to at-large election systems that enabled white voters to control all legislative seats in local governments and to redistricting plans that discriminated against African Americans and later Hispanics. Typically, I relied on my expertise as a quantitative historian to analyze voting patterns to gauge the discriminatory effects of electoral systems in place for state and local governments. I explored whether minorities voted cohesively as a bloc in support of preferred candidates and whether opposition bloc voting by whites usually denied minority voters the opportunity to elect these candidates to public office. I also analyzed remedial plans to assess how effective they were in surmounting obstacles to minority voting opportunities.

By the twenty-first century, the focus of my voting rights work had shifted to the analysis of partisan and racial gerrymandering and new forms of franchise restrictions such as laws that required the presentation of specified forms of photo identification for voting. Rather than consider only the discriminatory effects of voting laws and practices, I began deploying historical methods to determine whether states in their adoption of voter photo ID or other restrictive laws had violated the equal protection clause of the Fourteenth Amendment by intentionally discriminating against minority voters.

To date, I have worked as an expert witness in more than ninety voting rights cases. Nearly every case was fiercely contested, typically by white leaders battling to sustain the privileges that flowed from controlling politics in their states and communities. Discrimination creates winners as well as losers. My most gratifying experiences came in the early years, when our work as experts and lawyers helped local black people in the South defy the white power structure that had kept them subordinate for generations. At the risk of their livelihoods and their safety, African American citizens often joined the Justice Department and civil rights groups as plaintiffs in voting rights lawsuits.

Many decades of courtroom testimony and academic study have confirmed for me that although the players and the issues in voting rights change and evolve over time, the arguments remain familiar and the stakes are very much the same: Who has the right to vote in America, and who benefits from exclusion?

The Embattled Vote in America

INTRODUCTION

Voters and Nonvoters

The most significant civil rights problem is voting. Each citizen's right to vote is fundamental to all the other rights of citizenship.

—ROBERT F. KENNEDY, 1963

On February 18, 1965, advocates for the voting rights of disenfranchised African Americans organized a rare nighttime march in the small town of Marion, Alabama, part of the state's "black belt," to protest the jailing of James Orange. Prosecutors had charged Orange with contributing to the delinquency of minors after he enlisted students in voter registration drives. Alabama state troopers responded to the protest by beating peaceful demonstrators with billy clubs, sending terrified marchers fleeing into the night. Some sought refuge from police violence in a nearby restaurant, Mack's Café. State troopers followed them into the establishment, however, and one of those troopers, James Bonard Fowler, fatally shot an unarmed twenty-six-year-old black voting rights worker, Jimmie Lee Jackson. Insisting that Jackson had reached for his gun, Fowler claimed self-defense. Eyewitnesses told a different story: they said that Jackson was trying to protect his mother from police violence and that Fowler shot him deliberately, without provocation.

While Jackson languished in a hospital for eight days before dying from his wound, Alabama officials issued a warrant for his arrest for the assault of a police officer. They did not arrest, indict, or discipline Fowler, or even release his name to the public. Fowler remained on the state police force, and a year later he shot and killed another unarmed black man, Nathan Johnson, Jr., during an altercation at the Alabaster city jail. State police officials were quick to purge both killings from Fowler's personnel file but fired him in 1968 for assaulting his white police supervisor. In 2007, as part of a federal-state effort to reopen cold cases from the civil rights era, Alabama prosecutors indicted the seventy-three-year-old Fowler for murder. Two weeks before trial was set to begin in 2010, Fowler pleaded guilty to manslaughter and served five months of a six-month sentence. Fowler died in 2015, fifty years after killing Jimmie Lee Jackson.[1]

Americans were dying for the vote more than 175 years after their nation's founding because the framers made a consequential mistake when they drafted the Constitution and the Bill of Rights, the Constitution's first ten amendments. They failed to enshrine in these pivotal documents of our democracy the right to vote, not just for men or even only white men but for any American. Among many enumerated rights that the government cannot abridge, the right to vote remained conspicuously absent and remains so to this day. All subsequent amendments protecting the voting rights of racial minorities, women, and young people—the Fifteenth Amendment on race, the Nineteenth Amendment on sex, and the Twenty-Sixth Amendment on age—are framed negatively, stipulating not what the states must do to ensure people's voting rights in America's democratic republic but what they cannot do.

Jimmie Lee Jackson died, one could plausibly argue, because the political leaders who drafted these amendments perpetuated the framers' mistake of failing to establish an affirmative right to vote. Jackson died because white supremacists who controlled southern governments had circumvented the Fifteenth Amendment's prohibition against denying the right to vote "on account of race, color, or condition of previous servitude." They did so through patently discriminatory, although seemingly race-neutral, restrictions such as poll taxes and literacy tests.

As the pioneers of modern democracy, the founders understood that the right to vote grounds all other rights, that it empowers Americans to become participants in government, rather than mere petitioners. But it was their omission of voting rights that triggered a war over America's embattled vote that continues to rage in the halls of Congress and in the courtrooms of federal judges. Yet, as in Marion, Alabama, it has spilled into the streets too, with life and death at stake in the ongoing struggle for people's right to consent in their governing.

Opposition to voting rights for all Americans has revolved around three critical issues. Despite the revolutionary rallying cry of "no taxation without representation," for most of U.S. history, the American political leadership has considered suffrage not a natural right but a privilege bestowed by government on a political community restricted by considerations of wealth, sex, race, residence, literacy, criminal conviction, and citizenship. The notion of privileged access to the vote survives into our own time, albeit in subtler forms than before.

Since the early republic, proponents of a limited vote have waved the banner of voter fraud, in earlier times to justify the disenfranchisement of supposedly corruptible people such as propertyless workers, women, racial minorities, or immigrants. Today, it is allegations of such forms of alleged election fraud as voter impersonation, repeat voting, voting by noncitizens, or balloting in the name of dead people that are used to justify restrictive measures like voter photo ID laws or draconian purges of registration rolls. Numerous studies have documented that such voter fraud is vanishingly small in recent elections, but the outcry continues as loudly as ever.

Disputes over the vote have been intensely partisan, with principled justifications for voting restrictions functioning as thinly masked attempts to favor one party over another. From the end of Reconstruction through the early twentieth century, for example, it was the lily-white Democratic Party that benefited politically from suppressing the African American vote. In recent years the partisan calculations have reversed as African Americans have become the most reliable of Democratic voters, and Republicans have come to depend on the white vote.

Throughout much of American history, policymakers have managed to exclude most Americans from the community of voters. A firsthand observer of a 1799 congressional election in Virginia reported, "The parties were drilled to move together as a body; and the leaders and their business committees were never surpassed in activity and systematic arrangement for bringing out every voter. Sick men were taken in their beds to the polls; the halt, the lame and the blind, were hunted up, and every mode of conveyance was mustered into service."[2] However, while operatives in Virginia mustered infirm white propertied males to the hustings, they could forget about the disenfranchised women, African Americans, Native Americans, and white men without property who comprised most of the state's adult population.

Even today, in the world's oldest surviving democracy, voter identification laws, registration requirements, felon disenfranchisement, voter purges, and overcrowded polling places disenfranchise many millions of American citizens each year. Many other Americans either do not register at all, or if registered they do not vote. The racial and partisan gerrymandering of electoral districts by political bodies deprives most Americans of a meaningful vote for legislative offices.

Extreme polarization between the Republicans and the Democrats only intensifies battles over the vote. Political scientists studying voting in Congress found that polarization between the parties nearly reached its mathematical maximum in the second decade of the twenty-first century, with Republicans and Democrats almost never voting together on contested issues. In earlier times, both major parties were known for harboring liberal and conservative contingents. Not so anymore. Today, with very few exceptions, the most liberal Republicans are more conservative than the most conservative Democrats. Partisans on either side of this divide pillory their opponents as not only wrong on the issues but also immoral, corrupt, and un-American.

The partisanship underlying today's voter wars has lent itself to the creation of two separate democracies in the United States, one for red states, predominantly controlled by Republicans, and the other for blue states, predominantly controlled by Democrats. Red and blue states differ in their requirements for voting. In blue Maryland, for example, you can vote just by pointing to your name on the registration list. In red Georgia, you must present a form of government-issued photo ID. Red and blue states also differ in the opportunities for voters to choose their representatives for legislative seats in Congress, state legislatures, city councils, county commissions, and school boards. In states under their control, Republicans and Democrats have taken to crafting districts that discount and waste votes for the opposition party. The stakes in redistricting could not be higher, with voters now electing some 500,000 public officials in the United States, one for about every 500 American adults. By carefully designing the partisan composition of legislative districts with sophisticated mapping technology, the politicians who draw district lines largely decide the general election results of most legislative contests in the United States today, before voters cast a single ballot.

Throughout the American experience, the most critical fault line of American politics is not among competing parties, ideologies, issues, or personalities, but between voters and nonvoters. Nearly

90 million American citizens did not vote for president in the general election of 2016, and two years earlier the tally of lost votes included some 140 million citizens. Once the world's leader, the United States now trails most other developed democracies in voter participation. America's nonvoters are not a representative cross-section of the adult population, but disproportionately comprise people who are young and low-income. Within America's burgeoning minority population, only African Americans have come close to catching up with whites in voter participation.[3]

In exploring the consequences of America's constitutional omission on voting rights, it is easy to judge the founders too harshly. As men of the late eighteenth century, they shared the prevalent belief in a circumscribed political community limited to individuals with the independence and capacity to vote wisely and knowledgeably. They could have wreaked far more damage on voting rights by following the lead of the states and imposing in the Constitution economic requirements for suffrage. While not flawless, the U.S. Constitution and Bill of Rights were nevertheless far ahead of their time in establishing a democratic form of government, buttressed by the guarantee of many civil rights and liberties to the common people. Nearly a century later, the four-time British prime minister William Gladstone said that "the American Constitution is, so far as I can see, the most wonderful work ever struck off at a given time by the brain and purpose of man."[4]

Drawing on primary sources, recent scholarship, historical sources, and my own work as an expert witness in voting rights cases, I trace in this book the embattled history of the vote in America from the drafting of the Constitution through current-day debates over voter identification laws, purges of registration rolls, and gerrymandered legislative districts. I cover not just qualifications for casting votes but also the opportunities for Americans to cast meaningful votes. These issues include qualifications for holding public office; the uses and abuses of at-large and district systems for electing federal, state, and local legislators; and the procedures for conducting elections and identifying winners and losers.

America's default on the right to vote cannot be charged to the framers alone. Many subsequent generations of decision-makers have passed on the opportunity to establish a constitutional right to vote, even as they expanded the franchise for specified groups of Americans. The advancement of voting rights in the United States has not by any means followed a straight line of continued enfranchisement. Rather, the right to vote has both expanded and contracted over the course of American history, often at once and even sometimes in the same legislative halls or state constitutional conventions. Generations pass and the issues change, but the struggle for the ballot endures, as opponents of a broad suffrage continue to find new ways to suppress the right to vote.

The integrity of the vote in America now faces a dire and unprecedented threat: the manipulation of U.S. elections by hostile foreign powers. In 2016, the Russian government interfered in the American electoral process on behalf of Republican presidential candidate Donald Trump and Republican congressional candidates in select districts across the nation. Ironically, those who have advocated most strenuously for protecting the ballot from the spurious threat of voter fraud through such restrictive measures as voter photo ID laws and registration purges have resisted efforts to safeguard American elections from the real threat of future manipulation by Russia or other foreign adversaries. Russia's efforts to compromise American democracy continue without any hindrance from the incumbent American president, who has propagated the most outlandish claims of voter fraud.

THE FOUNDING FATHERS'
MISTAKE

A share in the sovereignty of the state, which is exercised
by the citizens at large, in voting at elections is one of the
most important rights of the subject, and in a republic
ought to stand foremost in the estimation of the law.

—ALEXANDER HAMILTON, 1784

After what George Washington called the "standing miracle" of
his victory over British arms, the general retired to his Mount
Vernon plantation, debilitated by bouts of smallpox, tuberculosis,
malaria, and dysentery, and years of warfare. He suffered from
aches and fevers and a "rheumatic complaint" so severe at times that
he was "hardly able to raise my hand to my head, or turn myself in
bed." Yet in 1787, the fifty-five-year-old Washington, who had already
outlived his father by seven years, decided to sacrifice his "love of
retirement" and "a mind at ease." He donned his best breeches and
frock coat, powdered his hair, and pushed his body to serve his
country once more, this time as the indispensable president of a
Constitutional Convention in the sweltering Philadelphia summer.[1]

Washington journeyed three days to Philadelphia, where he had
served in the First Continental Congress, to bolster the revolutionary

principles that he feared the loose alliance of states under the existing Articles of Confederation could not sustain. "The fabric which took nine years (at the expense of much blood and treasure) to erect, now totters to the foundation, and without support must soon fall," Washington lamented. "There are seeds of discontent in every part of this Union," which demand "a more vigorous, and energetic government, than the one under which we now live—for the present, from experience, has been found too feeble, and inadequate to give that security which our liberties and property render absolutely essential."[2] Washington's fellow Virginia delegate George Mason declared that only a new kind of revolution, written in ink not blood, could salvage America's republic. "The revolt from Great Britain," he said, "were nothing comparing to the great business now before us."[3]

Violence and the threat of violence pushed Washington and other nationalists to tear down and then reconstruct their government anew. An insurrection known as Shays's Rebellion, which ripped across Massachusetts in 1786, confirmed for Washington the combustible mix of popular unrest and feeble government that threatened the republic. Rural residents aggrieved by high state taxes and crushing debts turned to forms of democratic protest such as mass meetings, demonstrations, and petitions for tax reduction, debt relief, and paper currency. When these tactics failed, the protesters, known as Regulators, shut down the courts to prevent foreclosures. Authorities responded forcefully to what they viewed as lawless mob fury that perverted popular sovereignty. The legislature prohibited criticism of the government and any public gathering of twelve or more armed men. It suspended the writ of habeas corpus and empowered the governor to issue general search warrants. Eventually the governor of Massachusetts mustered militia forces, paid for with private funds, to crush the uprising.[4] Inflamed by overwrought reports of the events in Massachusetts, Washington wrote that we must "have a government by which our lives, liberties, and properties will be secured, or let us know the worst at once." Learning that other states had cut taxes, forgiven debts, and issued paper money to cheapen credit, Washington worried that "there are combustibles in every State which a spark might set fire to."[5]

The Articles of Confederation had lodged the national government in a unicameral (one-house) Congress. The state legislatures appointed members of Congress, termed "delegates," with a minimum of two delegates for the least populous and a maximum of seven delegates for the most populous states. State legislatures could recall and replace at will delegates who did not vote independently in Congress; states voted as a bloc with one vote per state, regardless of population. The government lacked an independent executive or judiciary, and critical powers of Congress turned on the consent of the states.

Only fifty-five of the seventy-four delegates that the states appointed to the Philadelphia Convention of 1787 attended even a single session, and only thirty-nine delegates eventually signed the document. These few men of privilege, talent, and erudition spurned their formal charge to amend the Articles of Confederation. According to Virginia governor and delegate Edmund Randolph, "The powers, by which alone the blessings of a general government can be accomplished cannot be interwoven in the confederation without a change of its very essence; or, in other words, that the confederation must be thrown aside." As president of the convention, Washington stayed mostly silent during delegates' debates, speaking only once at the end of the session on the number of inhabitants that each member of Congress should represent. Yet his presence alone validated the convention's audacious enterprise, and the final product suited his preference for a strong national government.[6]

In just under four months, behind closed doors and sealed windows, a few dozen delegates drafted a radically new frame of government that was powerful enough to tame the unruly passions of the crowd and protect their interests as property and slave owners, dealers in public securities, and participants in commerce. Still, their public statements, private letters, and transcripts of the convention debates reveal something more altruistic in their motives than a self-serving grasp of power. The founders were genuinely committed to the ideas of the Enlightenment, an intellectual awakening that put reason above faith, challenged inbred authority, and supported popular sovereignty, and the rights of common people.

The framers could not by decree replace the Articles with their new Constitution. Their secret labors would bear fruit only upon ratification by at least three-quarters of the states. Learned but pragmatic in their politics, the framers understood that the states would decline to ratify a Constitution that empowered an aristocracy of wealth. As John Adams observed, "Men are not only ambitious, but their ambition is unbounded: they are not only avaricious, but their avarice is insatiable. The desires of kings, gentlemen and common people, all increase.... It is necessary to place checks upon them all."[7]

The Philadelphia delegates created a government unique for its time. The Constitution, as amended in the first Congress by the Bill of Rights, balanced popular sovereignty and rights with the power and stability needed to protect property, secure public and private credit, attract foreign capital, regulate commerce, generate revenue, and protect the nation from enemies foreign and domestic. "Tis done. We have become a nation," wrote Benjamin Rush, who would lead the movement for ratification in Pennsylvania.[8]

In defiance of precedent, America transitioned from one form of government to another, not by sword and musket but peaceably, by the ballot in state conventions. Thomas Jefferson, who eventually backed the Constitution despite misgivings, wrote that "we can surely boast of having set the world a beautiful example of a government reformed by reason alone, without bloodshed."[9] "Governments, in general, have been the result of force, of fraud, and accident," wrote the influential framer James Wilson of Pennsylvania. "The United States exhibits to the world the first instance, as far as we can learn, of a nation, unattacked by external force, unconvulsed by domestic insurrections, assembling voluntarily, deliberating fully, and deciding calmly concerning that system of government under which they would wish that they and their posterity should live."[10]

To check unbridled ambition, the Constitution distributed power among legislative, executive, and judicial branches of government. It further divided authority between the national and state governments, while simultaneously establishing federal laws and treaties as the supreme law of the land. Among other prerogatives, the Constitution authorized the national government to tax, regulate interstate and foreign commerce, coin money, regulate naturalization, and raise an army. It broadly empowered government "to provide for the common Defense and general Welfare of the United States" and "to make all Laws which shall be necessary and proper" for carrying out such enumerated powers. The Constitution endowed a single president with extraordinary power as both the nation's chief executive and the commander in chief of its armed forces. Its Bill of Rights secured personal freedoms for the American people that a popular majority could not wash away. The Constitution could be amended only by a new convention called by two-thirds of the states or by the vote of two-thirds of both chambers of Congress, ratified by three-quarters of the states.

This fortified new government gained its authority from popular consent but not through direct democratic rule. The people would instead elect representatives within a republic to carry out the duties of state. A republic, said James Madison, is a "government which derives all its powers directly or indirectly from the great body of the people, and is administered by persons holding their offices . . . for a limited period, or during good behavior."[11] The founders may have loved the common people, but not well enough to entrust them with control over government. Drawing on the cautionary lessons of ancient Athens, they were firm in their belief that direct rule by a fickle and unreliable people begets corruption and chaos. An editorial in the Baltimore *Federal Gazette* warned, "There is a wide difference between power being derived from the people, and its being seated in the people. Disorder and tyranny, as in the ancient republics, must ensue from all power being seated in and exercised personally by all the people."[12]

National elections under the Constitution were typically indirect. Voters directly elected only members of the House of Representatives for two-year terms. The state legislatures chose members of the Senate for six-year terms and decided how to select members of an Electoral College that by majority vote chose the president for four-year terms. The president, with the "advice and consent" of the Senate, appointed federal judges for life terms. The Constitution stayed silent on the procedures for choosing state and local officials. Although all the original states elected members of legislative bodies, most of them appointed rather than elected governors, judges, and presidential electors, all powerful positions that the political leadership wanted to insulate from the public.

Still, the vote was the pivot point of popular sovereignty in the new constitutional order, affording ordinary Americans a say in governing. "The people can in no way exercise sovereignty but by their suffrages, which are their own will.... The laws therefore which establish the right of suffrage are fundamental to this government," wrote Pennsylvania Federalist Tench Coxe under the name "A Voter" in the *Centennial of Liberty* newspaper.[13] Another commentator styled "An American Citizen" echoed Madison in claiming that popular consent anchored all constitutional powers, even if indirectly: "The people will remain, under the proposed constitution, *the fountain of power and public honor.* The President, the Senate, and House of Representatives, will be *the channels* through which the stream will flow—but it will flow *from the people,* and from them *only. Every office,* religious, civil and military, will be either their *immediate gift,* or it will come *from them* through the hands of *their servants.*"[14]

Despite the primacy of popular sovereignty in their new government, the framers did not inscribe a right to vote in the original Constitution or Bill of Rights. Among other enumerated rights, the right to vote remained conspicuously absent. At the Philadelphia convention, delegates left recommendations on voting rights to the Committee on Detail and devoted only about 1 percent of their time to debating the vote, a shockingly brief consideration given its importance for the new constitutional order.

The delegates knew that every American state imposed economic requirements for voting. Most states required the ownership of real or personal property, which signified an enduring attachment to society and the financial independence needed to cast an uncorrupted vote. The prevailing wisdom denigrated individuals without property as dependents, lacking wills of their own and susceptible to corruption by demagogues or the wealthy few on whom their livelihoods rested. "Very few Men who have no Property," noted John Adams succinctly, "have any Judgment of their own."[15]

At Philadelphia, several delegates favored national property qualifications for voting that no state could annul. Some claimed that unlike the aristocratic, crowded states of Europe, America offered abundant land open to men of diligence and enterprise. Only the indolent and the profligate would forfeit the franchise. In an earlier pamphlet, Alexander Hamilton had written that disenfranchised men "are only under a conditional prohibition, which industry and good fortune may remove. They may, one day, accumulate a sufficient property to enable them to emerge out of their present state."[16]

Some delegates warned of a time when America's industries would spawn masses of corruptible, propertyless workers. "The time is not distant when this country will abound with mechanics and manufacturers, who will receive their bread from their employers," said Gouverneur Morris of Pennsylvania. "Give the vote to people who have no property, and they will sell them to the rich." Despite having doubts about overriding state discretion on suffrage, Madison agreed that "in future times," people without property will either combine to threaten "the rights of property & the public liberty . . . or which is more probable, they will become the tools of opulence & ambition."[17]

Others objected in principle to property qualifications that would bar from voting many patriotic and virtuous Americans. George Mason of Virginia said "that every man having evidence of attachment to & permanent common interest with the Society ought to share in all its rights & privileges" but provided no guidelines for sorting out such exemplars of virtue. In a convoluted disquisition, Benjamin Franklin generally opposed property qualifications that would "depress the virtue & public spirit of our common people; of which they displayed a great deal during the war, and which contributed principally to the favorable issue of it."[18]

Practical considerations halted debate on property qualifications short of a principled resolution. When specifying a property valuation responsive to the varying economic conditions of the states or fluctuations in the value of money, delegates struggled in vain for agreement. Wilson of Pennsylvania said, "It was difficult to form any uniform rule of qualifications for all the States." Setting the bar for suffrage too high or too low would also jeopardize the Constitution's ratification by the states. "The right of suffrage was a tender point," observed Oliver Ellsworth of Connecticut, "and strongly guarded by most of the [State] Constitutions. The people will not readily subscribe to the Natl. Constitution, if it should subject them to be disfranchised."[19]

That pragmatic and not philosophical restraints stayed the hands of delegates intent on limiting the vote to property holders was confirmed by the setting of suffrage requirements for unorganized western territories under federal control. Unlike the thirteen states, the western territories had no say in ratifying the federal Constitution and lacked preexisting suffrage rules. The Northwest Ordinance of 1787, adopted in the waning days of the Articles, untouched in the Philadelphia convention, and reaffirmed with marginal changes by the first federal Congress, restricted suffrage to adult males owning at least fifty acres of land.[20]

Delegates unanimously ratified the recommendation of the Committee on Detail (art. 1, sec. 2) that voters for the U.S. House of Representatives "shall have the Qualifications requisite for Electors of the most numerous Branch of the State Legislature." No delegate proposed making suffrage a constitutional right, even for a select demographic of men or just white men of adult age. When the first Congress debated the Bill of Rights, no member proposed a guarantee of suffrage rights. Convention delegates did not address the question of votes for free African Americans, perhaps because they comprised a very small component of the population and some states had already limited voting to whites. None addressed voting for women. Men of the time viewed women, like children, as dependents who fell outside the political community. So too did they regard Native Americans as citizens of "domestic dependent nations." Delegates did not broach the question of residency requirements or voting by non-naturalized immigrants (aliens), leaving resolution of these sensitive matters to the states.

In choosing not to decide on voting rights, the Philadelphia delegates made a choice, with profound, lasting consequences for American democracy. With voting qualifications left to the discretion of each state, Americans barred from voting by state property qualifications or other restrictions had no recourse to federal constitutional principles. They could appeal only to the lawmakers or the courts of their states. The Constitution's silence on voting qualifications also severed voting rights from citizenship. Most U.S. citizens in the early republic could not vote, because of gender, age, residency, race, or economic restrictions. Yet in many states, noncitizens could vote if they met other suffrage requirements.

The lack of a constitutional right to vote and the varying qualifications of the states reinforced the established view of the time that the vote, however essential to a popular government, was not a natural right but a privilege conferred by government and subject to constitutional and statutory limitations. Still, by not setting any national economic standards for voting, the Constitution opened a path for states to ease their property or tax-paying requirements without constitutional restraints.

During the ten months of ratification debates in the states, both the Federalists, who backed the new government, and their Anti-Federalist challengers paid little heed to voting rights. Apparently Anti-Federalists who opposed the Constitution's intrusions on states' rights found it sufficient to leave voting qualifications to the states. The Anti-Federalists' claim to represent the common people against the constitutional government's "oligarchy," "tyranny," or "aristocracy" did not extend to a national guarantee of voting rights.

Most states of the new union eased the property qualifications of the preconstitutional era or supplemented them with tax-paying qualifications. Inflation simultaneously reduced the stringency of the property valuations needed for suffrage. Still, the right to vote remained dependent on an American's place of residence. Of the sixteen states in the union as of 1800 (the original thirteen plus Vermont, Kentucky, and Tennessee), seven had property requirements (landed or personal property) for voting and six had tax-paying requirements or property requirements with a tax-paying alternative. Only three sparsely populated states with a paucity of voters—New Hampshire and the new states of Kentucky and Vermont—authorized voting without economic restrictions.[21]

Most states did not impose citizenship restrictions as of 1800, and only five states mandated white-only suffrage: Virginia, South Carolina, Georgia, Delaware, and Kentucky. A single state, New Jersey, extended voting to women, who like their male counterparts had to own real or personal property. Native Americans and slaves remained outside the political communities of all states.[22]

The idiosyncratic decision-making by the states resulted in a lack of any consistency among economic, racial, and citizenship requirements for voting. Of the five states with white-only voting, one had property requirements, three had mixed property and tax-paying qualifications, and one had no economic restrictions on voting. Only one of these racially restrictive states prohibited aliens from voting. Some states also had different suffrage requirements in voting for the lower and upper chambers of the legislatures and in voting for governor, when this position became elected rather than appointed. Within states, suffrage was often more tightly restricted for local than for state and national offices.[23]

Reliable political data for the early republic is hard to come by, and historians dispute the scope of the eligible electorate. Recent estimates indicate that by 1800 economic restrictions may have disenfranchised only about 20 percent of the adult white male population nationwide. However, citizenship, and state, county, and city residence requirements, which could run up to two years, further disenfranchised a substantial but unknown segment of white adult males. The actual turnout of voters nationwide markedly increased from 1788 to 1800, but likely remained below a third of the nation's adult white male population.[24]

Despite their distrust of direct democracy and insistence on checking human avarice, America's framers still optimistically hoped that the virtue of voters would sustain their new government. Constitutional checks and balances might forestall tyranny, but the framers looked for more from the nation's restricted community of voters and their representatives. Even James Madison, the expositor of balanced power, pinned his aspirations for republican government on individual virtue. "No theoretical checks—no form of government can render us secure," he wrote. "To suppose that any form of government will secure liberty or happiness without any virtue in the people, is a chimerical idea." Tench Coxe noted, "Tis not possible for any nation on earth, to hold their strength and establishment, when the dignity of their government is lost, and this dignity will forever depend on the *wisdom* and *firmness* of the officers of government, aided and supported by the *virtue* and *patriotism* of their citizens."[25]

For America's framers, the ideal voter chose candidates in contemplative solitude, insulated from the passions of the crowd and the allure of self-serving wealth. A supporter of the Constitution warned voters not to act "without cool and serious reflection in the hour of stillness and composure at your own houses. Take care of the flame which may be kindled in your minds at taverns, places of parade and public meetings."[26] In 1795, Samuel Adams, one of the more radical founders, commented, "All elections ought to be free, and every elector who feels his own independence as he ought, will act his part according to his best and most enlightened judgment." Yet the privacy of the vote was not generally protected in the early republic, as voters in most states voted by voice or eventually on paper ballots, preprinted and uniquely color-coded by the political parties.[27]

In turn, the ideal representative would similarly stop his ears to public clamor and act independently in the public interest. Madison pointed to the capacity of the Constitution "to refine and enlarge the public views, by passing them through the medium of a chosen body of citizens, whose wisdom may best discern the true interest of their country, and whose patriotism and love of justice will be least likely to sacrifice it to temporary or partial considerations."[28] If members of a legislature should deliberate in public, John Adams wrote, "the time of the whole assembly shall be wasted, and all the public affairs delayed, for days and weeks, in deliberating and debating, affirming and denying, contradicting and proving."[29]

In one stroke, Madison cut to the heart of his vision for America. The Constitution, he wrote, will endure unlike the failed Athenian democracy because of its "total exclusion of the people in their collective capacity."[30] A "Correspondent" in New York agreed that representatives are accountable only to the "free and independent exercise of their own judgment." Thus, *the people! the people!* is often the burden of the song to those who never gave any other evidence of their patriotism but a prostitution of every principle of honor at the shrine of popularity," the writer noted. "If Legislators are to be considered as the guardians of the public liberty, the upright patriot must stem the popular impulse."[31]

In formal recognition of the autonomous voter and representative, the Constitution replaced bloc-voting by states in the new bicameral Congress with voting by individual members. It was now every member for himself; senators and members of Congress from states with multiple members could split their votes without first reaching consensus. Jefferson wrote that among the Constitution's worthy provisions, "I am much pleased too with the substitution of the method of voting by persons, instead of that of voting by states."[32]

Leaders of the new republic rejected pleas to supplement the vote with such direct forms of democracy as recalling and replacing officials in the interim between elections, instructing them on policy, and subjecting them to public pressure. For most framers, public involvement with government began and ended with voting and elections. Voting provided an orderly and verifiable means of assessing the people's will; other forms of popular engagement risked imposing minority views on the majority and subverting lawfully elected governments. The people truly exercised sovereignty, wrote Benjamin Rush in 1787, "only on the days of their election." Once voting and counting is completed, sovereignty is "the property of their rulers." A few years later, a Federalist writer declared, "the sovereignty of the people is delegated to those whom they have freely appointed to administer that constitution, and by them alone can be rightfully exercised, save at the stated periods of election, when the sovereignty is again at the disposal of the whole people."[33]

Unlike the Articles, the Constitution did not authorize the states to recall and replace any national officeholder. Only their fellow legislators could expel members of either chamber of Congress, by a two-thirds vote for serious transgressions. Presidents and judges could be removed only through impeachment by a majority vote of the House and conviction by a two-thirds vote of the Senate. Notably, the voters would have at least an indirect say in impeaching and removing federal officials, because the framers placed these powers solely within political bodies, rather than the courts. Alexander Hamilton explained that impeachments broadly cover "the abuse or violation of some public trust" and are properly "denominated POLITICAL."[34]

During the ratifying debates, Anti-Federalists awoke from their slumber on voting qualifications to assail the lack of a constitutional recall as a flagrant betrayal of local democratic control. In Massachusetts, state legislator Martin Kinsley warned that we "cannot recall our members; therefore, our federal ruler will be masters and not servants."[35] Luther Martin, a Philadelphia delegate who soured on the Constitution, complained that even if national legislators abused their powers to "totally annihilate their state governments, their states could not recall them, nor exercise any control over them."[36] A commentator styled Amicus said that he preferred to retain the recall "and give the new government *unlimited powers* to act in the public good," than to abandon the recall and "give them *limited* powers."[37] The Federalists remained unmoved, agreeing with Hamilton that the recall would turn a legislator into "a slave to all the capricious humors among the people."[38]

After ratification, the first Congress debated a proposed addition to the Bill of Rights that would guarantee the people's right to issue binding instructions to their congressional representatives. This amendment, proposed by Anti-Federalist representative Thomas Tudor Tucker of South Carolina, did not specify the means for issuing instructions, although the power would most likely lodge in state legislatures. Pushing aside practicalities, Representative John Page of Virginia insisted that "under a democracy . . . the popular opinion ought to be collected and attended to" through instructions.[39]

Without instructions, legislators would heed popular voices as much as "the whistling of the wind," said an Anti-Federalist writing under the pseudonym John DeWitt.[40]

Instruction was no minor matter for members of Congress. The House spent more time debating instruction than any other proposed Bill of Rights amendment, and the majority Federalists who deplored direct democracy spoke out in vehement opposition. Representative Thomas Hartley of Pennsylvania argued that instruction would upset the special relationship between voters and their representatives: "At least it ought to be supposed that they have the confidence of the people during the period for which they are elected; and if, by misconduct, they forfeit it, their constituents have the power to leave them out at the expiration of that time." Echoing the common fear of the fickle crowd, he warned that instructions would subject members to the "many inconveniences and real evils [that] arise from the popular opinions on the moment." He continued, "Happy is the government composed of men of firmness and wisdom to discover, and resist popular error." James Madison questioned whether legislators should follow instructions "to violate the constitution" or "to patronize certain measures, and from circumstances known to him, but not to his constituents, he is convinced that they will endanger the public good."[41]

Representative John Vining of Delaware fretted about potential instructions "to make paper money" and debase the coinage: "Every honest mind must shudder at the thought." For Representative Michael J. Stone of Maryland, instruction "would change the Government entirely; instead of being a Government founded upon representation, it would be a democracy," an epithet that he believed needed no explanation.[42]

Congress decisively rejected instruction, forty-two to ten in the House and fourteen to two in the Senate. These votes in Congress rippled across the states. The practice of local government's instructing state legislators largely faded away in the early republic.

Formal recourse for officials alleged to have violated the public trust was limited to rejection by the voters at election time.[43]

Most founders envisioned no place in their constitutional order for grassroots organizations like the Sons of Liberty, which had spurred resistance to the British Crown's "taxation without representation," or the Committees of Correspondence, which linked patriots together across the colonies. In the 1790s, Americans organized Democratic Societies roughly modeled on these revolutionary groups. The societies urged popular demands on a government that they claimed served the "benefit of the *few* to the exclusion and depression of the *many*." The societies drew on techniques honed during the revolution: demonstrations, mass meetings, resolutions, petitions, and symbolic acts such as the erection of "liberty poles" and the burning of oppressive laws. "Patriotic vigilance alone can preserve what patriotic valor has won," proclaimed a New York society.[44]

Although the First Amendment to the Constitution guaranteed rights of assembly and petition, most newspapers joined founders like Washington and Hamilton in their condemnation of the societies for organizing popular resistance to lawfully elected governments. In their view, political engagement through the authorized channels of voting and representation did not squelch popular sovereignty but rather preserved stability in a fragile republic threatened by enemies internal and external. Only elected officials, "the constituted organs of the people," said Federalist Samuel Kendal, could properly express "the general will of the nation." They abetted their arguments by charging the Democratic Societies with complicity in the anti-tax Whiskey Rebellion that swept across western Pennsylvania in 1794, and which Washington labeled "the first *ripe fruit* of the Democratic Societies."[45] In his writing on the Constitution, Madison had warned against collective action by the people. However, in the 1790s, when he and Jefferson were organizing an opposition to the Washington administration, both defended the Democratic Societies. Many of their allies declined to do so, and the societies largely disappeared in the aftermath of the Whiskey Rebellion.

Yet suppression of the Democratic Societies did not quell informal bottom-up, popular participation in politics. Local activists still held public debates, orations, festivals, parades, and protests. They delivered politically charged sermons in churches, issued pamphlets and broadsides, and sent petitions and proclamations to Congress and state legislatures. In these unofficial spheres of expression, women, children, noncitizens, adult men without property or tax bills, and African Americans who lacked the vote could still engage with politics, at least as petitioners if not decision-makers. The rapid growth of political parties in the early republic enduringly breached the wall of separation between elected governments and outside groups. The rise of parties also spurred the proliferation of an unabashedly partisan press that packaged together news and opinion to discredit the opposition and promote its favored party, candidates, and policies. Newspapers had a broad reach among the unusually literate American people.[46]

Leaders of the new republic resolved other issues beyond suffrage qualifications that affected the opportunities for voters to participate in politics and elect candidates of their choice. These included qualifications for holding public office, the geographic base for electing federal and state legislators, and the procedures for conducting elections and identifying their winners and losers.

Unlike their nondecision on suffrage qualifications, the Philadelphia delegates set constitutional requirements for holding federal office. They aimed to balance voter choice with protections against foreign intrigue and the election of public officials lacking in character and wisdom. After considerable debate, delegates required that members of the U.S. House must be at least twenty-five years of age, a resident of the state they represented (not a congressional district), and an American citizen for at least seven years. They imposed similar standards for holding a Senate seat but upped the age qualification to thirty years and the citizenship standard to nine years. The more stringent eligibility standards for president included an age of at least thirty-five years, fourteen years of consecutive residence in the United States, and "natural-born" citizenship, a phrase that delegates did not define.

The framers immunized the Constitution's office-holding qualifications from irresponsible or corrupt interference by either state legislatures or Congress. In Federalist no. 60, Hamilton asserted that "the qualifications of the persons who may ... be chosen ... are defined and fixed in the Constitution, and are unalterable by the legislature." The U.S. Supreme Court has agreed, ruling that the constitutional requirements for holding federal office cannot be altered, supplemented, or diminished by state or federal law, but only by constitutional amendment.[47]

Beyond citizenship and age, the Constitution's rules for federal office-holding were less onerous than most qualifications for holding state offices. In addition to barring women—and in some states African Americans—from office-holding, states had economic requirements for office-holding in 1800 that were at least as restrictive as their suffrage qualifications and typically much more so. Marylanders, for example, could vote for members of the state's General Assembly if they owned fifty acres of land or property worth thirty pounds but could serve in the assembly only if they had real or personal property valued at more than five hundred pounds. In New Jersey people worth fifty pounds could vote for members of the state legislature, but only those worth five hundred pounds could serve in the lower chamber, and only those worth one thousand pounds could serve in the upper chamber. Residents of South Carolina could vote for state representatives and senators if they possessed an estate of fifty acres or paid at least three shillings in taxes. However, they could serve in the state house only if they possessed "an estate of five hundred acres of land and ten negroes, or a real estate of the value of one hundred and fifty pounds." They could serve in the state senate only if they had reached the age of thirty and amassed an estate worth three hundred pounds.[48]

The Constitution specified no racial, gender, economic, or religious impediments for office-holding. The issues of office-holding by women or racial minorities never reached the floor of the convention. Apparently, the delegates saw no danger that voters, state legislators, or electors would elevate such manifestly unfit people to federal office.

The disconnect between qualifications for voting and office-holding led to three great paradoxes of American constitutional government. Although noncitizens could vote and hold state or local office in many states, voters could only elect U.S. citizens to federal offices. States could impose any manner of restrictions on voting or office-holding, but federal office-holding qualifications could be tightened or loosened only through a constitutional amendment. Yet citizens barred from voting by property, tax-paying, racial, gender, registration, or literacy restrictions in their states could still constitutionally hold any elected federal office, if they met the residency, citizenship, and age requirements, and for president the special condition of "natural-born" citizenship. Under the Constitution, any American-born citizen, boy or girl, black or white, could grow up to be president of the United States, even if they could not vote or hold office in their home state.

Deference to the states also meant that legislatures could adopt two-tiered qualifications for voting, one for presidential electors and another for the state legislature and the U.S. House of Representatives. States could set different suffrage requirements for selecting their lower and upper legislative chambers and for their local offices.

The Constitution only partly determined how votes translated into representation. State legislatures would select members of the U.S. Senate, and electors from each state would select by majority vote the president of the United States. Each state could decide how to select members of the Electoral College, the U.S. House of Representatives, state legislatures, and local governing bodies. State legislatures in the early republic typically appointed members of the Electoral College, but some states elected members, winner-take-all, proportionally statewide, or winner-take-all within congressional districts.

Decisions made by each state on the geographic bases for Congress and state and local legislatures set the context for the choices open to voters and the impact of their votes. States differed among themselves on electing members of Congress at-large or in districts and on the apportionment of legislative districts at every level of government. The early Americans who qualified for the vote, like the inhabitants of George Orwell's *Animal Farm,* were all equal, but some were more equal than others.

The deference to the states on setting the rules for legislative elections began in Philadelphia in 1787. The convention's Committee on Detail recommended that each state should prescribe "the times and places and manner of holding the elections" for the U.S. House and Senate, but that Congress should retain the authority to "alter" state provisions. Delegates Charles Pinckney and John Rutledge proposed an amendment that would leave the regulation and administration of elections strictly to the state governments. Madison objected to this diminution of federal authority. Among "many other points," the controlling authority could decide "whether the electors should vote by ballot or vivâ voce, should assemble at this place or that place; should be divided into districts or all meet at one place, should all vote for all the representatives; or all in a district vote for a number allotted to the district." Madison insisted that Congress must retain power over the conduct of elections to avoid corrupt manipulation by the states. Gouverneur Morris of Pennsylvania argued that "the States might make false returns and then make no provisions for new elections."[49]

Swayed by these reservations, delegates rejected the Pinckney-Rutledge amendment and authorized Congress to "make" as well as "alter" provisions for the administration of elections. According to article 1, section 4, clause 1, the "Elections Clause" of the Constitution, "The Times, Places and Manner of holding Elections for Senators and Representatives, shall be prescribed in each State by the Legislature thereof; but the Congress may at any time by Law make or alter such Regulations, except as to the Place of chusing Senators."

At the state ratifying conventions, Anti-Federalists fought to retain sole state control over elections and keep Congress from setting rules that would purportedly favor wealthy Americans. Federalists responded by reiterating arguments made in the convention and citing the many checks on congressional discretion, such as the setting of fixed terms for U.S. representatives and the guarantee to every state of a "Republican form of government." Several states ratified the Constitution after adopting resolutions of understanding that Congress would intervene in the regulation of elections solely under dire circumstances.

Such resolutions had no force in law, and the first Congress rejected a constitutional amendment that would have sharply restricted any federal intervention in the conduct of elections. Nonetheless, Congress only sparingly exercised this authority. In 1792, Congress set the first Wednesday in December as the uniform date across the nation for balloting by electors for the president and vice president. It would not intervene again in the conduct of elections until the 1840s, and its most significant involvement did not come until well into the twentieth century.[50]

While the Constitution dictated the apportionment of congressional seats *among* the states, it let the states apportion congressional, state, and local legislative seats *within* their boundaries. Congressional seats would be allocated to states in proportion to total population as gauged each decade by a mandatory federal census, with two loopholes. Apportionment rules excluded "Indians not taxed" and counted slaves as "three-fifths of other persons." This "three-fifths clause" ended a standoff between southerners, who wanted to count slaves fully to pad their congressional and Electoral College representation, and northerners, who did not want to count slaves at all. Every state, regardless of population, would have at least one member of Congress. A state's representation in the Electoral College turned on its allocation of House seats, with the number of electors equal to its number of House seats plus its two senators. This system guaranteed that every state would have at least three electoral votes. It boosted the electoral strength of slaveholding states, because slaves, under the three-fifths rule, counted at least partially in their allocation of electoral votes but as nonvoters would not have counted at all under a popular voting system for electing the president.

Each state chose the method for electing its congressional delegation and state and local legislatures, with its decision-making having a profound influence on the political power of various economic, demographic, and geographically defined groups within each state. For Congress, the states had to decide first whether to elect members in distinct geographic districts or at-large by all voters in the state. Proponents of at-large elections argued that voters statewide would elect the best men the state had to offer. A district system, they said, would deprive voters of the widest range of choice and splinter Congress into factions responsive to local rather than state or national interests. A 1791 editorial in the Philadelphia *Federal Gazette* warned that "it is to be dreaded that the Representatives of the respective States, in Congress, will too often be influenced by local views, and will consult the partial interests of their own districts, in preference to the general advantage of the Union."[51]

Backers of district elections countered that the wealthy few would control at-large elections, whereas district winners would represent the state's diverse interests. District voters would choose among well-known local candidates, accountable to small constituencies, rather than strangers intent on exploiting office for selfish ends.

A commentator from Philadelphia asked, "How would you like that six or eight men, whom you know not, and perhaps living in Philadelphia . . . should be elected to represent you in Congress, and afterwards proceed to tax you to pay themselves?"[52]

These disputes produced no consensus in the republic's early years. The original states with more than one representative were about evenly divided between at-large and district elections for Congress. States with district elections had to decide whether to base representation on population or geography. America's revolutionaries had rejected Britain's self-serving notion of "virtual representation," which posited that the British Parliament could represent the people of its North American colonies. Although population-based apportionment seemed to fit best with the ideal of direct representation, the British tradition of representation by geographic communities, which could speak with a single voice for a common interest, still held sway in many states and fit the model of apportioning two senators to each state regardless of population.[53]

After the nation's first census in 1790, most states with district-based congressional elections established at least roughly equal populations for each district. However, some states still upheld geographic representation through, for example, requirements that counties not be split in drawing congressional districts. Some states established in urban areas multimember districts that elected more than one representative.

States confronted again the push and pull of geographic- versus population-based representation in drawing districts for their legislative seats. Seven of the original thirteen states apportioned their state senate seats equally by county, county groupings, or towns, regardless of population. In Georgia, for example, Wilkes County, with 8,095 nonslave inhabitants, and Camden County, with 782 nonslaves, each elected the same number of senators, for a ratio of more than 10 to 1. The Rhode Island town of Newport, with 6,739 inhabitants, and the town of James Town, with 501 inhabitants, each elected the same number of senators, for a ratio of about 13 to 1. The remaining states either apportioned districts according to taxable inhabitants or had mixed systems of apportionment.[54]

Even for their lower houses, supposedly "the people's house," states still vacillated between population and geographic representation. The result was a hodgepodge of apportionment rules, some of them nearly indecipherable. A few states based House districts on geographic units irrespective of population, but most states had mixed population and geographic representation.[55]

The Constitution's deference to the states led as well to disparities in the issues of election versus appointment of public officials and in the frequency and timing of elections. Although all states elected members of their state legislatures, fewer than half elected their governors, and none elected state judges. Six of the original thirteen states elected members of their upper legislative chamber annually, whereas South Carolina held such elections every two years; Delaware, New York, and Virginia every three years; and Maryland held its indirect election of state senators by electors every five years. Some states had no fixed election day. Other states held elections on different months and days: Massachusetts on the first Monday in April, Maryland on the first Monday in October, and Pennsylvania and New Jersey on the second Tuesday of October. Virginia had different dates for electing state officials, members of Congress, and presidential electors. To participate in each election, voters had to journey three times to their county courthouse.[56]

States differed too in the nomination of candidates, in voting by ballot or voice, and in the number and location of polling places. In some states, candidates self-nominated by declaring their intention to run for office. In others, coteries of prominent men, county conventions, open meetings, or caucuses of officeholders nominated candidates. Most states relied on paper ballots, although prior to the widespread use of preprinted party ballots by the 1830s, voters often had to write down the names of their chosen candidates. Voters in

Maryland and Virginia and in parts of other states announced their choices openly by voice, shouting out the names of their preferred candidates for all to hear.

New England states had but one polling place per town, which was their unit of local government rather than a county. Most other states divided counties into voting districts and townships, with separate polling locations. Delaware, however, restricted voting to the single county courthouse until 1811, and Virginia until 1830. The importance of polling place numbers and locations cannot be overstated. The greater the number and diversity of polling locations, the greater the opportunity to vote in elections, particularly for people of lesser means. Commenting on the expansion of polling locations in New Jersey after 1788, the pioneering scholar of early American voting Chilton Williamson wrote, the "bringing of the poll closer to the voters was, possibly, as important an event as the prior abandonment of the freehold qualification for voting." Decisions about the number and location of polling places remain consequential and controversial today.[57]

The states had diverse practices for identifying eligible voters, resolving election disputes, and certifying results. Although the state governments held the final authority on voter qualifications, polling place responsibilities fell on many hundreds of localities (today more than ten thousand). In New England, town selectmen primarily oversaw elections; in New York and Pennsylvania, locally elected judges and election inspectors; and in most southern states, the county sheriff.

Local officials typically had the authority to open and close the polls, judge whether individuals were qualified to vote, and certify the final tally. Pennsylvania relied on state-level property and tax rolls for verifying the eligibility of voters, but in most states local governments maintained such records and inconsistently enforced suffrage qualifications. Contemporary newspapers are filled with allegations of how election officials either countenanced illegal voting or conversely barred legal voters from the polls. However, few such allegations had enough credibility to invoke a formally contested election, at least for members of the U.S. House, which kept track of such disputes. Only one contest led to the vacating of an election during the first five sessions of Congress.[58]

The one uniform practice across states was winner-take-all elections. Massachusetts and New Hampshire had majority vote requirements, but in other states a plurality of the vote—what became known as the "First Past the Post" system of elections—sufficed. No state authorized any form of proportional representation. A candidate had to win an election by plurality or majority vote to gain a public office, then, as today.

The enlightened thinking that had guided the founding of America's functioning, if imperfect, democracy had international reach. The push for popular sovereignty, human rights, and the reasoned reconstruction of government rocked a European continent encumbered by hereditary privilege. Democratic ideals little penetrated Czarist Russia, the cobwebbed kingdoms of central and eastern Europe, or the reactionary Bourbon dynasty in Spain. Nonetheless, like the United States in the late eighteenth century, France, England, and the Netherlands all grappled with issues of voting and representation.

Even in these nations, however, the tide of democratic reform soon receded, leaving the United States in the early nineteenth century as the exemplar of a functioning constitutional democracy, with voting rights that extended beyond a small, entrenched elite. Unlike other societies, America lacked feudal traditions, a hereditary monarch and aristocrats, or a nationally established church. Its expanding western settlements helped diffuse the social conflict that wracked more crowded lands. It had fought a successful revolution to break free from an external imperial power and establish a government responsible to its people. Thousands of ocean miles shielded the fledgling nation from the foreign intervention that had first upheld and then dismantled democracy in Holland. America stood as a beacon to the world.

Yet circumstances alone do not drive history. Democracy emerged in Britain's former American colonies only through the energy and creativity of the framers and their critics who insisted on a Bill of Rights. As Shakespeare wrote, "Tis in ourselves that we are thus or thus."[59] Beyond self-interest, constitutional-era debates addressed high principles, respected competing perspectives, and typically ended in compromises that sealed in place a lasting frame of government. With ratification by all the states the framers could credibly claim that the Constitution represented the will of the people, not just a bargain between rulers and subjects.

These worthies were still men of their time, committed to a restricted political community of independent, adult men that ruled out any universal right to vote. In a federal system, with many Americans loyal to states and communities, the framers were content to leave voting qualifications and the conduct of elections to the states. Like most revolutionaries and reformers in Europe, American leaders opposed grassroots popular engagement with government and believed that the direct and indirect election of public officials served the new republic well. The contentious issue of slavery also shaped representation. Southern slave states rejected the popular election of the president because their slaves would count for nothing in the popular tally. Instead, they accepted selection by the electors chosen in each state, with slaves accounting for three-fifths of a person in apportioning each state's representation in Congress and the Electoral College.

Framers of the Constitution could have tightened elite rule by following the model of the Northwest Ordinance and stipulating property-holding requirements for voting and office-holding. They could have inserted into the Constitution racial and gender qualifications. Given the constraint of ratification by the states, certain concessions to rule by popular consent in the interests of social stability seemed preferable to stifling dissent with repression.

The early onset of democracy in the United States has been both a blessing and a curse. The United States possesses the world's most deeply rooted democratic traditions and has enjoyed stable politics and the peaceful transfer of power since the Civil War. Beyond voting rights, the American constitutional tradition includes elements essential to a functioning democracy: a free and independent press; rights of assembly, petition, and speech; civilian control of the military; and checks and balances on rogue power.

Still, American democracy remains tethered to such precedents as state discretion over the conduct of elections, local administration of elections, political gerrymandering of districts, and indirect election of the president, all of which hinder democratic practice. Most critically, the United States has yet to overcome the founding fathers' ambivalence about voting and to guarantee a constitutional right to vote and hold public office, a step that would enable all citizens to participate fully in a representative government of their own choosing.

· 2 ·

A WHITE MAN'S REPUBLIC

I believe this government ... was made by white men, for the benefit of white men and their posterity forever, and was intended to be administered by white men in all time to come.

—STEPHEN A. DOUGLAS, U.S. SENATOR, ILLINOIS, 1858

In the early nineteenth century, opinion makers began to question the fitness of African Americans to vote. In a story that made headlines across New England and New York, disgruntled losers of the 1803 elections in the town of Wallingford, Connecticut, complained that election officials "had the effrontery to bring forward a Negro fellow by the name of Toby" (no last name provided), who voted for their winning opponents. The critics did not claim that Toby lacked the legal qualifications to vote. Rather, they leveled a charge that became familiar over time: that "a few years hence" this "*man of colour*," this "Black night walker," had attempted to rape a white woman.[1]

They said that Toby had been whipped for this crime, even though eleven years earlier, the state had mandated imprisonment for attempted rape. Even if true, conviction for this alleged crime would not have barred him from voting because Connecticut law did not disqualify former felons. Still, by trivializing this black man as child-

like, using his first name only, and yet stereotyping him as a pred-
ator of white women, Toby's detractors insinuated that he should be
excluded from the political community of the state. In 1818, Connecticut replaced its property qualifications with minimal tax-paying
requirements. Four years earlier it had snuffed out black voting by
limiting the franchise to "whites" only. In 1845, Connecticut abolished all economic qualifications for voting by white people. Yet two
years later, when voters had the opportunity to reestablish black
voting rights by referendum, they rejected black suffrage by nearly
4 to 1: 19,495 to 5,616.[2]

By expanding voting opportunities for whites while extinguishing
suffrage for African Africans, Connecticut followed a pattern typical
for the states in antebellum America. By the eve of the Civil War,
standards for voting based on people's intrinsic qualities had largely
supplanted standards based on external possessions. As American
economic life became more open and fluid for white men in the early
nineteenth century, so too did access to the vote for this privileged
slice of the population. In 1800, only five of sixteen states mandated
white-only voting. In 1860, twenty-eight of thirty-three states, com-
prising about 97 percent of the nation's free black population, had
adopted such racially restrictive suffrage. Only five New England
states with minimal black populations—Maine, Massachusetts, New
Hampshire, Rhode Island, and Vermont—authorized voting by
African Americans and other nonwhites. Yet in 1860, no state imposed property qualifications for voting, and only a half-dozen
had tax-paying requirements.[3]

The development of political parties, the rise of new racialist ideologies, and the increasing separation between home and work led to
a belief in a "white man's Republic." Pursuit of this ideal expanded
suffrage for white males while denying voting rights to people deemed
unfit for political life: women, noncitizens, Native Americans, African Americans, and in some states felons and allegedly mentally
incompetent individuals. By rules of inclusion and exclusion, white

men were the winners in this new political order. Members of this privileged group, despite divisions among them, gained the advantage of shaping the nation's laws and policies without regard to the great majority of the American people.

The movement toward a white man's republic took place in an increasingly open polity, dominated by political parties that shattered the traditional ideal of autonomous voters and representatives. In his farewell address near the end of his two presidential terms, George Washington reaffirmed the fading vision of a public sphere fenced in by the formal processes of voting, representation, and law-making. He denounced parties as likely "to become potent engines by which cunning, ambitious, and unprincipled men will be enabled to subvert the power of the people." The spirit of party, he said, "agitates the community with ill-founded jealousies and false alarms; kindles the animosity of one part against another; foments riot and insurrection. It opens the door to foreign influence and corruption."[4]

Washington was the last American president to rise above partisan squabbling. As the nation grew and diversified, white manhood suffrage expanded, and the scope of government increased. The model of the isolated, virtuous voter and representative dedicated only to the common good could no longer hold. Instead, parties became an indispensable link between voters and government, mobilizing constituents and turning them out at the polls in support of partisan candidates and policies.[5]

By the time Washington left office in 1797, one faction known as the Federalists had coalesced around Alexander Hamilton and John Adams. The Federalists backed a strong and active national government, promotion of commerce and industry, and support for Great Britain. Another faction known as the Democratic-Republicans centered on Thomas Jefferson, Washington's former secretary of state, and James Madison, now serving in Congress. The Democratic-Republicans supported limited government, low taxes, states' rights, an agrarian-based republic, and revolutionary France. The rise of political parties and their diverse platforms and constituents would make voting qualifications and the basis of representation an unending source of partisan conflict.[6]

After defeating Jefferson in America's first contested presidential election in 1796, Adams and his Federalists led an effort to restrict suffrage and office-holding through federal law, although indirectly. Consistent with the emerging consensus of the time, they sought not to impose economic requirements for voting and holding office. Instead, they made it much more difficult for aliens to become citizens of the United States. Only citizens were constitutionally eligible for federal office. While just a few states at the time explicitly barred noncitizens from voting or competing for public office, other states de facto barred aliens from political life and would enshrine citizen-only suffrage into law.

In 1798, the Federalist Congress passed, and President Adams signed, the Alien and Sedition Acts. The Sedition Act made it a criminal offense to "write, print, utter or publish" false statements critical of the government. It expressed the Federalist view of an inviolate government that, once elected, should be immune to public clamor. The Alien Acts required immigrants to register with federal authorities and granted the president latitude to deport aliens judged as threatening to national security or originating from enemy nations in times of war. The president could order deportation, with no judicial recourse, even in the absence of an overt act by the alien. This provision had the potential to reduce dramatically the number of immigrants eligible to become naturalized American citizens.

The Alien Acts further restricted immigrant voting and office-holding through stringent waiting periods for naturalized citizenship. The acts extended the waiting period for declaring the intention to become a citizen from three to five years and the residency period for final citizenship from five to fourteen years. Partisan politics, not just ideology, in post-Washington America drove the Federalists to constrain opportunities for naturalized citizenship. Adams and his allies believed that their Democratic-Republican opponents in 1796 relied on votes from Irish, French, and French-Canadian immigrants. The deportation provisions of the Alien Acts, although renewable, would expire in 1800, but the naturalization requirements would persist unless repealed by Congress.[7]

Raising still familiar claims, proponents of the Alien Acts condemned aliens as loyal to foreign governments, hostile to American traditions, and prone to vice and crime. Federalist representative Harrison Gray Otis warned of "wild Irishmen" and "the turbulent and disorderly of all parts of the world" who came to the United States "with a view to disturb our own tranquility after having succeeded in the overthrow of their own governments."[8] William Cranch, Adams's nephew by marriage, said that without the Alien Acts, "A Horde of unprincipled foreigners will rush in upon us" and will "scatter in every direction the seeds of immorality & irreligion, of modern philosophy & democratic disorganization—We shall have French patriots & united Irishmen among our secretaries, our Senators and our Representatives. Law and order would disappear and America would witness the grossest scenes of rapine & plunder, murders & rapes."[9]

Even the retired George Washington weighed in, calling for protection from aliens "who acknowledge *no allegiance* to this Country, and in many instances are sent among us (as there is the best circumstantial evidence) for the *express purpose* of poisoning the minds of our people." He feared that alien participation in government threatened "to dissolve the Union" and negate "the fair and happy prospects which were unfolding to our View from the Revolution."[10]

The fate of naturalized citizenship turned on the election of 1800 between Adams and Jefferson. Neither man openly campaigned for office. Presidential candidates in the early republic, following the precedent set by Washington, held that personal campaigning demeaned the dignity of the office and the need to represent all Americans. Their respective supporters, meanwhile, showed no such restraint and campaigned vigorously in the states. Even though most states then in the union still appointed members of the Electoral College, Jefferson's Democratic-Republicans proved adept at securing electoral votes, organizing at the local level and tarring Federalists as uncaring aristocrats. Merited or not, the Federalists took on the image of a party of the privileged elite and the Democratic-Republicans the party of the common folk. This was a battle that the Federalists could not win, especially as America moved toward broad white male citizen suffrage after 1800. As Abraham Lincoln later quipped, "God must love the common man, he made so many of them."[11]

Jefferson seemingly won the presidency with an Electoral College majority of seventy-three votes to sixty-five for Adams. But did he? With each elector casting two votes, Jefferson's de facto vice-presidential running mate, Aaron Burr of New York, also received seventy-three electoral votes. The prevailing constitutional rules empowered the House of Representatives to choose the president in the event of such a tied vote. Each state would cast one vote, not in the new, heavily Democratic-Republican House, but in the lame duck House that lacked a clear state-by-state partisan majority. It took thirty-six ballots for the House finally to elect Jefferson as president on February 17, 1801, barely two weeks before the commencement of the new presidential term on March 4. Burr became vice president, but his failure to remove himself from consideration for president left him isolated within the Jefferson administration.

The election of 1800 profoundly changed voting and elections in the United States. After the fiasco of an Electoral College tie, Congress passed and the states ratified the Twelfth Amendment to the Constitution before the next presidential election of 1804. This amendment transformed the election of presidents by creating the modern presidential ticket system of a president and vice president, with separate balloting for each office in the Electoral College. If no presidential candidate gained an Electoral College majority, the House would again elect the president. As before, each state, no matter the size of its population, would cast a single vote for president. However, the choices open to House members would now be limited to the top three rather than the top five finishers in the Electoral College vote. Decision-makers at the time viewed the Twelfth Amendment as much more important than just a patch for a flawed electoral system. In their view it represented fundamental changes in popular versus communal sources of popular sovereignty and in the balance of power and authority between the national government and the states.

Congressional debates on the amendment delved deeply into these decisive issues of American democracy. Opponents of the amendment like Representative Gaylord Griswold of New York argued that the Constitution "was a compact formed by the several states" that no amendment should annul. He valued election both by the Electoral College and by the House of Representatives as equally sound means for choosing a president that balanced popular sovereignty with the wisdom of communal decision-making by elected representatives. The proposed new system, he warned, would entrench the odious "power of party." With diminished prospects for House elections of the president, only major organized parties would have the resources and expertise to garner a majority of electoral votes in the states; independent candidates and nominees of minor parties would be relegated to the role of spoilers.[12]

Proponents countered that the amendment clarified the distinction between president and vice president and moved the choice of a president closer to the people. It avoided Electoral College ties that pitched elections into the House of Representatives, which they viewed as an evil, not a benefit, because of the intrigue and corruption that allegedly plagued legislative bodies. The amendment, they claimed, guarded against the election of fringe candidates by reducing the House's choice from the five to the three leading competitors in electoral votes. Without a hint of irony, Representative John Clopton of Virginia affirmed, "It must be a consideration of primary importance that the modes of election be so established that in their event they may always secure a full expression of the public will." Elections that defaulted to the House, he warned, "may terminate contrary to the public will."[13]

Jefferson's victory recalibrated the relationship between immigration and citizenship. In 1781, Jefferson had penned his own worries that aliens would "warp and bias" American democracy "and render it a heterogeneous, incoherent, distracted mass." He hoped that "our government be more homogeneous."[14] However, as president, he understood the political advantage to his party of moving aliens quickly to citizenship. His administration declined to renew the deportation provisions of the Alien Acts, and the new Jeffersonian-controlled Congress adopted a naturalization law that reduced the period for notice of intent to apply for citizenship from five to three years and slashed the waiting period for final approval from fourteen to five years.

Alexander Hamilton, writing under his pen name of the renowned orator of ancient Rome Lucius Crassus, lamented the easing of citizenship requirements, which would grant aliens premature voting rights. He thought the dangers of "admitting foreigners to an immediate and unreserved participation in the right of suffrage ... is verified by the experience of all ages." This grave error, he cautioned, led to the downfall of ancient civilizations. A similar fate awaited America once foreigners "get too early footing in [the] country."[15]

Within the states, Democratic-Republicans pushed to eliminate economic qualifications for voting, expecting political benefits from an expanded electorate and their common-man appeal. Although many Federalists defended the stake-in-society rationale for property ownership for voting (as did some Democratic-Republicans), they tended to tread lightly for fear of antagonizing new classes of voters.

However, the Democratic-Republicans failed to apply the logic of an expanded political community to African Americans and other "nonwhites," who they believed favored the Federalists and lacked the capacity for full participation in American life. Consistent with the rising ideology of a white man's republic, the new Jeffersonian naturalization law continued to limit citizenship only to "free white persons." The law both deprived nonwhites of the rights and privileges of naturalized citizenship and implicitly acknowledged their inferiority to whites. However, in leaving the meaning of "white" undefined, the law potentially denied citizenship to immigrants from Africa, Asia, the Middle East, Hawaii, Latin America, and perhaps even dark-skinned people from parts of Europe. The issue of how to distinguish between "whites" and "nonwhites" emerged during antebellum debates in the states over inserting "white only" voting requirements into their constitutions. It became a vexed issue for the courts and for immigration officials responsible for the adjudication of applications by aliens for U.S. citizenship.

The shrunken Federalist Party, although more sympathetic to black rights than were their opponents, still cautiously approached the contentious issue of black voting, and many of the party's leaders still upheld economic qualifications for voting. In the face of these hard politics, proponents of black suffrage relied mainly on such abstractions as the inherent rights of man and a suffrage that reflected fully the popular will. Yet contradicting this conception of a "universal suffrage" were widely accepted restrictions aimed at women, paupers, felons, noncitizens, transients, and the young. "I cannot clearly comprehend what is meant by the phrase Universal Suffrage," wrote the canny old Federalist John Adams. "Is the whole human species to be allowed an equal vote—are all the Women and Children to turn out? are all the parish paupers to come to the Hustings? are all the gaols to be emptied and all the Prisoners to appear? are all the Gypsys and beggars in the town streets and the fields to be assembled?" The answer to his questions was a resounding "no." Proponents of "universal suffrage" typically meant no more than adult white male suffrage, free of property and tax qualifications.[16]

Opponents of black suffrage played on the common belief that the inherent moral and mental deficiencies of African Americans rendered them ill-equipped for the vote. They charged that unscrupulous men of wealth would buy the black vote and corrupt elections with voter fraud. The opposition raised the specter of blacks flooding into states not just for voting but also for holding public office. A white-only suffrage, such people argued, would preserve the integrity, independence, and virtue of the vote.

Maryland pioneered the movement toward realizing the ideal of a white man's republic. In 1802, the Maryland state legislature advanced the conventional vision of "universal suffrage." For local and state offices it abolished economic requirements for voting by adult white males, which it then extended in 1810 to federal elections.[17] In response, Federalists in Maryland launched a never-ending debate, which reverberated nationwide, over expanding the electorate versus guarding against voter fraud. They warned that fraud would proliferate in tandem with the extension of the vote to a lower-class electorate. At the turn of the nineteenth century, in a precursor to contemporary disputes over voter identification laws, Federalists sought without success to combat alleged fraud by requiring each potential voter to present at the polls documentary proof that he met the state's property qualifications for voting.[18] Democratic-Republicans responded with a broad ideal of popular voting rights, at least for men, whites, and citizens. They dismissed the claim that a more expansive white, male suffrage would propagate fraudulent voting. One Democrat complained that despite the lack of tangible evidence, the "Gentry, with their usual consistency, prate about illegal votes." Such complaints would continue unabated across the centuries.[19]

While expanding the vote for white males, Maryland contracted the vote for African Americans. The state constitution of 1776 had

granted suffrage to all freemen who met property-holding requirements, irrespective of race. However, to forestall voting by a growing
free African American population, the state legislature in 1783 and
1796 selectively disenfranchised former slaves freed after 1783 as
well as their free-born children. As of 1802, the legislature banned
all African Americans from voting. Poll-book data from Annapolis
in 1800 showed that despite earlier restrictions, African Americans
had been voting in Maryland prior to the extinction of their franchise. In 1851, Maryland also abolished voting by noncitizens.[20]

New Jersey quickly followed suit in restricting the vote to white
males. Until 1807, New Jersey had the nation's most liberal suffrage
requirements. The constitution of 1776 had authorized voting by "all
inhabitants," with the minimum requirement of real or personal
property valued at fifty pounds or more. New Jersey was the only
state to open voting to women, along with free blacks and aliens.
Harking to fears of voter fraud, critics charged that New Jersey's liberal suffrage led to voting by unfit people who corrupted elections. In
1799, the prominent lawyer William Griffith wrote, "It is corruption
perfectly disgusting to witness the manner in which women are
polled at our elections. Nothing could be a greater mockery of this
invaluable and sacred right than to suffer it to be exercised by persons who do not even pretend to any judgment on the subject."
Equally objectionable was a suffrage that let "our polls swarm with
the very refuse of English, Irish, Dutch, and French emigrations and
transportations." In 1802, a petition challenging a local election
in Trenton charged that "Negroes and actual slaves voted," "that
aliens voted," and that "married women voted." In a contested 1806
election for the location of the Essex County courthouse, both
sides charged the other with fraudulent voting by women, blacks,
and aliens.[21]

In 1807, in the wake of the Essex County controversy, the New
Jersey state legislature voted overwhelmingly for limiting the vote
to white male citizens, while retaining the property requirements.

In a preamble to the new law, the legislators lumped together categories of people that they deemed inherently unfit for the vote: "Doubts have been raised and great diversities in practice obtained throughout the state in regard to the admission of aliens, females, and persons of color, or negroes to vote in elections." Restricting such voting "is highly necessary to the safety, quiet, good order and dignity of the state." In 1844, New Jersey eliminated economic qualifications for voting but retained its racial, gender, and citizenship restrictions.[22]

In 1821, New York adopted a new constitution that eliminated property qualifications and granted the vote to male adults who paid taxes, worked on public roads, or served in the militia. Thus, New York, like several other states, viewed service to society through means other than finance as a legitimate source of suffrage rights. Still, New York had its defenders of property qualifications. Convention delegate Elisha Williams debunked the idea of universal suffrage, noting that proponents would still exclude the young and women "who cannot be, and never have been supposed, in the most extravagant theories of equality, capable of expressing their wills independently and intelligently." Advocates of universal suffrage would also exclude "all foreigners, all paupers, and all felons." Given that sovereignty "could not be conferred alike on all," voting was not a natural right but a privilege earned by property-holders through "industry, frugality, and character." Such fine points of logic did not move the majority, who reasoned that "there is no privilege given to property, as such; but those who contribute to the public support, we consider as entitled to a share in the election of rulers."[23]

Simultaneously, the new constitution contracted voting rights, imposing without dispute a citizenship requirement for suffrage. More controversial was the convention's suffrage committee's recommendation for restricting voting to whites, washing away forty-five years of black voting under the prior 1777 constitution. Committee member John Z. Ross said that African Americans "are a peculiar people incapable, in my judgment of exercising that privilege with any sort of discretion, prudence, or independence." He noted that "your jails and penitentiaries" are filled "by the very race, whom it is now proposed to clothe with the power of deciding upon your political rights." Black votes, he warned, would be "at the call of the richest purchaser," and "the blacks will claim to be represented by persons of their own colour, in your halls of legislation." When other states began freeing their slaves, black suffrage in New York would "invite that kind of population to this state."[24]

Other delegates conceded the alleged inferiority of black people but blamed their plight on ill-treatment that could ultimately be cured only through full black participation in American life. Abraham Van Vechten said, "As to their degradation, that had been produced by the injustice of white men, and it does not become those who have acted so unjustly toward them, to urge the results of that injustice as a reason for perpetuating their degradation." The emancipation of slaves in the state, "by necessary implication, admit their title to the native and acquired rights of citizenship." Peter Jay argued that the presumption of black inferiority was a mere prejudice "that arises from an association of ideas. Slavery, and a black." But, "with the diminution of slavery, the prejudice has already diminished, and, when slavery is no longer known among us, it will perhaps disappear."[25]

Beyond principle, debate in the New York convention centered on the conundrum of distinguishing "whites" from "nonwhites." Robert Clark charged that "by retaining the word 'white,' you impose a distinction impracticable in its operation." Among so-called whites, he said, "there are many shades of difference in their complexion. Then how will you discriminate." Also, "men descended from African ancestors, but who have been pretty well white-washed by their commingling with your white population, may escape your scrutiny; while others, whose blood is as pure from any African taint as any member of your Convention, may be called upon to prove his pedigree, or forfeit his rights of suffrage, because he happens to have a swarthy complexion." Samuel Young responded that "the common sense of mankind would sufficiently direct, who were to be admitted, and who were to be excluded, by such a general provision." This supposed "commonsense" view of whiteness would later reemerge in federal court decisions that struggled to construe the meaning of "white" in federal naturalization law.[26]

By a narrow margin, delegates declined to limit the vote explicitly to whites, but in practice the new constitution disenfranchised African Americans by imposing on every "man of color" a prohibitive suffrage requirement of a free and clear estate valued at $250, "which we know they cannot comply with," said Jonas Platt.[27] The voters overwhelmingly approved the constitution in January 1822. Under the new property qualification, only sixty-eight of the more than twelve thousand free African Americans in New York City could vote in 1825.[28]

During the 1821 New York convention, a controversy arose with national implications for suffrage rights: whether the Constitution had indirectly guaranteed voting for all citizens, including African Americans, through its clause affirming that "the citizens of each state shall be entitled to all *privileges and immunities* of citizens in the several states." James Kent, the distinguished chancellor of the New York courts, said that "it deserved consideration whether such exclusion [of African Americans] would not be opposed to the constitution of the United States." Another jurist, New York Supreme Court chief justice Ambrose Spencer, countered that "this clause regards mere personal rights," not political rights. "It was intended by the constitution to admit persons of other states to purchase property, and enjoy the personal rights of the states whence they claim." Rufus King objected that the clause includes no such limitation: "Such is not the text; it is to all rights."[29]

The debate over the "privileges and immunities" clause ended inconclusively in New York, but two years later, the 1823 federal circuit

court case *Corfield v. Coryell,* presided over by Supreme Court justice Bushrod Washington, sustained Spencer's reservations. The
decision limited the scope of the "privileges and immunities" clause
in the original Constitution only to rights that are "fundamental;
which belong, of right, to the citizens of all free governments; and
which have, at all times, been enjoyed by the citizens of the several
states which compose this Union, from the time of their becoming
free, independent, and sovereign." Such unfettered fundamental
rights did not include voting, which the court considered a right constrained by "the laws or constitution of the State in which it is to be
exercised."[30]

When New York convened another constitutional convention in
1846, a new American party system had emerged in the states and
nation. After 1800, the dominant Democratic-Republican Party had
relied on a caucus of members of Congress to nominate a single candidate for president. Nomination by "King Caucus" was tantamount
to election given the feeble Federalist opposition. This system disintegrated in 1824, marking the start of a transition to a new era of
relatively balanced competition among reorganized and strengthened parties.

During the election of 1828, war hero Andrew Jackson easily defeated the incumbent president John Quincy Adams and became the
first president from the newly emerging West and the leader of a
Democratic Party that superseded the prior Democratic-Republicans
of Thomas Jefferson. Styling himself as the champion of the "common
man"—which for this Indian fighter and slaveholder meant the white
man—Jackson proposed to expand American democracy. He called
for replacing the Electoral College with a popular vote for president,
limiting the presidency to a single term, and restricting federal ap-
pointments to four years. "As few impediments as possible should
exist to the free operation of the public will," Jackson said. Although
he failed to win enactment of these sweeping reforms, the states did
follow the precedent of "Jacksonian Democracy" by opening many

new offices, including governorships and judges, to popular election.[31]

In 1828, for the first time in U.S. history, more than half the states chose electors by the "general ticket" method, that is, winner-take-all by a statewide vote. By the subsequent election of 1832, all but two states had adopted the general ticket procedure. As opposed to the district system, which splintered the state's Electoral College votes, the general ticket system increased the state's impact on presidential elections by unifying its electoral votes. In 1832, Maryland was the last holdout to maintain a district system, and South Carolina remained the final state to appoint electors by votes of the state legislature. The conversion to general ticket elections strengthened the two-party system; it diminished prospects for third parties and independent candidates, who lacked the resources to campaign statewide or the broad appeal needed to defeat the majority parties and win a statewide plurality.[32]

By 1834, Jackson's opponents had coalesced into a new Whig Party led by Henry Clay and Senator Daniel Webster of Massachusetts. The Whigs backed an activist government that would impose tariffs on foreign goods, promote education, build the nation's infrastructure, and enforce moral standards. The Whigs opposed the Democrats' aggressive approach to the territorial expansion of the United States. Until the early 1850s, when the Whig Party disintegrated, Democrats and Whigs fought largely to a standstill across the nation. Unlike later party systems, partisan allegiances did not closely follow sectional lines, and neither party gained a lock on the presidency or a decisive advantage in Congress. Close partisan competition, a rising number of elected offices, and new forms of popular mobilization expanded voter turnout and led Democrats and Whigs to continue easing suffrage qualifications for white males. Neither party wanted to fall behind in the enfranchisement of new voters.

At a high tide of competition between Democrats and Whigs, the New York constitutional convention of 1846 dragged on from June 1 to October 9, again pondering the reform of voting and elections. Consistent with the ideal of an expanded democracy, delegates from both parties agreed to eliminate economic qualifications for white voters and for the first time to elect mayors and justices of the peace. Voting rights for blacks, however, remained controversial. Delegates opposed to black suffrage mustered on their behalf the power of religion, science, and constitutional law. John Leslie Russell insisted that white-only voting was not "the expression of a prejudice. It was but the expression of the sentiment of the Almighty, who had ordained the colored man to be inferior to the free white race." Bishop Perkins observed "that the great offence which brought the flood on the earth" was "the intercourse of one race with another that God had separated." John Kennedy further asserted, "We are informed by physiologists, that the human family was divided into five races: all of which had distinctive characteristics. Those two which had the fewest points of resemblance were the Caucasian and Ethiopian. . . . Let not government dare to counteract and overthrow the distinctions and divisions that nature designed should exist." As irrefutable proof of black inferiority, he cited the disproportionate number of colored men in the state's Sing Sing and Clinton prisons. Consistent with Justice Washington's construction of the Constitution's "privileges and immunities" clause in the *Corfield* case, Kennedy insisted that "the elective suffrage was a privilege,—a franchise—a civil right, and not a natural right; and the governing power may limit, restrict, or extend the exercise of it in such manner as to it might seem wise and proper."[33]

Delegates also debated whether to demand literacy as a condition of voting. Alpheus Greene agreed that "the right to vote is not a natural or inalienable right; but is a right conferred by the government on its members for a specific purpose," that of choosing public officials. Given that everyone's rights are affected by each vote cast, the community must "have a right to demand that the voter should be intelligent." However, most delegates found persuasive William

Taylor's argument that although "we should do everything we could for the education of the rising generation," a literacy test would "disfranchise many intelligent men—well qualified to discharge all the business of life—but who had never learned to read or write."[34]

The convention dropped all economic requirements for white voters. It submitted a proposition on eliminating the stringent freehold qualifications for people of color to the voters, who rejected it by nearly 3 to 1: 224,336 to 85,406.[35] Delegates declined to adopt a literacy test but required voters to provide proof of eligibility and authorized the legislature to enact laws to exclude "all persons who have been or may be convicted of bribery, larceny, or of any infamous crime."[36]

Pennsylvania followed the lead of other states in revising its constitution to erase voting by African Americans. The state's constitution of 1790 had authorized voting by all citizens twenty-one years of age or older who paid a state tax. It included no racial restrictions. The route to black disenfranchisement followed a circuitous path that led from the courts to a constitutional convention in 1837–1838.[37]

In 1835, William Fogg, an African American who election officials had turned away from the polls, filed America's first voting rights lawsuit, *Hobbs v. Fogg*. Fogg was a free citizen of Pennsylvania, a state founded on the principle that "all men are born equally free and independent." He charged that election officials had barred him from voting in violation of the state's color-blind constitution simply because he looked black. Fogg won his case in a lower court, but the Pennsylvania Supreme Court upheld the state's appeal in 1837, in effect by writing black people out of American democracy. The court ignored the state constitution and found that "no coloured race was party to our social compact," and that there was no basis on which "to raise this depressed race to the level of the white one." The court did hold out some hope for future generations, noting that a black man's "blood, however, may become so diluted in successive descents to lose its distinctive character; and, then, both policy and justice require that previous disabilities should cease."[38]

This idea of excluding blacks from the "social compact" reemerged when the commonwealth adopted a new constitution in a convention that began on May 2, 1837, and lasted until February of the following year, nearly tripling the time spent at the Philadelphia convention that drafted the nation's Constitution. The convention maintained tax-paying qualifications for voting while abolishing the vote for nonwhites and continuing the exclusion of aliens. With Tennessee having outlawed nonwhite voting in 1834 and North Carolina in 1835, Pennsylvania's new "white-only" provision meant that none of the sixteen pre-1800 states outside of New England authorized voting by blacks or other nonwhites.

Delegate Phineas Jenks argued to the Pennsylvania delegates that the commonwealth should replace its tax-paying requirements for suffrage with property qualifications, which he said better assured responsible voting than "white only" suffrage. He pointed to prosperous colored men of substantial means including one with riches of "a hundred thousand dollars." He did not believe it would "be proper for an individual who has so deep a stake in society to be excluded from the exercise of the elective franchise." Benjamin Martin responded for the majority, saying, "It is altogether futile and useless to pursue the experiment of making the African and Indian equal to the white citizen." Perhaps thinking about the Fogg suit, Martin continued that voting rights would ill-serve blacks, because an aroused public would turn them away from the polls, thus "holding out expectations to them which could never be realized." He warned of attracting African Americans to the state. Look to Philadelphia, he said, where blacks congregate "from all the southern States, and have so corrupted each other, that they are now in a situation far worse than the bondage from which they have escaped. It is impossible to walk through Cedar ward, in a clear warm evening, for the black population."[39]

Although delegates upheld the tax-paying requirement for suffrage, they initially voted down the "whites only" clause with about 20 percent of Democrats joining a near unanimous Whig delegation. However, events intervened to reverse this verdict. On October 10, 1837, Democrats lost five of six local elections in Bucks County. They raised the issue of voter fraud, charging that the opposition had prevailed through illegal black votes and filing suit to overturn the elections. In January 1838, Judge John Fox of the Bucks County Court issued an opinion on black voting in these elections that paralleled the reasoning of the state supreme court in *Hobbs v. Fogg* to exclude people of color from the state's political community.[40] Although *Hobbs* had been decided earlier, that opinion was not published until after the end of the convention. By a vote of seventy-seven to forty-nine, delegates added a "white only" suffrage clause to the constitution.[41]

With a resounding protest entitled "The Appeal of Forty Thousand Citizens Threatened with Disenfranchisement to the People of Pennsylvania," black leaders condemned the new constitution for denying "that all men are born equally free by making political rights depend on the skin in which a man is born? Or to divide what our fathers bled to unite, to wit, TAXATION and REPRESENTATION." They said that the freedom of all depended on the freedom of the least powerful and that "when you have taken from an individual his right to vote, you have made the government, in regard to him, a mere despotism, and you have taken a step toward making it a despotism for all." Their appeal fell on deaf white ears in Pennsylvania. Without a federal guarantee of the vote, the disenfranchised black people of Pennsylvania and other states had no recourse to any authority higher than their discriminatory state constitutions and hostile state courts.[42]

Across the nation, black people protested their exclusion from the vote, with no more success than the free African Americans of Pennsylvania. In 1840, a "Convention of the Colored Inhabitants of the

State of New York, to Consider Their Political Disabilities," issued its own proclamation on behalf of black voting rights. The proclamation appealed to the ideology of American republicanism, citing the injustice of granting political rights to foreign-born citizens but not to native-born blacks:

> We are Americans. We were born in no foreign clime. . . . We have not been brought up under the influence of other, strange, aristocratic, and uncongenial political relations. In this respect, we profess to be American and republican. . . . We call upon you to return to the pure faith of your republican fathers. . . . For no vested rights, for no peculiar privileges, for no extraordinary prerogatives, do we ask. We merely put forth our appeal for a republican birthright.[43]

More than forty conventions of black people seeking political rights followed this New York conclave, echoing similar arguments in states across the nation. Black advocates spread their message to a wide but largely unreceptive audience. A commentary in Frederick Douglass's newspaper *The North Star* noted that in Ohio, "Our Colored Fellow Citizens" have "made very spirited and commendable efforts to secure the Right of Franchise. They have held conventions, sent forth addresses, passed resolutions, and delivered lectures with a view to dispose the public mind favorably to their object." African Americans in Ohio gained voting rights only with passage of the Fifteenth Amendment in 1870.[44]

Unique among antebellum conventions, Virginia's constitutional convention, which met from October 5, 1829, through January 15, 1830, pitted distinct parts of the state against each other in a dispute over linkages among suffrage, slavery, and representation in government. "The elective franchise looks to two objects: first the *persons* who are to exercise it, that is, *suffrage;* secondly to the *effect of suffrage,* that is *representation*," observed delegate Robert B. Taylor of Norfolk. With white-only voting a settled issue since colonial times, delegates debated Virginia's stringent property requirements for suffrage and the apportionment of the state legislature. Urban delegates from Williamsburg, Richmond, and Norfolk and rural delegates from the newly settled, largely nonslaveholding western counties clashed with eastern tidewater slaveholders. Delegate Chapman Johnson observed that beyond principled arguments about the rights of man or the basis of sound government, "We are engaged . . . in a contest for power."[45]

Slaveholding elites defended both strict property requirements for voting and the inclusion of slaves in the population base for apportioning legislative seats. They feared that any diffusion of political power to urban and western areas could result in taxing their slave properties and even challenging slavery itself. In defense of property qualifications, Philip Pendleton Barbour noted that given Virginia's abundant land, a fifty-acre freehold was "within the reach of every man in the community, who possesses ordinary industry and economy. From such an arrangement, no danger can arise to the liberties of the people." The young and brash delegate Benjamin Watkins Leigh loudly sounded the alarm against embarking on "an adventurous career of experimental reform" in abandoning the freehold qualification. He warned of the chaos that would follow from the enfranchisement of landless Virginians, whom he compared to the degraded "peasantry of Europe" and to "drunken vagabonds," and condemned as dangerous "rabble." "The poor and dependent," said Philip N. Nicholas, would submit "to the seductions of wealth. The extreme rich and the extreme poor, if not natural allies, will become so in fact."[46] Defenders of the undemocratic status quo in this star-filled convention included Chief Justice John Marshall of the U.S. Supreme Court, a diehard Federalist, and past Democratic-Republican presidents James Madison and James Monroe, all of them holders of slaves.

Reformers rejected all arguments by slaveholders as pretext to seal in place eastern control of state government by restricting the suffrage. The vote "is the substratum, the paramount right upon which all these [others] rest for protection, preservation, and safety," said Lucas P. Thompson. A "minority of one class have taken possession of this right," he observed, "not by the consent of the majority, but by consent among themselves." A petition from the "non-freeholders of the City of Richmond" declared that many citizens of Virginia are engaged in pursuits with "no less integrity, requiring as much intelligence . . . as agricultural pursuits." Rather than advancing virtue, the privileging of wealth "corrupts and vitiates the very persons it is intended to benefit," said Robert B. Taylor.[47]

The base of representation in the state legislature underlay this regional power struggle. In a reprise of controversies at the Philadelphia Convention of 1787, delegates debated whether to include slaves in the basis of legislative representation. The Virginia debates, however, occurred in the context of a state that recognized slaves only as property, raising the question of whether property should be included with people in apportioning state legislative districts.

Eastern delegates insisted on basing representation according to both people and property, because both required protection under the law, they claimed. On the eve of the convention, Justice Marshall said that slave property "is among the most productive funds for taxation, it bears a great portion of the burthens of government and has peculiar claims of that body which is to be entrusted with the power of imposing taxes." Slave representation, he insisted, was "perhaps the only security against oppressive taxation." Like slaves, he added, "females, minors, &etc are excluded from the polls, but are included in the enumeration of persons on whom representation is apportioned."[48] John Randolph of Roanoke conceded that he spoke for "the great tobacco-growing and slave-holding interest." He railed against the tyranny of "King Numbers," represented by the more numerous nonslaveholders who would oppress those who held slave property with "their monstrous claims of power."[49]

The Richmond contingent argued instead for representation based only on people to the exclusion of slaves, the so-called white basis of representation. Otherwise, the slave power would "preponderate and oppress the rest. . . . Its safest check, its best corrective, is found in a general admission of all upon a footing of equality." Robert B. Taylor added that just representation must consider only "*the people represented*. . . . Property cannot vote; it cannot delegate power; and yet we are told that is to have a representative."[50]

Reformers fell two votes short of adopting universal white male suffrage and apportioning the legislature into districts of equal white populations. Instead, the convention compromised on limited economic requirements that modestly increased the pool of eligible voters. It marginally adjusted the apportionment of state legislative seats, with representation still lodged disproportionately in the slaveholding east.[51] Former president Monroe pronounced himself satisfied with the new arrangement, saying he supported "some tie which shall connect the voter to the soil," but that a leasehold still represents "some hold on the land" and gives "security by it to our system of Government."[52] Two decades later, at the constitutional convention of 1850–1851, Virginia slid into conformity with most other states in eliminating its remaining economic qualifications for suffrage. A compromise on representation gave the western part of the commonwealth a majority of seats in the Virginia House of Delegates and the east a state senate majority.[53]

Rhode Island adopted a new constitution in 1842 in the wake of a domestic insurgency known as Dorr's Rebellion, which demanded voting rights for disenfranchised whites. By 1840, the state's stringent property-holding qualifications had excluded about 60 percent of adult white males in a state that led the nation in its urban percentage. Rhode Island's apportionment of the state legislature by towns cemented control of state government by a rural-based elite minority. Under the leadership of Thomas Wilson Dorr, insurgents, mostly affiliated with the Democratic Party, convened a People's Convention.[54]

The Dorrites insisted that democracy did not begin and end with elections but included the right of a sovereign people to abolish and reconstruct their frame of government. The delegates drafted a new constitution that eliminated economic requirements for voting, but to mute criticism against a movement branded as radical and dangerous, upheld a practice established by statute in 1822 of restricting voting to whites only. Thus, the tensions between popular sovereignty and racial exclusion that had marked American antebellum politics emerged full blown in Rhode Island, creating what one abolitionist decried as a "glaring inconsistency" in the Dorr movement for expanded democracy.[55]

Once the Dorrites steered this "People's Constitution" to ratification in a statewide popular plebiscite, newly enfranchised voters elected Dorr governor. The state's old guard mobilized in opposition as a "Law and Order" party that returned incumbent governor Samuel Ward King to office in a separate election under prior suffrage rules. After King declared martial law, Dorr's followers attempted an unsuccessful armed uprising. On the run from militia forces, the Dorrites disbanded. Among the 3,500 militiamen were more than 200 African Americans disillusioned with the reformers' exclusion of their race from voting. Ultimately, the rebels gained only limited concessions for a broadened suffrage. Rather than continue to repress an insurgency, the old guard compromised and enacted a new constitution. It established a complex, multitiered system for qualifying voters. It retained property qualifications for naturalized citizens while imposing only tax-paying requirements for native-born Americans. These provisions somewhat expanded suffrage but not substantially enough to threaten the power of the state's elite.

The "Law and Order Constitution" restored the voting rights of African Americans, about 3 percent of the state's population. Rhode Island thus became the first—and through the onset of the Civil War the only—American state to have rescinded and then restored black suffrage. However, many African Americans could not have afforded to pay the poll tax of one dollar, about equal to two days' pay

for an unskilled laborer. The constitution precluded alien voting
and imposed formidable barriers to voting by naturalized citizens,
who comprised a considerable portion of the state's working class.
The people of Rhode Island "would rather have the Negroes vote
than the damned Irish," wrote Elisha Potter, a leader of the Law and
Order movement.[56]

The Dorr Rebellion led to federal litigation with important implications for voting rights. The aptly named Dorrite Martin Luther
challenged the "Law and Order" Constitution. He claimed that by retaining economic restrictions on voting, it violated the provision of
the U.S. Constitution (art. 4, sec. 4, clause 1) that guaranteed "to every
State in this Union a Republican Form of Government." He petitioned
the courts to strike down the Law and Order Constitution and in effect default to the Dorrite Constitution adopted by voters without
economic constraints on their suffrage.

The case reached the U.S. Supreme Court, which declined in 1849,
long after the rebellion's end, to consider enforcing the "republican
form of government" clause. Chief Justice Roger Taney's opinion for
the Court held that "the power of determining that a state government has been lawfully established" did not rest with the courts but
with the Congress and president. Taney ruled that with the prom-
ulgation of the Law and Order Constitution, "the contest was over"
regarding which constitution governed the state. Any further resolution of the matter, he found, was a political question beyond the
scope of judicial resolution. Thus, the Court must "examine very
carefully its own powers before it undertakes to exercise jurisdiction." Until the 1960s, the courts generally followed Taney's precedent and avoided intervention into what later became known as the
"political thicket" of voting rights and representation without a clear
legal standard. Although weakened considerably, the doctrine still
holds some sway in today's courts.[57]

New states of the union closely followed the pattern of older states
in excluding people of color from the ballot while avoiding economic

requirements entirely or imposing only tax-paying qualifications for white males. Beginning with Ohio in 1803, seventeen states entered the union through 1860, bringing the total to thirty-three. In establishing white-only suffrage, as well as eventually eliminating all economic requirements, Ohio set the pattern for other new states. In November 1802, thirty-five Ohio delegates, mostly Democratic-Republicans, drafted a constitution for the emerging state in less than a month. The constitution, which Congress quickly approved, limited voting to white men who paid taxes or labored on state roads. Delegates narrowly agreed to the exclusion of nonwhites from voting, although they outlawed slavery. The constitution apportioned both houses of the state legislature per the number of adult white male inhabitants.[58] When a second constitutional convention convened in 1850, delegates decisively rejected suffrage rights for nonwhites but dropped the tax-paying requirement for voting by adult white men.[59]

In referenda votes, the broader electorate in new states, not just convention delegates, rejected voting rights for nonwhites. Illinois in 1848 defeated nonwhite voting by a 70 percent majority, Michigan in 1850 defeated nonwhite voting by a 71 percent majority, and Iowa in 1857 defeated nonwhite voting by an 85 percent majority. Wisconsin held three referenda over the course of a decade. Voters defeated nonwhite suffrage by 66 percent in 1847, then reversed this verdict by a 56 percent majority in 1849. After the state courts nullified this referendum because its low turnout of 9,340 failed to meet minimum state law standards, voters again rejected black suffrage in 1857 by 59 percent.[60] A few of these new states enfranchised Native Americans as a special category of nonwhites. But these paper rights for Indians came with tight restrictions that nullified their effect. Some states, for example, allowed voting by so-called civilized Indians who "were not a member of any tribe."[61]

To reconcile the ideal of "universal suffrage" with the disenfranchisement of nonwhites, political leaders insisted that certain people, like women and children, fell outside the political community, given their inherent inability to vote wisely and independently. Still, on the eve of the Civil War, the ideal of a "white man's Republic" remained America's unfinished work. American lawmakers came close but never quite achieved the finality of granting voting rights universally to adult white males. Property qualifications for voting had disappeared, and only a handful of states had tax-paying requirements. But decision-makers hedged their backing of universal suffrage even for white males by excluding people deemed unfit for political participation on grounds of moral or mental deficiency, dependence on the state, lack of a stable residence, or alien affiliation.

These exclusions were widespread. About half the states disenfranchised felons, and nearly a quarter denied the vote to individuals of unsound mind, variously defined, and to paupers, commonly defined as people dependent on state welfare. Virtually every state had residency restrictions, typically ranging from one to two years of residence in the state and three months to a year of residence in the county or town. Residency qualifications were onerous in America's highly mobile society. Analysis of census data shows that 26 percent of white, native-born men aged twenty to twenty-nine and 11 percent of men aged forty to forty-nine moved from one state to another during the 1850s.[62] Only a handful of states, mostly in the West, permitted aliens to vote. Other states either limited voting to citizens in their initial frames of government or in revised constitutions.[63]

Two states concluded that only the literate had the fitness to vote. In the 1850s, Massachusetts and Connecticut adopted literacy tests for voting, a sword wielded against Irish immigrants, not African Americans. Although estimates are uncertain, these many noneconomic restrictions likely disenfranchised some 10 to 15 percent of America's adult white male citizen population.[64]

Most states in the antebellum period expanded the eighteenth-century roster of elected offices to include judges and governors.

They also eliminated or refrained from establishing economic requirements for holding state office. However, nearly all established more stringent age and residency qualifications for office-holding than for voting, especially for state senates and governorships. States generally restricted their state senates to people aged twenty-five years old or more and their governorships to those aged thirty years or above. Residency requirements for the state senate ranged primarily from two to four years and from four to six years for governors.

Typically states adopted some form of population-based apportionment for state legislative and congressional districts, usually based on the number of qualified electors, although regional imbalances in the base of representation remained. Apportionment by population rather than fixed geography created new biases in the voting for Congress and state and local legislatures. Given the lack of clear principles or court supervision, state legislatures had a relatively free hand in drawing the boundaries of population-based districts.

Although the term "gerrymander" had not yet been coined at the time of the Constitutional Convention, James Madison warned delegates there, in support of Congress's authority to make or alter state election practices, that "whenever the State Legislatures had a favorite measure to carry, they would take care so to mould their regulations as to favor the candidates they wished to succeed.... Besides, the inequality of the Representation in the Legislatures of particular States, would produce a like inequality in their representation in the Natl. Legislature."[65]

When Madison ran for the first U.S. House of Representatives from Virginia in 1788, he became the target of what we now term a political gerrymander. Led by Patrick Henry, Madison's Anti-Federalist opponents, who controlled the Virginia legislature, manipulated the drawing of congressional district lines to place Madison within a geographically extended district filled with political opponents.

The legislature required a year's residence in a congressional district, so he could not run in a more favorable district. Madison survived the gerrymander by personally campaigning across the district and appealing to Anti-Federalists by promising to support the addition of a Bill or Rights to the Constitution. Ironically, Anti-Federalist efforts to deny Madison a congressional seat contributed to their goal of obtaining a Bill of Rights as the first amendments to the new Constitution.[66]

Partisans in some state legislatures across the nation continued to design electoral districts for statehouses and Congress that favored their preferred candidates. Even town councils and county commissions began to design districts for partisan advantage. Although as Madison proved, the practice of custom-designing districts was not infallible, it still diluted people's votes by minimizing their opportunities to elect candidates of their choice.

In 1812, when Elbridge Gerry, the governor of Massachusetts, signed a redistricting plan for the state senate biased toward his Democratic-Republican Party, critics decried one contorted district as a "monster," "the spawn of the devil," or "Beelzebub come to life." Mostly they thought it resembled a salamander, which led them to coin the epithet "gerrymander" as a merger of the district's shape and governor's last name. The gerrymandering of districts became more widespread over time as party systems matured during the early nineteenth century and partisan conflict intensified.[67]

With minimal success some states adopted measures designed to curb the widely recognized evil of the gerrymander. These included requirements that districts must be compact and contiguous (connected at all points), that counties should not be divided, and that reapportionment must not occur more frequently than once every ten years. Some states ended the district-level election of congressional representatives and reverted to at-large elections of the state's delegation by all voters in the state. This meant, however, that in the new age of partisanship, the dominant political party in the state could sweep the entire congressional delegation. In response, Congress passed the Apportionment Act of 1842, which required states with more than one representative to elect members of Congress in single-member, contiguous districts. Nonetheless, it did not act to curb the gerrymandering of districts, and disputes over the 1842 regulations led several states to postpone their congressional elections until the following year. Congress repealed the district election requirement in 1850 but restored it in 1862.[68]

Both Congress and state governments in the antebellum period left largely untouched the eighteenth-century practice of local control over the administration of elections. Decision-makers in both older and new states continued to defer to local election officials, with minimal state oversight or efforts to harmonize differing local practices. Delegates to the many constitutional conventions held prior to the Civil War either ignored or briefly and inconclusively discussed issues related to the administration of elections even as they engaged in bracing debates over laws governing suffrage and legislative apportionment. In a history of local election practices, historian Alec C. Ewald concludes, "I find not a single instance in which delegates seriously considered stripping local officials of the responsibility to decide how, when, and where American ballots would be cast and counted." Congress likewise failed to exercise its constitutional powers to take control over the loose and inconsistent conduct of elections for federal office.[69]

With their eyes wide open to the enfranchisement of masses of workers without property of their own, the men who made and remade state constitutions in antebellum America adopted the model of white man's suffrage largely unencumbered by economic requirements.[70] As early as the Constitutional Convention of 1787, delegate Gouverneur Morris, a supporter of property qualifications, warned that "the time is not distant when this Country will abound with mechanics & manufacturers who will receive their bread from their employers." James Madison backed this view, saying, "In future times a great majority of the people will not only be without landed, but any other sort of, property."[71]

Defenders of property qualifications in the states made similar claims, without success. In 1800, a year before the Maryland legislature struck down property qualifications, the Federalist-controlled state senate warned that in "future times . . . a considerable proportion" of the state's population "will probably be, as we find it in other countries, destitute of property, and without sufficient virtue and knowledge to resist the arts, the corruptions and the impositions of ambitious men, desirous of raising themselves to power, even on the ruins of public liberty and happiness." The electorate dismissed the prior senate in the next election, and the new body, controlled by Democratic-Republicans, joined the House in eliminating economic qualifications.[72]

During New York's constitutional convention of 1821, Chancellor James Kent futilely defended property qualification with the warning,

> We are no longer to remain plain and simple republics of farmers. . . .
> The growth of the city of New York is enough to startle and awaken those who are pursuing the *ignis fatuus* [deceptive goal] of universal suffrage. It is rapidly swelling into the unwieldy population, and with the burdensome pauperism, of an European metropolis. New York is destined to become the future London of America; and in less than a century, that city, with the operation of universal suffrage, and under skillful direction, will govern this state.

Most delegates at the New York convention accepted broad suffrage, not because they disagreed with this vision but, as historian Chilton Williamson explains, because "it would make for repose and stability," whereas its rejection would "shake the very foundations of society."[73]

The men who wrote laws and enacted constitutions in antebellum America chose to incorporate the nonagricultural working class in the political system rather than assume the costs of exclusion and repression. Among older states, the elimination of property qualifications did not turn on the balance between those with and without an attachment to the soil. The still predominantly agricultural states of Connecticut, New York, and Maryland abolished property qualifications before 1825, whereas New Jersey, Rhode Island (largely), and Virginia did so only after 1840, when their industrial and commercial workforce outnumbered those engaged in agriculture. Among the seventeen new states entering the union after 1800, none imposed property qualifications for voting and only three required the payment of a tax.

The extinction of nonwhite voting was the essential counterpoint to the simultaneous expansion of white, working-class suffrage. The inclusion of whites and the exclusion of nonwhites from the political community reinforced the erasure of class distinctions by distinctions of race. No matter how downtrodden a white male voter, he could still look down with race pride on the disenfranchised black people beneath him. John C. Calhoun, a U.S. senator from South Carolina and former vice president of the United States, captured in 1849 the idea of white privilege that prevailed in the South and North: "With us the two great divisions of society are not the rich and the poor, but white and black." Only whites, "the poor as well as the rich, belong to the upper class, and are respected and treated as equals."[74]

Even with the limitations of its model of a white man's republic, the United States in 1860 remained the world's leader in opportunities for voting and representation across social classes. In Europe and Latin America, the push for democracy generally failed to overcome the power of entrenched elites, monarchs, and self-made despots. Despite the founding of independent nations in Latin America and the upheavals of the democratic revolutions of 1848 that swept across many European nations, suffrage reform in every democratic nation through the first six decades of the nineteenth century was incomplete, leaving most ordinary citizens without voting rights. Yet, despite the relative expansiveness of American democracy in a world still ruled by privileged elites, the United States maintained a racially exclusive franchise that would become fiercely contested during the Reconstruction that followed the Civil War and the liberation of the slaves. The nation grappled with the question of whether it could redeem the sacrifices and promises of the war without according full citizenship rights, including the franchise, to its now free black population. Even more vexing was the question of whether the principle of voting rights for blacks extended to other excluded Americans.

CONSTRUCTING AND
DECONSTRUCTING THE VOTE

The policy that emancipated and armed the negro—now
seen to have been wise and proper by the dullest—was not
certainly more sternly demanded than is now the policy
of enfranchisement.... It will be found that the nation
must fall or flourish with the negro.

—FREDERICK DOUGLASS, 1866

Nearly a decade before the Civil War, controversy over slavery
shattered the American party system with the Whig Party's
demise. The Whigs had united moderate but generally proslavery
southerners with northern Protestants, who formed the vanguard
of antislavery, temperance, and anti-immigrant movements. This alliance failed when southern Whigs deserted the party as northerners sought, in vain, to use antislavery to salvage the party in
their region. Like Oliver Wendell Holmes's one-horse shay that
"went to pieces all at once," the Whigs fell apart not gradually but
quite abruptly and suddenly, after the party decisively lost the
presidential election of 1852. "We are slayed. The party is dead-dead-
dead!" said Whig representative Lewis Davis Campbell of Ohio.[1]

By 1856, two new parties had arisen to compete with the ruling Democrats. The American, or Know-Nothing Party, appealed to voters who feared that Catholics, blacks, and immigrants were debasing American culture and politics. One leader who denounced the Know-Nothing appeal was the former Whig turned Republican Abraham Lincoln. He wrote in 1855, "How can anyone who abhors the oppression of negroes, be in favor of degrading classes of white people? Our progress in degeneracy appears to me to be pretty rapid. As a nation, we began by declaring that *all men are created equal.* We now practically read it 'all men are created equal, *except negroes.*' When the Know-Nothings get control, it will read 'all men are created equal, except negroes, *and foreigners, and catholics.*'"[2]

The Republican Party opposed the expansion of slavery and, like the defunct Whigs, backed an activist government that promoted industry, commerce, and education. Although the Republican nominee for president, the famed explorer John C. Frémont, lost to the Democrat James Buchanan in the election of 1856, he nevertheless finished in second place, well ahead of the Know-Nothing nominee, former president Millard Fillmore. The results of 1856 installed the fledgling Republican Party as the opposition to the still-surviving Democrats in a new two-party system.

Democratic Party leaders in the 1850s sought to apply their idea of a white man's republic to resolve the conflict over the expansion of slavery. The Democrats would leave the decision up to the voters of each territory as it entered the union whether it would become a slave or free state. During the campaign of 1856, James Buchanan lauded this policy of popular sovereignty as "founded upon principles as ancient as free government itself," which stemmed "from the original and pure fountain of legitimate political power, the will of the majority." This expedient, however, satisfied neither the proponents nor the opponents of slavery's expansion. As applied to the territory of Kansas, the doctrine led to a bloody civil war, termed "Bleeding Kansas," between pro- and antislavery forces.[3]

The Democratic Party's compromise position on slavery failed to prevent its regional splintering in the pivotal election of 1860, when the party fielded two presidential candidates, the regular Democrat, Senator Stephen Douglas of Illinois, and the bolting southern Democrat, Vice President John C. Breckinridge of Kentucky. Although Republican Party candidate Abraham Lincoln won only 40 percent of the popular vote, the split within the Democratic Party let him carry every northern state and sweep the Electoral College vote.

After his election through the dissolution of the old political order, Lincoln faced the cheerless task of presiding over the near dissolution of the nation itself. Many southerners refused to accept the legitimacy of a president from a party they perceived as committed to the extinction, not just the limitation, of slavery. Even before Lincoln took the oath of office on March 4, 1861, seven southern states had seceded from the union. Tensions were so high in America that president-elect Lincoln had to steal into the capital under cover of darkness. Just five weeks later, on April 12, 1861, the Civil War began with the bombardment of Fort Sumter in South Carolina.[4]

Unlike the Whigs, the Democrats withstood sectional divisions and endured to oppose Lincoln's commitment to military victory and Republican efforts to establish political and civil rights for the freed slaves after the war. Partisan conflict over racial issues in the 1860s would give Republicans a sizable advantage in northern states, create a solidly Democratic South after the demise of Republican-run Reconstruction governments, and define voter loyalties for another seventy years. Republicans emerged as the party of activist government in the late nineteenth century, whereas Democrats continued to defend limited government and states' rights, principles that party leaders invoked to oppose constitutional amendments that sought to provide federal guarantees of voting and other civil rights.

Four long and bloody years of Civil War had little effect on voting rights in Union states. Three new states entered the union from 1861 to 1865: Kansas in 1861 (just before the war), West Virginia in 1863, and Nevada in 1864. All three followed the model of a white man's republic, limiting suffrage to white males with certain modest exclusions. These votes portended a long and bitter postwar struggle to jettison the ideal of a white man's republic and secure voting rights for black Americans.[5]

In 1865, the ratification of the Thirteenth Amendment abolished slavery, but the final northern victory in the Civil War, shortly after Abraham Lincoln's assassination, left unresolved the big questions of Reconstruction: Under what terms would states be restored to the union? To what extent would the federal government provide civil rights and liberties, economic security, and suffrage to newly freed slaves?

It would remain for lesser leaders than Lincoln to decide the future course of American democracy. During his reelection campaign in 1864, Lincoln had dumped his vice president, Hannibal Hamlin, and put a Democrat, Andrew Johnson, the wartime governor of Tennessee, on his ticket in a show of national unity. In his second inaugural address, Lincoln spoke of how the great and bloody war was a divine retribution for slavery, visited on a guilty people both north and south. If the bloody war "continue until all the wealth piled by the bondsman's two hundred and fifty years of unrequited toil shall be sunk," he declared, "and until every drop of blood drawn with the lash shall be paid by another drawn with the sword, as was said three thousand years ago, so still it must be said, 'the judgments of the Lord are true and righteous altogether.'" Andrew Johnson listened but failed to comprehend the meaning of Lincoln's words.[6]

Johnson loved the union but not the black people that it had liberated from slavery. Although later in life a moderately wealthy slaveholder, Johnson had risen from the lower ranks of white society, what some at the time called "mudsills," the humble white farmers, laborers, tradesmen, and mechanics that he championed in his political campaigns. However, like John C. Calhoun, Johnson believed that race transcended class and that any white man, however humble, could look down on any black man. If blacks were given the right to vote, Johnson said in 1844, that would "place every splay-footed, bandy-shanked, hump-backed, thick-lipped, flat-nosed, woolly-headed, ebon-colored Negro in the country upon an equality with the poor white man."[7]

Johnson was an odd man in his time. He was an apostate Democrat assuming the incumbency of a Republican president. He lacked allies in either party and prided himself on being an outsider untethered to a capital city that he called "12 square miles bordered by reality." By opposing efforts to reconstruct the nation and integrate newly freed slaves into American life, Johnson quickly fell afoul of a Congress controlled by Republicans with southern states still in limbo. He pardoned thousands of wealthy planters from the consequences of rebellion, including disenfranchisement, and pushed to restore southern states swiftly to the union with no controls on race relations and no federal guarantee of the right to vote. He lambasted the "Radical Congress" for giving blacks privileges "torn from white men." He proclaimed himself to be protecting America not from ex-Confederates but from radical Republicans and their black allies. At an outdoor rally, Johnson told a crowd of cheering white men that he was their Moses who would lead "the emancipation of the white man" from his slavery under postwar Reconstruction. He forced Congress to override his vetoes on legislation aimed at protecting black rights and safety in the South, and exploited his powers as president to evade and obstruct the enforcement of these laws.[8]

In a remarkable White House colloquy held in February 1866 with a delegation of prominent African Americans led by George T. Downing of Washington, DC, and the renowned Frederick Douglass, Johnson justified his continued commitment to a white man's republic and his disdain for African American suffrage. The end of slavery, Johnson said, was never a goal of the war and claimed that "Lincoln himself has pointed out" that abolition only arose "as an incident to the suppression of a great rebellion." The freeing of the slaves, he insisted, did not mandate voting rights for black people, whom he continued to exclude from America's political community. "The first great principle of government," he said, "is the right of the people to govern themselves," that is, implicitly white people. To include blacks as voters, he claimed apocalyptically, would be "to adopt a policy that I believe will end in a contest between the races, which if persisted in will result in the extermination of one or the other. God forbid that I should be engaged in such work!"[9]

After the disappointed delegates departed, Johnson reportedly disparaged in private what he called the "darkey delegation." He said, "Those damned sons of bitches thought they had me in a trap! I know that damned Douglass; he's just like any nigger, and he would sooner cut a white man's throat as not."[10]

Judging by the results of state-level referenda on black voting rights, most northern voters shared Johnson's continued support for the white man's republic. From 1865 to 1870, blacks gained voting rights through referenda only in three states: Iowa in its second referenda, and Michigan and Minnesota in their third. Black suffrage failed to win a popular majority in New York, Wisconsin, Connecticut, Ohio, Kansas, Nebraska, the Colorado Territory, Missouri, or Washington, DC.[11] Faced with such futility, African Americans pressed Congress for a constitutional amendment that would override state suffrage restrictions. "Slavery is not abolished until the black man has the ballot," Douglass said. He and his allies brushed aside objections that voting would lead down the slippery slope to social equality or even intermarriage across the races. Federal intervention to enfranchise African Americans, they argued, only guaranteed their rights as citizens and accorded no special privileges to black people. They compared themselves favorably to naturalized immigrants, who had voting rights across the nation.[12]

Despite the lack of voter support at home and misgivings about black inferiority, northern Republicans in the U.S. House and Senate eventually embraced racially neutral suffrage as a legacy of the war and emancipation. African American votes held out the only prospect for competitive Republican parties in the South, once the eleven former Confederate states rejoined the union. Congress took its first step toward guaranteeing black suffrage in late 1866 and early 1867 when it mandated black voting rights in the District of Columbia and required race-neutral suffrage for Nebraska's and Colorado's admission to the union. The Reconstruction Acts of 1867, which Congress enacted over President Johnson's veto, required black suffrage within the former Confederate states.[13]

Still, adoption of the landmark Fourteenth Amendment to the Constitution disappointed African Americans because it failed to guarantee voting rights for members of their race. The amendment gained the requisite two-thirds vote in both chambers of Congress in June 1866, before the midterm elections. Ratification remained in doubt until Congress required its approval by former Confederate states as another condition for readmission to the union.

Although it fell short of protecting black voting rights, this complex, 435-word amendment—the most prolix of all constitutional additions—still had important implications for voting and representation. Section 1 reversed the *Dred Scott* decision that had declared slaves property, and granted national and state citizenship—in most states a prerequisite for voting—to "all persons born or naturalized in the United States." Birthright citizenship in the United States applied not just to former slaves but also to the American-born children of immigrants, whether their parents were documented or not. It reinforced this citizenship status by declaring that "no state shall make or enforce any law which shall abridge the privileges or immunities of citizens of the United States," with the phrase "privileges and immunities" borrowed from the original Constitution. This provision enshrined in the Constitution the guarantee of African American citizenship that Congress had established by law in the Civil Rights Acts.

Debates in Congress indicate that members did not intend to include the right to vote among a citizen's "privileges and immunities." By a wide margin, the Joint Committee on Reconstruction rejected drafts of section 1 designed to assure political equality for citizens of color.[14] The full Senate rejected by a vote of thirty-seven to ten a similar provision, which said that "no state, in prescribing the qualifications requisite for electors therein, shall discriminate against any persons on account of color or race."[15] In presenting the proposed draft of the Fourteenth Amendment, Republican senator Jacob Howard of Michigan quoted from Bushrod Washington's 1823 opinion to explain that voting was a state-granted privilege, not an inherent natural right encompassed within the "privileges and immunities" of citizens. The Republicans still balked at mandating black suffrage nationwide and risking the wrath of the many voters in northern states hostile to black rights.[16]

Section 1 further prohibited the states from denying "to any person within its jurisdiction the equal protection of the laws." At least indirectly this clause could be construed as prohibiting any racially discriminatory voting laws. However, it was not so understood by legislators at the time, and narrow court constructions limited its application to suffrage until well into the twentieth century. In recent years, however, this clause has assumed powerful meaning by protecting voting rights from intentional or purposeful voting discrimination by states or localities. In the second decade of the twenty-first century, for example, courts struck down voter photo identification laws and congressional redistricting plans adopted by state legislatures that were deemed as intending to suppress the votes of minorities.[17]

Still, some Republican legislators in the 1860s regretted a lost opportunity to rectify an omission in the Constitution and explicitly ensure voting rights through the Fourteenth Amendment. Representative James Garfield of Ohio, later the twentieth president of the United States, issued a ringing defense of the vote, which even "if it be not indeed one of the natural rights of all men is so necessary to the protection of their natural rights as to be indispensable, and therefore equal to natural rights." Although he lamented Congress's failure to "imbed" the right to vote "in the imperishable bulwarks of the Constitution," Garfield supported the amendment as the only practical option at the time. "I am willing," he said, "when I cannot get all I wish to take what I can take.[18]

Members of the House and Senate focused less on section 1 than on sections 2 and 3 of the proposed amendment. Section 2 had potentially weighty implications for suffrage and representation. Although it did not compel the former Confederate states to enfranchise blacks, it seemed to punish racial disenfranchisement through reduced representation. Under section 2, if the right to vote is "denied to any of the male inhabitants of such state, being twenty-one years of age, and citizens of the United States, or in any way abridged, except for participation in rebellion, or other crime, the basis of representation therein shall be reduced in the proportion which the number of such male citizens shall bear to the whole number of male citizens twenty-one years of age in such state."

This provision, proponents said, would keep the white South from unduly benefiting from the elimination of the three-fifths clause of the Constitution and the full counting of former slaves for purposes of representation in Congress and the Electoral College. The far-reaching effect of section 2, said Radical Republican representative Thaddeus Stevens, co-chair of the Joint Committee on Reconstruction, "will be either to compel the States to grant universal suffrage or so to shear them of their power as to keep them forever in a hopeless minority in the national Government, both legislative and executive."[19]

Section 2, which was not limited to race but covered all forms of suffrage restriction other than sex, age, crime, and rebellion, had the potential to compel revolutionary changes in suffrage laws both in the South and across the rest of America. In principle, it would have docked the representation of states for denying the vote not just to people of color but also to paupers, the mentally ill, and those who failed to pay poll taxes or pass a literacy test. However, Congress never followed through with a mechanism for implementing this explosive section of the Fourteenth Amendment; it remains unenforced to date. The federal courts have rebuffed efforts to enforce the provision judicially, terming enforcement a "political question" outside their purview.[20]

Section 3 of the amendment punished secessionists by denying public office and voting rights for president to former U.S. government officials who had backed the southern rebellion. In 1872, under powers authorized by the amendment, Congress softened its impact by allowing nearly all secessionists, expect for several hundred former top officials, to hold public office and vote. It ultimately extended political rights to all former Confederates.

Paradoxically, while most northern states denied black people the ballot, in former Confederate states many southern blacks voted in the presidential election of 1868 under the protection of northern troops and the aegis of permissive southern state constitutions that Congress had required via the Reconstruction Acts. By this time, however, the North had lost much of its leverage over seven of the eleven rebellious states that Congress had restored to the union. Supporters of black suffrage worried that voting rights would not last in the South and had yet to take hold in the North.[21]

In January and February 1869, the lame duck session of the 40th Congress debated a Fifteenth Amendment to the Constitution proposed by the House Judiciary Committee for black voting rights. It asserted that "the right of citizens of the United States to vote shall not be denied or abridged by the United States or by any state on ac-count of race, color, or previous condition of servitude." The fate of the amendment and many alternative versions was by no means certain. Republicans dominated both chambers of Congress, but not all were radicals committed to an advanced view of black rights.

Deliberations over the proposed voting rights amendment raised large philosophical and practical questions about the vote in Amer-ica. What constitutional revision was needed to justify the sacrifices of the Civil War and secure rights for former slaves? What was the proper balance of sovereignty between the state and national gov-ernments? Should a voting rights amendment establish an affirma-tive right to vote or impose prohibitions on the states? Could a negative prohibition against race-based disenfranchisement truly protect black voting rights? If framed negatively, should an amendment transcend race and in effect mandate nearly universal male suffrage by prohibiting states from denying voting rights on the basis of religion, economics, literacy, or education? What form of an amendment would likely gain the assent of three-quarters of the states, with many skeptical of black suffrage?

In adopting the committee's version of the Fifteenth Amendment, Congress compounded the framers' mistake of passing on the oppor-tunity to transform American politics by enshrining an affirmative right to vote in the Constitution as some Republicans proposed. Con-gress failed to safeguard against the de facto disenfranchisement of African Americans through devices such as poll taxes and literacy tests. Yet these criticisms may too harshly judge the legislators of the time. If Congress had expanded the committee's draft amend-ment to mandate universal suffrage or even proposed safeguards beyond race, the amendment would likely not have passed muster with three-quarters of the states. Echoing James Garfield's com-ments on the Fourteenth Amendment, the proposal's Republican author, Representative George S. Boutwell of Massachusetts, said, "I believe that if we adhere to the proposition to protect the people of this country against distinction on account of race, color, or previous condition of slavery, we undertake all that is probably safe for us to undertake now." The bloodshed in the war vindicated only the elimination of race-based suffrage restrictions, not broader extensions of voting rights.[22]

In defense of Boutwell's draft, Republican senator William Stewart of Nevada said that "it is the only measure that will really abolish slavery" and redeem the promise of the war and the Thirteenth Amendment. With the new amendment, "we shall have peace. Until then there is no peace." Opponents countered that Republicans had at most justified intervention in the former Confederate states only, not uniformly across all states. The Republican platform of 1868, said Senator James Dixon of Connecticut, a former Republican turned Democrat, called for only protecting suffrage rights in the South, in distinction to "the loyal states," where voting qualifications would be left "to the people of those States."[23]

However, Republicans could not credibly protect the voting rights of black people only in the formerly rebellious states. Backers of the amendment pointed to a broader platform provision that applauded the "immortal Declaration of Independence as the true foundation of Democratic Government" and favored making its "principles a living reality on every inch of American soil."[24] They cited the sacrifices of war made by black Americans and the opposition of Democrats to the Reconstruction laws and amendments. Republican senator Orris F. Ferry of Connecticut evoked the image of northern black soldiers "shattered and maimed" in defense of the union and asked whether anyone could "look these scarred veterans in the face and tell them that it is doing no wrong to deprive them of all share in the government for which they have made this horrible self-sacrifice." Senator Oliver P. Morton, formerly Lincoln's "war governor" of Indiana, charged that the Democratic Party "cherished slavery while it lived, and now that slavery is dead it has taken to its embrace its odious and putrescent corpse." He said that "in defiance of that party we are about to plant in the Constitution the great principle of impartial suffrage."[25]

Republicans insisted that given white people's antipathy to African Americans across the country, principle, not politics, prompted them to protect black suffrage. "Our many struggles on behalf of the Negro," said Republican senator Henry Wilson of Massachusetts, "has cost the party with which I act a quarter of a million votes. There is not today a square mile in the United States where the advocacy of the equal rights and privileges of those colored men has not been in the past and is not now unpopular." Presciently, he added, "That the cause of the poor, wronged, and oppressed negroes has been, now is, and for some years will continue to be an unpopular cause." Nonetheless, Republicans knew that the survival of their party in a post-Reconstruction South depended on black votes, which could also help Republicans in northern states with substantial black populations.[26]

Opponents assailed the committee's amendment for intruding on the rights of the states. This controversy over state sovereignty blazed in 1869 because, unlike other emerging democracies and constitutional monarchies in the nineteenth century, America remained fixed in the eighteenth-century practice of defaulting voting qualifications to the states, rather than setting national standards. The states had retained sovereignty as "independent Republics" under a federal system of government, argued Senator Dixon. "Because the doctrine of State's rights has been carried to an extreme, and a dangerous extreme at the South, shall we go to the other extreme and say there are no State rights?" An independent republic "must necessarily control the question of suffrage in its own elections. This lies at the very foundation of all government."[27]

Senator Morton asked incredulously how anyone could claim that "after the culmination of a war that cost this nation six hundred thousand lives, that we were not a nation." He said, "The states have certain rights guaranteed to them by the Constitution," but "we have no state sovereignty," and by propagating this canard, his opponents have declared "a war on the Constitution." The antislavery veteran Republican senator Charles Sumner of Massachusetts expressed his "sense of sadness" that "after a bloody war with Slavery, and its defeat on the battle-field," we must "be compelled to meet the champions of a kindred pretension. . . . Nobody ever vindicated Slavery" through states' rights, and "now nobody can vindicate Caste, whether civil or political, the direct offspring of Slavery." He warned that "the old champions reappear, under other names," but the intent of "establishing a Caste and an Oligarchy of the skin" remained.[28]

Echoing arguments made in antebellum state constitutional conventions, Democrats and a few Republicans reached to history, common experience, science, and scripture to prove that African Americans lacked the fitness to vote. Senator James R. Doolittle of Wisconsin, the harshest Republican critic of black suffrage, proclaimed that "six thousand years and the whole history of the race" and "natural philosophy, all ethnologists, all historians" proved the "incompetency" of blacks for the vote. Any attempt to force "an amalgamation of the races [is] against nature and against the laws of God. Those who attempt to do it are warring against all history and warring against the laws of Him that made history and made the races of men." The only solution, he said, to the eternal conflict of the races was to dispatch America's former slaves to "the islands of the West Indies" where "the white race is not adapted to the climate and cannot live there."[29]

Democratic senator Garrett Davis of Kentucky expressed his view that the black "is inferior in physical condition, in mental and moral endowment, to the white race or the yellow race. Every ethnologist knows it. Every man who is acquainted with the negro practically and from experience knows it." The African American is "in a condition of brutalized, ferocious, and ignorant barbarism. That is the condition as proven by all history, and by the modern travelers in the interior of Africa." Proposing an argument that has not yet died in America today, he even claimed that slavery was a blessing for blacks in America, insisting that "they are indebted to slavery for all that they know, all their intellectual and moral elevation from the condition of the most ignorant barbarism."[30]

Senator Doolittle played on antiforeign sentiments, notably the hostility of West Coast legislators to the Chinese. If we establish equality of the races, he argued, "it may be hundreds of thousands of laboring men from China, and Japan, and the great fountain of human population in Asia, will be brought to the United States. In ten years, there may be as many Chinamen as there are white men on our western coast.... How can you contend in favor of giving this power [of political equality] to the African race if you deny it to the Chinese?"[31]

Despite this inflated rhetoric, the friends of black suffrage recognized the loophole in the committee's draft that accorded too much, not too little, discretion to the states, which could disenfranchise blacks on grounds other than their race. Legislators cited such deceptively race-neutral suffrage qualifications as freehold possessions, poll taxes, and literacy tests that would in practice exclude most colored citizens. Even Representative Boutwell conceded this flaw:

> MR. WALKER: I desire to inquire whether there is anything in this bill that will prevent any of the States from requiring of voters a property or educational qualification?
>
> MR. BOUTWELL: I do not suppose there is.
>
> MR. WALKER: Then the State may, under this bill require such a qualification?
>
> MR. BOUTWELL: I suppose they may.[32]

As always in America, debates about race also transcended race. Some of those who had backed the war and equal rights for freed slaves now pushed the boundaries of "universal suffrage" beyond old limits. They swept aside concerns of the founding fathers about imposing suffrage rules on the states and enfranchising the dependent and the foolhardy. They would for the first time imbed an affirmative right to vote in the Constitution, either for all citizens or in the predominant view for all male citizens, with perhaps limitations only for age, residence, mental competence, and crime.

Republican representative Samuel McKee of Kentucky recognized the failure of the Constitution and its amendments to guarantee any American the right to vote. He said that the voting rights amendment under debate "should be affirmative and not negative, and by that means we will have the right of the citizen to the elective franchise clearly defined, and behind which no state can go." Republican senator Willard Warner of Alabama agreed that "the question before us is not one of negro suffrage. It is the question of suffrage itself. . . . The sovereign power, belongs to the people, not to a portion of the people, not to the learned, not to the ignorant, not to the rich, not to the poor, not to the great, not to the weak, but to all the people." Still, the idea of affirmative voting rights even for men only lay beyond the consensus of the time, and lawmakers rejected all such drafts of the amendment in preference for a negative prohibition detailing what states could not do.[33]

The Senate ultimately backed a negatively framed but still sweeping amendment that Senator Henry Wilson proposed. This self-made former shoemaker and early abolitionist, known as the "Natick Cobbler," proposed to go beyond race and prohibit states from denying or abridging voting rights "on account of nativity, property, education, or religious belief." Republican senator George Henry Williams of Oregon said in support that if "the white people of a state should be disposed to having the power to disfranchise the colored citizens of that State, could they not put the legislation accomplishing that purpose upon some other ground than upon race or color?" For example, a state might "provide that no person should vote or hold office who did not have a freehold qualification. Apparently, that would operate equally upon all citizens, but it might practically operate to exclude nine-tenths of the colored people from the right of suffrage."[34]

Republican senator John Sherman of Ohio added, "We ought to deny to states the right to discriminate between citizens on account of anything except age, residence, and sex. In all other respects citizens should have an equal right to vote." He asked, "Why should you protect only and seek to extend only the right of suffrage to the colored race?" On February 9, 1869, the Senate voted down Wilson's amendment nineteen to twenty-four with twenty-three not voting; then on the same day it reversed itself to pass the amendment by an equally narrow vote of thirty-one to twenty-seven with eight not voting. The House rejected the Wilson amendment on February 15, but five days later adopted a more limited version that added "nativity, property, and creed" to the prohibited grounds for denying the vote. The Senate declined to adopt this amendment. Finally, after this odd and inconclusive back and forth, the House on February 25 and the Senate a day later took the path of least resistance and adopted by the requisite two-thirds vote Boutwell's original proposal with no substantive changes.[35]

Republicans in Congress broadly agreed that the inherited color of a man's skin should not bar him from voting and that black suffrage redeemed the sacrifices of war. However, most still believed that acquired abilities, especially literacy, remained legitimate qualifications for voting that could not be assailed by waving the bloody shirt of war. A literacy restriction "is no wrong done to the voter," said Republican senator James W. Patterson of New Hampshire, "for it simply protects the purity and integrity of the Government under which all his rights are secured." To deny suffrage "on account of race or color or want of property is doing violence to the civilization of our age, and insults Christianity, but to protect and guard it against floods of ignorant barbarism is simply to preserve the jewel of liberty."[36]

Agreement by two-thirds of both chambers of Congress did not end the battle for the Fifteenth Amendment, which wended its tortuous way for a year through the states. Ironically, the obstacle that advocates of black suffrage faced in obtaining ratification by the necessary twenty-eight of thirty-seven states was not the South. The seven former Confederate states already admitted to the union had been compelled by Congress to establish voting rights for African Americans and were largely controlled by Republican officeholders. All but Tennessee ratified the amendment, and Congress made ratification a precondition for admission of the remaining four erstwhile Confederate states.

The problem was in the North and border regions, where Senator Wilson had predicted the cause of African Americans would languish. Early in the ratification struggle an editorial in the *New York Times* warned that "in Indiana as well as in Ohio, New York, and perhaps some others of the larger and more powerful old states the sentiment of the people is opposed to the amendment." Republicans won ratification in barely enough northern and border states through support from newly elected president Ulysses S. Grant and by uniting in a fragile party coalition. Republican leaders whipped together radicals committed to racial justice with moderates who recognized the amendment's limited scope. Republican leaders sought to deprive Democrats of a wedge issue by putting black suffrage behind them. They also hoped to benefit from an influx of black voters.[37]

Still, ratification was precarious. The New York legislature ratified the amendment on April 14, 1869; rescinded its ratification on January 5, 1870; and ratified it again on March 30, 1870, after the amendment had already won approval nationwide. The amendment languished for more than two months in the Indiana legislature and passed only after a failed effort by Democratic legislators to prevent a voting quorum by resigning their seats. The northern states of California, Delaware, New Jersey, and Oregon and the border states of Kentucky, Maryland, and Tennessee first rejected and then post-facto ratified the amendment. Except for New Jersey, these states ratified the amendment only in the twentieth century, with Tennessee delaying until 1997.[38]

African American activists embraced even a flawed Fifteenth Amendment as the only practical option at the time and a landmark achievement for black freedom. The *Christian Recorder,* an influential black newspaper, hailed the amendment as the "crowning one" among all constitutional amendments, saying that at last "the nation has proclaimed political freedom."[39] African Americans expected the federal government to enforce the amendment, but they could not have been expected to foresee "the return to power of the Democrats in the southern states and the U.S. House of Representatives, the Republican retreat from Reconstruction, and the resurgence of Jim Crow, with its inventive and unjust measures designed to deny blacks the vote on grounds other than race, color, or previous condition of servitude."[40]

A riot in 1874 foreshadowed the end of Reconstruction and the beginning of black disenfranchisement in the South. In the majority-black Barbour County, Alabama, black voters had been electing local Republican officials since the early years of Reconstruction. Then on election day in 1874, a mob of armed whites stormed the county polling place near the town of Eufaula. The men fired their weapons at the black voters, killing at least seven, wounding some seventy more, and driving many others from the polls. The election supervisor Elias M. Keils heard the white men shouting, "kill him, damn him, kill him." But they misfired and killed Keils's sixteen-year-old son, who was standing at his side. The murderers escaped conviction by silencing witnesses, and few blacks dared to vote again in Barbour County, defaulting control of its government to white Democrats. In that same election, Democrats regained control of the Alabama state government when they added a Democratic governor to their majority in the state legislature.[41]

The effective end of Reconstruction came just a year later with the failure of an election bill in 1875 designed to protect black political rights. Republicans in the 1870s could not prevent the unraveling of Reconstruction and the "redemption" of southern states by Democrats committed to the extinction of black voting. The harsh depression that began in 1873 and endured until 1876 made it difficult for Reconstruction administrations in the states to govern effectively. In every southern state by the mid-1870s, white supremacists predominated in numbers of voters and economic power. White vigilante groups like those that perpetrated the Eufaula massacre terrorized and intimidated black voters and their white allies, assuring so-called Redeemer control of elections. The self-styled "Redeemers" were the white Democrats who sought to overthrow the Reconstruction governments and suppress the black vote.

Public opinion in the North lacked the will for continued intervention in southern affairs on behalf of blacks. In the early 1870s, Congress passed a series of enforcement acts designed to curb violence perpetrated by the Ku Klux Klan. Despite the suppression of the Klan, white violence and intimidation of black voters continued while enforcement waned. In early 1875, after Republicans had lost control of the U.S. House and Democrats were surging into power in southern states, Ulysses Grant and the lame-duck Republican Congress worked to enact a new election bill that would protect voters from violence and coercion.[42]

Members of Congress knew that they stood at a turning point in their nation's democracy. The great question before them was whether the federal government would redeem the promise of the Fifteenth Amendment by acting to assure access to the vote across racial lines. Opponents of the proposed election law turned reality on its head and blamed Republican Reconstruction and unruly blacks for racial turmoil in the South. They said that racial harmony and the rule of law would prevail under the benevolent and watchful eyes of white people fit to vote and hold public office. Democrats are "more sincere in caring for the real interests of the lowly and colored," claimed Democratic representative Samuel Cox of New York, "than those who use them to their hurt and to the distress, impoverishment, and dishonor of southern people and State governments." Democratic representative John K. Luttrell of California charged that "the whole scheme of securing Federal interference was gotten up by the leaders of the Republican Party in manufacturing outrages that did not exist, or where they did exist, it was only in the camps of the Republicans." An editorial in the *Atlanta Constitution* blamed the Eufaula massacre on violence not by whites but by black Republicans against black Democrats. "The affair in Eufaula and other occurrences," the editorial said, "have taught the negro that he can no longer safely resort to intimidation. The whites have resolved to protect the colored democratic voters."[43]

Opponents challenged any robust construction of the Reconstruction amendments, arguing that they did not authorize federal interference in the affairs of sovereign states. "These amendments, if rightly construed, as they have been by the United States Supreme Court, are only intended to deny powers to the States and not to grant or enlarge the Federal powers," said Representative Cox. "They furnish no authority for such bills as the present one."[44] Cox was referring to the Court's 1873 decision in the *Slaughter-House Cases,* which narrowly construed the Fourteenth Amendment as protecting only a very few rights of national citizenship and none of the broader rights of state citizenship. Even some allegedly sympathetic voices insisted that racial equality in the South could not be achieved by the force of law. "Let the general government refrain from all further legislation or interference on behalf of the negro as such," said the editors of the *Chicago Tribune.* "A taste, a sentiment, a feeling, an instinct, a prejudice, these pass the bounds of all legislation, and the attempt to rectify or regulate these by law serves only to irritate opposition."[45]

Proponents of the election bill pointed to the findings of federal investigations and the petitions of black southerners as proof that white supremacists intended to wipe out black suffrage by all available means, including terror. "We cannot shut our ears against the testimony that comes up from the South," said Republican representative Lyman Tremain of New York. "We cannot shut our ears against the appeals made by Representatives on this floor of four millions of emancipated freedmen asking us for protection of lives, property, and their political rights." The election bill was necessary, he insisted, to protect "the rights of the people, the preservation of law and order, and the protection of the ballot-box and its purity. It is to secure to men who have been emancipated and to their political friends the right to enjoy the elective franchise."[46]

Supporters claimed that section 2 of the Fifteenth Amendment, which granted Congress the "power to enforce this article by appropriate legislation," and the constitutional authority to regulate elections provided ample grounds for federal protection of voting rights. The adoption of the Reconstruction amendments, said Republican representative Joseph Gurney Cannon of Illinois, "implies necessarily the duty to do all things by legislation or otherwise necessary to enforce the same," including "appropriate legislation." Republican representative Charles G. Williams of Wisconsin asked, "Will we protect these men [African Americans] or will we leave them to be overborne and butchered? . . . If the sacred right of choice through the ballot-box may be ruthlessly trampled underfoot, what vestige of free government remains in this country that is worth preserving?" The House eventually passed the election bill but too late in the lame-duck session for a Senate vote.[47]

Reconstruction died with this failed effort to enforce the Fifteenth Amendment. "The colored men, who compose the body of the Republican Party, have been made 'peaceful' by the shot-gun of the raiding white leaguer, the bowie-knife of the southern desperado or the whip-lash of the ex-slave master," said Representative Charles Hays of Alabama, a former Confederate soldier turned Republican. If this continues, "Our doom is sealed.... What we do want is a fair chance to express ourselves at the ballot-box for the men of our choice."[48]

A year later, the U.S. Supreme Court further undercut efforts to protect black voters and their allies from white vigilantes. The Court ruled that only the states, not the federal government, could protect private citizens from denying the rights of other citizens. It said that the Fourteenth Amendment "adds nothing to the rights of one citizen as against another.... The duty of protecting all its citizens in the enjoyment of an equality of rights was originally assumed by the States, and it still remains there." White terrorists could thus intimidate black voters without fear of retribution from federal authorities and with the knowledge that white supremacist governments supported efforts to suppress the black vote by any necessary means.[49]

The disputed presidential election of 1876 symbolically ended the already doomed Reconstruction of the South. Although Democratic candidate Samuel J. Tilden, the governor of New York, won the popular vote against Republican governor Rutherford B. Hayes of Ohio, the outcome of the election turned on disputed Electoral College votes in Florida, South Carolina, and Louisiana. With the Constitution silent on the resolution of such disputes, Congress improvised by forming a special electoral commission that ultimately consisted of eight Republicans and seven Democrats. The commission voted along party lines to award all disputed electoral votes to Hayes, which gave him a one-vote victory in the Electoral College.

Democrats derided the president-elect as "Rutherfraud B. Hayes" or "Old 8 to 7," and claimed that Republicans had stolen the election by altering returns and stacking the electoral commission. Hayes's backers countered that they had thwarted a Democratic plot to steal the election by suppressing the black vote. A similar scenario would unfold 124 years later in the disputed election of 2000, after the partisan affiliation of blacks and whites had flipped in the South. This time, Democrats accused Republicans of suppressing black votes in the disputed state of Florida and benefiting from a partisan-driven Supreme Court decision that, again by a one-vote margin, prematurely stopped the recount in that state.

Upon assuming the presidency, Hayes withdrew federal troops from the South and ended efforts to protect black voting rights. By the 1880s, white Democrats in every southern state firmly controlled their U.S. House and Senate seats, their state legislatures, and their governorships, creating a solidly Democratic South. Politics in the late nineteenth century revolved around a regional division of power growing out of Civil War alignments and a national stale-mate between Republicans, who dominated the North, and Demo-crats, who controlled the redeemed South. The stalled politics of America's late nineteenth-century "Gilded Age" resulted in a seesaw series of close elections: with neither party gaining a firm hold on government or the electorate, the White House changed hands in every contest of the era except 1880, when Republican James A. Gar-field won by fewer than ten thousand votes. During this period, the difference between Democratic and Republican percentages of the national popular vote for president averaged only about 1 percent; differences in the vote between the North and South averaged about 25 percent.[50]

Freed from the shackles of federal enforcement of the Fifteenth Amendment, white supremacists in the South attempted to wipe out the gains of Reconstruction for black voters, through repeated acts of terror and economic coercion, claiming the need to protect peace-able whites from bloodthirsty blacks. As the New York Times observed in 1880, "Singularly enough, the propensity to riot, incendiarism, and murder which was charged against the negroes never alarmed the 'defenseless white people,' except during political campaigns and on the eve of important elections. Still more singularly, every 'negro uprising' on record in the South resulted in the butchery of from five to one hundred and fifty of the 'bloodthirsty blacks,' while not one hair of the head of any of the 'peaceable and defenseless whites' was ever harmed."[51]

Although black voting declined after redemption, it is a testament to the courage and determination of African Americans in the South that many continued to vote through the Gilded Age despite the very real threat of ongoing state-tolerated or -sponsored violence and intimidation by the white majority. Some African Americans continued to win election to state legislatures, and three African Americans served in Congress in 1890.

By the 1890s, however, white southerners had devised new means for disenfranchising black people through revisions of their state constitutions and election laws. Between 1890 and 1910, every former Confederate state purposely disenfranchised black voters through measures that appeared racially neutral on their face but were anything but in practice. The states adopted stringent residency re- quirements, poll taxes, white-only primaries, and literacy tests with discretion for interpretation by white registrars. Some states adopted "Grandfather Clauses" that exempted individuals from literacy tests whose ancestors had previously voted, essentially ruling out black people. Even earlier, the southern states began adopting and ex- panding laws disenfranchising felons and ex-felons, with appli- cable crimes often tailored to African American offenders, such as larceny and "moral turpitude." These suffrage restrictions not only burdened African Americans but to a lesser extent poor whites too, whom southern elites feared could join insurgent movements that challenged the dominant Democratic Party in their states.[52]

As advocates of black suffrage had warned, court rulings immu- nized these laws from the Fifteenth Amendment because they did not on their face explicitly target voters "on account of race." In 1870, a federal district court judge in Oregon ruled that the Fifteenth

Amendment "does not take away the power of the several states to deny the right of citizens of the United States to vote on any other account than those mentioned therein." The judge said that "any State may deny the right of suffrage to citizens of the United States on account of age, sex, place of birth, vocation, want of property or intelligence, neglect of civic duties, crime, &c."[53]

The U.S. Supreme Court further affirmed that "the Fifteenth Amendment does not confer the right of suffrage upon any one." Rather, it only protects individuals from explicit "discrimination in the exercise of the elective franchise on account of race, color, or previous condition of servitude." Laws that applied equally to all races, like poll taxes and literacy tests, regardless of their de facto discriminatory effects, fell outside the amendment's scope, as legislators recognized when they enacted the amendment in 1869.[54]

In 1884, the Alabama Supreme Court upheld the catchall provision of the Alabama constitution that disenfranchised people convicted of specified crimes, including petit and grand larceny, and any "crime punishable by imprisonment in the penitentiary." The court ruled that "political suffrage is not an absolute or natural right, but is a privilege conventionally conferred upon the citizen by the sovereignty. There can be practically no such thing as universal suffrage." Rather, the right to vote "is one conferred by constitutions and statutes, and is the subject of exclusive regulation by the State, limited only by the provisions of the Fifteenth Amendment to the Federal Constitution." Thus, the state had the prerogative to disenfranchise criminals through a race-neutral provision "to preserve the purity of the ballot box, which is the only sure foundation of republican liberty."[55]

Under the leadership of President Benjamin Harrison, Republicans in Congress made another push in 1890–1891 to defend the voting rights of African Americans. Legislation introduced by Representative Henry Cabot Lodge and Senator George Frisbee Hoar, both of Massachusetts, would have authorized federal district courts, upon petition from a small number of constituents, to appoint federal supervisors of registration and voting in congressional elections—anticipating a provision of the landmark Voting Rights Act of 1965. "There is absolutely nothing in this bill except provisions to secure the greatest amount of publicity in regard to elections and to protect the ballot-box by making sure the punishment of those who commit crimes against the suffrage," wrote Representative Lodge. Although the House passed the bill, proponents could not overcome a Senate filibuster led by Democrats and joined by a few Republicans. This was the first major legislation to date supported by the president and a majority of both Houses to be killed in the Senate by filibuster. With the failure of the Lodge Bill, Congress would not enact new voting rights legislation until the 1950s.[56]

The historian J. Morgan Kousser found that although white terror had reduced black suffrage in elections before the adoption of legal disenfranchisement in the 1890s, it declined much more steeply thereafter, accompanied by a less dramatic decline in turnout by poor whites. Another study by Kent Redding and David R. James finds that black presidential turnout in the eleven former Confederate states tumbled from an average of 61 percent in 1880 to but 2 percent in 1912.[57]

African Americans in the South did not passively concede this dismissal from southern politics. Black activists united to press for the restoration of the vote and other civil rights and liberties. In 1890, T. Thomas Fortune, editor of the preeminent black newspaper *New York Age,* rallied other prominent African Americans to form the National Afro-American League, America's first national civil rights organization. The league dissolved in 1893, but its leaders reestablished it in 1898 as the National Afro-American Council, which brought men and women together in the struggle for black rights. "We are not to be eliminated," declared the council's first statement. "Suffrage is a federal guarantee and not a privilege to be conferred or withheld by the States." The council too proved to be short-lived and collapsed in 1907.[58]

These path-breaking civil rights groups and other organizations such as the Niagara Movement, founded in 1905, sought to sponsor litigation, move public opinion, educate voters, and lobby and petition political leaders. Although the groups suffered from meager funding, internal dissension, neglect by the Republican Party, and a lack of mass support, they established a protest tradition that culminated in the founding of the interracial National Association for the Advancement of Colored People (NAACP) in 1909 and its strategy of battling discrimination in the courts.

The NAACP's most prominent African American cofounder, the intellectual and writer W. E. B. Du Bois, had said in his 1903 book of essays, *The Souls of Black Folk,* that "Negroes must insist continually, in season and out of season, that voting is necessary to modern manhood." Du Bois and the NAACP dissented from the approach taken by Booker T. Washington, founder of the Tuskegee Institute, who advocated for black progress through entrepreneurship and education instead of directly challenging legal segregation and disenfranchisement. The NAACP's 1911 charter listed among its goals "impartial suffrage" for black people.[59]

The disenfranchisement of southern blacks had profound implications for policy and politics in the South and across the United States. It established southern and border states as an essentially one-party system dominated by the nearly all-white Democratic Party. Southern blacks' lack of the vote or leverage within the Democratic Party left them incapacitated to stop or even slow down the far-reaching imposition of the Jim Crow racial caste system of discrimination across education, religion, transportation, employment, law enforcement, and access to public facilities and accommodations. White southern Democrats came to dominate seniority-based committee assignments in Congress, with their tenure uninterrupted by competition from the minority Republicans in their states. The nonenforcement of section 2 of the Fourteenth Amendment also meant that the white Democratic South would benefit from the counting of the disenfranchised black population for congressional seats and membership in the Electoral College.

Meanwhile, in the opening decade of the twentieth century, both in the United States and internationally, there remained the question of whether the political community of voters included women. At the time that Congress passed the Fifteenth Amendment to prohibit voting discrimination against blacks, America's political leaders had never seriously considered suffrage for women, creating a breach between the struggles for racial and gender rights. Women went on to pursue the achievement of suffrage independently through movements of their own.

· 4 ·

VOTES FOR WOMEN

Women, we might as well be dogs baying the moon as
petitioners without the right to vote!

—SUSAN B. ANTHONY, 1895

To protest the Fifteenth Amendment's omission of voting rights
for women, Susan B. Anthony of New York State voted in the
presidential election of 1872, defying the state constitution that
limited the ballot to male citizens. Officials arrested, prosecuted,
and convicted Anthony of casting a ballot "without having a lawful
right to vote." The presiding judge fined her one hundred dollars—a
considerable sum at the time—but she refused to pay, and the government never collected. Anthony used what she called this unjust trampling by men upon "my natural rights, my civil rights, my
political rights" to bolster her case for women's suffrage.[1]

Women voted in the early days of the republic in the single state
of New Jersey. The suffrage provision of the New Jersey constitution of 1776 made no mention of sex but authorized voting by "all
inhabitants" who met age, property, and residence requirements.
Through election laws passed in 1773 and 1783, the state seemed to
back off women's voting by referring to voters as "he." Then in 1790, a
new law for seven counties referred to voters as "he or she." Seven

years later, in 1797, yet another law for the full state again labeled voters as "he or she," making New Jersey the only American state to authorize voting by women. The state's property requirements, however, denied the ballot to married women who lacked control over property under the laws of the time. Only unmarried women or widows who controlled property could vote. An editorial in the *Washington Federalist* praised the unique New Jersey system: "The ladies of New Jersey are very handsome and very federal; and they have a privilege which none of their sisters in other states enjoy. By the constitution of New Jersey, the unmarried women and the widows of that state, who are of full age and are worth $133 clear estate, have a right to vote in all elections."[2]

That privilege was rescinded, however, in 1807, when New Jersey fell in line with other states. It added a tax-paying option to its property requirement for voting but disenfranchised both women and African Americans. Historians have puzzled over New Jersey's exceptionalism in granting women voting rights. Perhaps lawmakers believed that property requirements blocked all but a few women from voting. More predictable was the elimination of female suffrage. Women had purportedly backed the Federalist Party, and their Democratic-Republican opponents controlled New Jersey's government in 1807. Opponents of women's suffrage typically claimed that women lacked the independence and strength of mind and body to cast a responsible vote. Yet, they also pointed to the special moral virtues of women that sustained the home and nurtured the future citizens of the republic. Participation in the nasty world of politics, the opposition said, would only corrupt women and weaken the American home and family.[3]

Opponents of women's and black suffrage raised the specter of voter fraud, claiming that white men had exploited dependent women and ignorant blacks to cast illegal votes. An anonymous opinion writer in the *Trenton Federalist* praised the legislature for ending "what has made our elections disagreeable, contentious, and corrupt; all Females and Negroes being now deprived of a vote, who, not being eligible to nor much acquainted with the affairs of government, need not any longer be made use of to answer a party purpose, and this restriction I am persuaded is entirely agreeable to the generality of women." Several decades later, in 1884, a historian of New Jersey, William A. Shaw, asserted without evidence that "women vied with the men, and in some instances surpassed them, in illegal voting."[4]

The commentator in the *Trenton Federalist* correctly predicted that women would little protest their exclusion from the ballot. Still, women across the land managed to influence politics, not as decision-makers but as petitioners. To apply the virtues of the home to reforming society, women formed voluntary groups that pressed for temperance, prison reform, and economic rights for married women. American women became mainstays of the abolition movement, eventually gaining full membership in the American Anti-Slavery Society, but were excluded from full participation in the World Anti-Slavery Convention held in London in 1840. The European delegates still clung to the traditional view that women should not take part in political activity of any kind.[5]

Philanthropic engagement by women led to agitation for suffrage rights. In 1846, two years before the widely acknowledged emergence of a women's movement at the Seneca Falls Convention of 1848, six women from Jefferson County petitioned the New York Constitutional Convention for the vote. The women insisted on their right to consent in governing, no less than men. Their petition said that women's "equal, and civil and political rights with men" involved "no new right but only . . . those . . . which have ungenerously been withheld from them."[6] The all-male delegates were quick to dismiss the women's concerns. They pointed to the now-universal disenfranchisement of women and minors across the nation as proof that voting was not an inherent right of citizenship. "If suffrage were a natural right," said delegate John Kennedy, "women and children were among your electors."[7]

In 1848, Lucretia Mott and Elizabeth Cady Stanton, two anti-slavery activists, frustrated by their second-class status in the World Anti-Slavery Convention, banded together to organize America's first women's rights convention. An estimated two hundred or more women and some forty men, including the prominent black abolitionist Frederick Douglass, gathered at Stanton's farm near Seneca Falls, in upstate New York. The convention's "Declaration of Sentiments," signed by one hundred of the participants, proclaimed, "We hold these truths to be self-evident: that all men and women are created equal." It charged that "the history of mankind is a history of repeated injuries and usurpations on the part of man toward woman, having in direct object the establishment of an absolute tyranny over her."[8]

The convention passed a dozen resolutions, all unanimously except for women's suffrage rights, which some delegates thought too controversial. Only an eloquent plea by Douglass, the convention's only African American, carried the majority for voting rights. He said, "In this denial of the right to participate in government, not merely the degradation of woman and the perpetuation of a great injustice happens, but the maiming and repudiation of one-half of the moral and intellectual power of the government of the world."[9]

Although the Seneca Falls Convention did not lead directly to enduring women's rights organizations or immediate change, it would take on symbolic importance for suffragists and inspire women and some men to gather at local and national conventions from 1850 to 1860, before the Civil War intervened. The conventions promoted women's suffrage, economic equality between the sexes, reform of marriage and divorce laws, and opportunities for women's education and employment. Yet white and black activists had already begun to diverge in their backing for gender and racial equality. No black women attended the national women's conventions held in 1859 and 1860.[10]

Within the states, women continued to petition constitutional conventions for the vote. When Ohio held a second convention in 1850, several hundred women signed petitions for suffrage rights, and one delegate, the perhaps aptly named Norton Strange Townshend, spoke up in support. "Woman has by nature," he said, "rights as numerous and as dear as man.... She is man's equal in intelligence and virtue, and is therefore as well qualified as man to share in the responsibilities of government; and I can see no justice in making her a subject of government rather than a party to it." So minimal was the sentiment for women's suffrage in the convention hall that no delegate bothered to rise in response. The convention then rejected by a vote of seventy-two to seven an amendment to remove the word "male" from the constitution's voting qualifications.[11]

At the Massachusetts constitutional convention in 1853, Abigail May Alcott, mother of famed author Louisa May Alcott, petitioned the male delegates to grant equal suffrage rights to women. "On every principle of natural justice, as well as by the nature of our institutions," she wrote, a woman "is as fully entitled as man to vote, and to be eligible to office." Another petitioner, Abby Hills Price, challenged the conventional assumption that politics would corrupt women. She observed, should women "yield a natural right, and be placed in an inferior position, because those who have assumed power over her have become corrupt? Perhaps she can govern herself better."[12]

The petitions gained no traction in the convention, a result that Price had accurately prophesied: "But alas! It will, I fear, be weary years before ere so much is granted." In 1869, the Massachusetts house voted against granting women suffrage rights, 133 to 68. In 1879, Massachusetts granted women the right to vote in school committee elections, but the commonwealth would do nothing more until after ratification of the Nineteenth Amendment in 1920.[13]

Controversy arose in Kansas during its founding Wyandotte Convention in 1859, not only over slavery but also over voting rights for women. Clarina Howard Nichols of the Moneka Women's Rights Association lectured across the state for women's rights and presented enough petition signatures to win the chance to speak before the convention's suffrage committee—a signal accomplishment for a woman at the time. Although delegates rejected women's suffrage, they moved ahead of other states in adopting property and child custody rights for married women and gender equality in "the formation and regulation of schools."[14]

After the Civil War, politically engaged women believed that their moment for equal suffrage had arrived with the egalitarian impulse of Reconstruction for voting rights across racial lines. If former slaves could vote, they reasoned, why not women as well? But postwar male reformers opposed the coupling of black's and women's rights. Even Republicans sympathetic to women's suffrage feared that support for such a radical proposition as female voting would doom the goal of rights for the freedmen, an essential vindication of the war. Wendell Phillips, president of the American Anti-Slavery Society and a mainstay of the prewar women's movement, said in his 1865 keynote speech, "As Abraham Lincoln said, 'One war at a time,' so I say one question at a time. This hour belongs to the Negro."[15]

Elizabeth Cady Stanton challenged Phillips's proclamation of the "Negro hour" in a letter to the *National Anti-Slavery Standard*. Without abandoning the ideal of universal voting rights across racial and gender lines, she pivoted to arguing for the superior qualifications of white women as compared to black men. She questioned why egalitarian reformers would elevate black men "far above the educated women of the country." She asked whether women should "stand aside and see 'Sambo' walk into the kingdom first?" Although Stanton would vacillate between arguments from principle for universal suffrage and expediency for women, her pejorative contrast between black men and white women opened the predominantly white northern women's movement to continuing charges of racism and complicated any potential alliance with African Americans.[16]

Phillips struck back, likewise arguing from expediency, not principle, that "we cannot agree that the enfranchisement of women and the enfranchisement of the blacks stand on the same ground, or are entitled to equal effort at this moment." He continued, "Mrs. Stanton must see" that there is a good chance for Congress to adopt suffrage for black men but no chance "for an amendment to the Constitution which should include women."[17] Radical Republican leader Senator Ben Wade of Ohio, who upheld women's suffrage in theory, agreed. "I know that the time will come" for women's voting, Wade said, "not to-day, but the time is approaching."[18] Senator Wade could hardly have imagined at the time of his comments just how slow that approach would be; the guaranteeing of votes for women would not come until forty-two years after his death in 1878.

The dispute between Phillips and the women leaders became so bitter that he withheld from them funds that had been available for prewar female activists. Lacking other sources of funding, the women had few resources to pursue their campaign for suffrage.[19]

Philosophical and pragmatic objections to women's suffrage guided decision-making in Congress on the Reconstruction amendments that reshaped America's democracy. During debates over the Fourteenth Amendment, Susan B. Anthony implored Republicans to "hold the party to a logical consistency that shall give every responsible citizen in every State equal right to the ballot" and heed a petition for women's suffrage that notable women leaders, including Stanton, Anthony, and Lucy Stone, had signed.[20] Stone was the first Massachusetts woman to earn a college degree. She became a leading abolitionist and women's rights organizer, and among suffrage leaders she was the most steadfast supporter of votes for black men. Four months later, in May 1866, suffrage advocates united in the American Equal Rights Association, dedicated to a "second Revolution" that would secure "equal Rights to all American citizens, especially the right of suffrage, irrespective of race, color, or sex."[21]

This effort to link voting rights for women and African Americans failed. Section 2 of the Fourteenth Amendment penalized states for disenfranchisement only of "male inhabitants," inserting for the first time the word "male" into the Constitution. In 1867, the Equal Rights Association petitioned a New York constitutional convention both to enfranchise women and abolish the burdensome property qualifications for black men. The women organized meetings across the state and secured twenty thousand petition signatures.

Yet another former ally, newspaper editor and later the 1872 Democratic presidential candidate, Horace Greeley, turned against the suffragists. He chaired the New York convention's suffrage committee, which approved the removal of property requirements for black voters but rejected demands for women's suffrage. Greeley echoed the pragmatism that had limited the scope of Fifteenth Amendment protections for black voting. He said, "We shall have very hard work to ratify any Constitution that enfranchises the blacks. Had we extended the suffrage to women we should have been voted down by hundreds of thousands. It seems but fair to add that female suffrage seems to me to involve the overthrow of the family relation as it has hitherto existed." Stanton and Anthony lamented, "This campaign cost us the friendship of Horace Greeley and the support of the New York Tribune, heretofore our most powerful and faithful allies."[22]

Also, in 1867, referenda for women's and black suffrage failed in the relatively favorable state of Kansas. This was the first state referendum on women's suffrage and led to recriminations by activists for women's and black suffrage, each of whom blamed the other for their Kansas defeats. The losses splintered the women's movement between leaders who wanted to remain loyal to the Republican Party and those who would abandon a party that seemingly had forsaken their cause.

The women's suffrage movement endured additional dispiriting setbacks two years later in 1869. Legislation to grant women the right to vote in the District of Columbia died that year in Congress, and in the debates over the Fifteenth Amendment male advocates of women's suffrage deferred to the practicalities of the moment. Republican senator Willard Warner of Alabama said, "I would have [women] share with us all the powers, the duties, and the responsibilities of government.... But I know that woman's suffrage is not now attainable, and I would not as a practical legislator, jeopardize the good which is attainable by linking with it that which is impossible."[23]

Without forsaking her commitment to women's suffrage, Stone supported the Fifteenth Amendment and the Republican Party, but Stanton and Anthony refused to back any amendment that excluded voting rights for women. Again arguing from expediency, not principle, Stanton widened her invidious comparison between women and unfit men to include immigrants along with blacks: "American women of wealth, education, virtue and refinement, if you do not wish the lower orders of Chinese, Africans, Germans and Irish, with their low ideas of womanhood to make laws for you and your daughters ... awake to the danger of your present position, and demand that woman, too, shall be represented in the government!"[24]

In a departure from the prior rhetorical emphasis on the common humanity of all peoples, male and female, Stanton sought to turn on its head the ideology of separate spheres for men and women by extolling the unique and valuable contribution that women in distinction to men could make to politics. "With the black man you have no new force in government—it is manhood still," she said. "But with the enfranchisement of women you have a new and essential element of life and power." An 1869 suffrage convention argued that the "extension of suffrage to woman is essential to the public safety and to the establishment and permanence of free institutions," because, "as woman, in private life, in the partnership of marriage, is now the conservator of private morals, so woman in public life, in the partnership of a republican State ... will become the conservator of public morals."[25]

In the wake of disputes over the failures in Kansas and Congress, suffragists fragmented into competing organizations in 1869 to replace the irreparably fractured American Equal Rights Association. Breaking from the Republican Party and the movement for black rights, Stanton and Anthony formed the National Woman Suffrage Association (NWSA), which fought for women's rights beyond suffrage and maintained its independence from mainstream party politics. It eschewed male participation and sought to win suffrage nationally through a constitutional amendment. Lucy Stone and Julia Ward Howe formed the American Woman Suffrage Association (AWSA). It allied with the Republican Party and continued to back voting rights for African Americans. It actively sought male participation, limited its focus to the vote, and worked for women's suffrage rights in the states.[26]

The NWSA opposed ratification of the Fifteenth Amendment because of its singular focus on race. In June 1869, during the ratification struggle, the group passed a resolution authored by Anthony that declared, "*We repudiate* the Fifteenth Amendment, because by its passage in Congress the Republican Party proposed to substitute an *aristocracy of race*" that excluded women. "We know that what was apparently *meant* to protect the oppressed and help them on in life really aims at the 'most odious distinction ever proposed since nations had an existence.'"[27]

During a more than two-decade period of dueling women's rights organizations, only the state of Wyoming authorized suffrage for women. As a territory in 1869, Wyoming had become the first state or territory since New Jersey to establish women's suffrage, which carried over into its statehood in 1890. Otherwise, only Utah and Washington Territories established voting for women. Thus, through 1890, women had gained voting rights in just a few, lightly populated western jurisdictions. These newly settled areas needed women settlers and lacked an established male elite. Wyoming, for example, had just 9,118 settlers enumerated in the census of 1870, with men outnumbering women by about 4 to 1.[28]

In response to their lack of political success, suffragists pursued what became known as the "New Departure," arguing that the Constitution already guaranteed women's suffrage, albeit indirectly. In 1872, election officials in Missouri barred Virginia Minor, an American-born citizen, from voting because the state constitution restricted the vote to men. On behalf of his wife, attorney Francis Minor filed suit in state court alleging that Missouri's prohibition of female voting had violated the Fourteenth Amendment's provision that "no State shall make or enforce any law which shall abridge the privileges or immunities of citizens of the United States." Minor argued that because the fundamental right to vote was among these privileges and immunities, no state could deny suffrage to women citizens. The case reached the U.S. Supreme Court in 1874. Consistent with their narrow reading of the Reconstruction amendments and Bushrod Washington's restrictive ruling on the original Constitution's "privileges and immunities" clause, the justices unanimously rejected Minor's plea.

The Court found that the "privileges and immunities" clause did not substitute for the lack of a right to vote in the Constitution. The decision held that "the Constitution has not added the right of suffrage to the privileges and immunities of citizenship as they existed at the time it was adopted." It continued, "It cannot for a moment be doubted that if it had been intended to make all citizens of the United States voters, the framers of the Constitution would not have left it to implication" but "would have been expressly declared." The decision added that "for nearly ninety years the people have acted upon the idea that the Constitution, when it conferred citizenship, did not necessarily confer the right of suffrage." Thus, citizenship was not coterminous with suffrage, which was not a natural right. Each state had to decide, subject to limitations in the Fifteenth Amendment, which of its citizens were to be included within its political community of voters and officeholders. This decision ratified the long-standing practice in the United States of severing voting rights from citizenship, making some citizens more equal than others in choosing the representatives who governed their states and nation.[29]

In another disappointment for suffragists, their victories in the territories of Utah and Washington soon faded away. In 1887, through the Edmunds-Tucker Act, which restricted polygamy and other Mormon practices in Utah, Congress abolished acts of the territorial legislature, including votes for women. In Washington, the territorial supreme court struck down the women's suffrage law on the thin technicality that its title did not fully express the subject of the legislation. After the legislature reinstated women's suffrage in 1888, a territorial court again nullified the statute, holding that in the act establishing the territory, Congress intended the term "citizen" to mean only male citizens. The all-male constitutional convention for statehood that met the following year sidestepped the question of women's suffrage by authorizing a popular referendum. The male voters resoundingly rejected voting rights for women by a vote of 35,527 to 16,613. Utah reestablished women's suffrage when it achieved statehood in 1896, but women did not regain voting rights in Washington until 1910, twenty-one years after it joined the union.[30]

In the busy year of 1887, the U.S. Senate finally voted on a constitutional amendment on women's suffrage that California Republican senator Aaron A. Sargent had introduced in 1878. This was the first time that either chamber of Congress held a clean vote on women's suffrage not entangled with race. Yet arguments and sentiments had changed little since women first began petitioning for voting rights in the 1840s.

Republican senator Joseph N. Dolph of Oregon made the case for suffrage, saying that sex is the "least defensible" of all distinctions. Women "have sufficient capacity to vote intelligently." They "have ruled kingdoms" and "commanded armies. They have excelled in statecraft, they have shone in literature, and, rising superior to their environments and breaking the shackles with which custom and tyranny have bound them, they have stood side by side with men in the fields of the arts and the sciences." If suffrage were an issue of capacity, then let any requirement "be applied to women and to men alike."[31]

Democratic senator George G. Vest of Missouri countered that women's suffrage would add emotionally driven and corruptible voters to the electorate and upset the divinely ordained sex roles that preserved social order and harmony. If American government, he said, "shall ever be destroyed it will be by injudicious, immature, or corrupt suffrage." He warned his colleagues, "If we are to tear down all the blessed traditions, if we are to desolate our homes and firesides, if we are to unsex our mothers and wives and sisters and turn our blessed temples of domestic peace into ward political-assembly rooms, pass this joint [suffrage] resolution." Vest dismissed the precedent of women voting in western territories as irrelevant to national policy. "It is not upon the plains of the sparsely-settled Territories of the West that woman suffrage can be tested," he said. "Wyoming Territory! Washington Territory! Where are their large cities? Where are the localities in those Territories where the strain upon popular government must come?" He concluded by presenting a letter from an anti-suffrage woman, Clara T. Leonard of Massachusetts, who wrote, "One sex lives in public, in constant conflict with the world; the other sex must live chiefly in private and domestic life, or the race will be without homes and gradually die out."[32]

Most senators sided with Vest, not the pro-suffrage Dolph. Only sixteen senators voted for the suffrage amendment; thirty-four voted against, with twenty-six not voting, including fourteen senators paired yes and no. An editorial in the *New York Times* said that women should not despair over a vote that "at the present stage of the agitation is not a desperate showing by any means."[33] Elizabeth Boynton Harbert, president of the Illinois Equal Suffrage Association, said more cynically, "If the Senate will not allow women to vote," the women should all "emigrate to Wyoming and leave them in their lonely bachelorhood occupying the Senate." Lillie Devereaux Blake, representing women's suffrage groups in New York, commented, "When you see a little skinny, wizened-up man you may know he will oppose women, because he thinks if he gives women a chance they will overshadow him."[34]

Three years later, in 1890, women's rights advocates healed their split and merged their competing groups into the single National American Woman Suffrage Association (NAWSA). The new association, with Stanton as symbolic president and Anthony as de facto leader, had about seven thousand members and focused on suffrage as the fount of all other rights. Still, unity did not portend victory for suffrage. Just eight months after NAWSA's founding, voters in South Dakota crushed a women's suffrage referendum by a two-to-one margin. During the next twenty years, only a few lightly populated western states adopted women's suffrage, and Congress held no additional votes on a constitutional amendment.

Especially bitter for suffragists was their failure to gain momentum for the cause by winning voting rights in the nation's most populous state, New York, at its constitutional convention of 1894. Suffragists failed to get women seated at the convention, which the legislature called for the express purpose of curbing political corruption, and faced opposition from both men and women arrayed into anti-suffrage leagues across the state. Stanton wrote that "one of the most interesting features of the present agitation for woman suffrage is the organization of the women who are opposed to the demand." She noted the irony that these women, like the suffragists, were engaging in politics by drafting and signing petitions, canvassing door to door, lobbying convention delegates, holding meetings, and making public speeches. She hoped, largely in vain, that the anti-suffrage women would come to learn of "the helpless condition of women in this Republic," and that "universal suffrage is the first truth and only basis of a genuine republic."[35]

Even before the New York convention convened, the *Baltimore Sun* noted that women's suffrage had suffered a "Waterloo defeat" when the New York suffrage committee voted unanimously against enfranchising women, and sixteen to one against holding a popular referendum on women's suffrage.[36] The committee warned that women's participation in politics would introduce "political dispute and party work in family life, which will develop and increase estrangement, separations, infidelity, and divorce, and the consequent destruction of the home." The full convention voted ninety-seven to fifty-eight in support of the committee's recommendation against a suffrage referendum.[37]

Jean Brooks Greenleaf of Rochester, president of the New York State Woman Suffrage Association, tried to snatch a small victory from the jaws of this defeat saying, "Our vote of 58 was a great improvement on the 19 votes which we had in the convention of 1867." But the *New York Times* observed that after the convention, suffrage leaders "could not be found" in New York City, and "the equal-suffrage headquarters at 10 East Fourteenth Street were closed and no one could be found there to speak upon the matter."[38]

Prospects for women's voting rights picked up in 1911, when voters in California approved a suffrage amendment to the state constitution by a bare majority of 50.7 percent. In the nation's twelfth most populous and most rapidly growing state, suffragists, who ranged from socialists to wealthy socialites, overcame widespread opposition from an anti-suffrage movement financed by the liquor industry, which conflated suffrage with Prohibition, given women's preeminence in the anti-alcohol movement. According to one historian of the California campaign, "suffragists engaged in precinct canvassing and organization, soapboxing, automobile campaigns, staging pageants and parades, coordinating press work, producing literature, advertising and slogans for mass distribution, and holding public outdoor meetings and rallies." The women "pushed the battle for woman suffrage 'out of the parlors and into the streets.'"[39]

As before, the women mixed arguments from stances of principle and prejudice. Enfranchised white women, they said, would offset the state's dangerous minority vote. California suffragist Maud Younger warned that "women of California are in daily competition with Asiatics. . . . In different parts of the country the vote has been given to negroes, Indians, Hindoos, and other Asiatics. Have they greater interests to protect than have the American women? Are they more capable of citizenship?"[40] Not until 1926 did California repeal the provision of its 1879 constitution prohibiting any "native of China" from voting.[41]

In California and elsewhere, women tapped into the burgeoning movement for progressive reform. The loose coalition of reformers known as progressives believed that government should serve the public interest by steering a middle course between unchecked corporate greed and socialist remedies. The progressives backed economic reforms such as corporate regulation, progressive income taxes, restrictions on child labor, and public ownership of utilities. They demanded moral reforms such as Prohibition and immigration restriction.

Politically, progressive reformers sought both to purify politics and, most critically for disenfranchised women, to expand the impact of the vote. Beginning with South Dakota in 1898, some twenty-two states by 1918 had adopted the initiative, which authorized the electorate by petition to vote directly on legislation and in some jurisdictions on constitutional amendments. Most states also adopted the referendum, which authorized either the legislature or a petition of the electorate to place enacted legislation on the ballot to be voted up or down at a subsequent election.[42] Some states adopted the recall of public officials as well—a form of direct democracy that the first Congress had rejected for federal officeholders in the late eighteenth century. After the path-breaking recall of Mayor Hiram Gill of Seattle in 1911, reform advocate H. S. Gilbertson said, "No elected public officer in this country was ever before relieved of his authority and emoluments without a legal process, before the end of a definite term. But now, public office subject to the recall becomes a public trust." Not coincidentally, the successful recall of Mayor Gill marked the first election for Washington women after the achievement of statewide suffrage in 1910.[43]

For the first time in the early twentieth century, voters gained the opportunity to supersede nominations by closed party conventions and caucuses, and instead elect nominees for public offices. By the 1920s, nearly every state had required direct primaries for at least some positions. For presidential nominations, a 1928 compilation found that seventeen states had binding primaries for selecting delegates to national nominating conventions. The rules for conducting primaries varied markedly among the states. Closed primaries authorized voting only by those voters who registered with a party or pledged their loyalty to party nominees. Open primaries posed no restrictions on a voter's choice of primaries, whereas partially open primaries authorized this option only for unaffiliated voters.[44]

The direct primary diminished party discipline in elections, encouraged candidates to form their own political organizations, and expanded candidate-centered voting by the electorate. It contributed to increased ticket-splitting by voters and to the consolidation of support by candidates in areas of strength in the primaries. Even for presidential nominations, with party organizations still appointing most national convention delegates, primaries became important for selecting delegates and testing the popular appeal of competing candidates.[45]

Through the Seventeenth Amendment to the Constitution, ratified in 1913, reformers succeeded in gaining the election of U.S. senators directly by popular vote, supplanting 125 years of selection by state legislatures. Echoing the arguments made for the Twelfth

Amendment more than a century earlier, proponents of direct elections said that the reform would bring government closer to the people and avoid the corruption of vote-trading and -buying in legislatures. The report of a U.S. House Committee endorsing the Seventeenth Amendment noted "the instances of bribery and corruption which have taken place in the legislatures of the different States in the last 25 years, and which could not have occurred had popular elections prevailed." Popular elections would rest the choice of senators "securely upon the judgment and wisdom of the individual voter" and avoid the legislative deadlocks that at times deprived states of full representation in the Senate.[46]

In this newly receptive climate, suffragists deemphasized arguments from pure egalitarian principle and instead turned around the claim that politics would corrupt women. They insisted instead that virtuous women would uncorrupt politics and bolster reform. These liberal, maternalist women shared conservative assumptions about sex differences but sought to raise socially conscious children and apply principles of the household economy to political and social reform as engaged voters. During the California campaign, suffragist leader Mary Swift said that votes for women "will be a benefit to society," and that women voters "knew what justice means for humanity, [have] minds and hearts big and kind enough to be a great help in forming the policy of our government, of any government." An advertisement called "I Can Handle Both," published in the *San Francisco Call,* stressed that women were capable of shouldering responsibilities as mothers and as voters who would bring the morality of the home into politics. The Equal Suffrage League of Baltimore pointed to the adoption in Denver, Colorado, of progressive reforms, proclaiming, "The women voters led!"[47]

Women in the anti-suffrage movement drew on similar maternalist ideology for opposite effect. These conservatives, who formed the backbone of the National Association Opposed to Woman Suffrage, urged women not to repudiate custom and tradition by barging into politics but instead to maintain their motherly responsibilities of rearing courageous sons and domesticated daughters. Women's suffrage, they argued, would confuse sex roles, weaken families, and instigate a destructive "war of the sexes." An "Iowa Woman," writing in the preeminent anti-suffragist newspaper *The Woman Patriot*, said women "cannot take on the affairs of government and political life, without neglecting or abandoning vital duties that they are foreordained to accomplish. They are the Mothers of all mankind, and the home makers for the world. No man can fill that place. . . . The Mother and the Home is the making of the man."[48]

In the South, both white and black women fought for suffrage, although largely independent of one another as black suffragists forged their own organizations. White suffragists in the South had varying views on race. Some mirrored the anti-Asian arguments made by suffragists in California, claiming that votes for women would strengthen white supremacy by countering the black vote. A 1906 statement by the Conference of Southern Women Suffragists said, "We ask for the ballot as a solution of the race problem. There are over 600,000 more white women in the southern states than all the negro men and women combined."[49] Anti-suffrage women and their male allies responded that any expansion of voting rights threatened the South's restriction of black voting. A statement by Virginia anti-suffragists noted, "Every argument for sexual equality in politics is, and must be, an argument also for racial equality. . . . If the white woman is entitled to vote because she bears, has borne, or might have borne children, the Negro woman is entitled to the same right for the same reason."[50]

Particularly troubling for southern suffragists was the fear that a constitutional amendment for women's suffrage would validate federal intervention in southern race relations. Laura Clay of Kentucky, a leader of NAWSA and a nationally prominent advocate of state-level suffrage for women—although with a literacy requirement to restrict the black vote—opposed what became known as the Susan B. Anthony Women's Suffrage Amendment to the U.S. Constitution. Clay premised her arguments on states' rights, not race, decrying the proposed amendment as the "Anthony Force Bill," the pejorative that southerners applied to bills that would enforce voting rights for African Americans. In mustering opposition to a federal amendment, she wrote to western members of Congress who, she said, also had a "race problem." She warned that adoption of the Anthony Amendment might threaten anti-Asian laws. At the 1919 NAWSA convention, she was one of only three delegates, all from the South, voting against a resolution supporting the Anthony Amendment. *The Woman Patriot* gleefully cited her opposition. After Congress adopted the amendment in 1919, Clay opposed its ratification by the states.[51]

In the North, the lobbying and grassroots campaign for suffrage drew its vitality from the same ethnic, racial, and religious forces that backed Prohibition. Suffragist Florence Kelley told Congress in 1906, "I have rarely heard a ringing suffrage speech that did not refer to the 'ignorant and degraded' men or 'ignorant immigrants' as our masters."[52] In twenty-seven suffrage and prohibition referenda held in northern states from 1906 to 1918, white, mostly evangelical Protestants overwhelmingly lined up behind both Prohibition and suffrage, irrespective of their economic standing, literacy, occupation, or urban or rural residence.[53]

By 1911, the suffrage movement had advanced in numbers and in the sophistication of its political organization. California alone boasted more than fifty local women's suffrage groups active at the time of the referendum. Independent organizations such as the Women's Christian Temperance Union, the Women's Trade Union League, the American Federation of Labor, and the National Federation of Women's Clubs came to back the previously isolated suffrage movement. A Mrs. John O'Connor, president of the Chicago Women's Club, explained in 1912 that the concerns of club women had expanded from "the home and its needs" to "all matters pertaining to the growth and welfare of the city and its people. These awakened interests and the work which they demanded made these women feel the need of the ballot."[54]

Since the formation of NAWSA, women had become more educated and more likely to work outside the home. In most states, married women had gained control of their own earnings, the right to own property, and expanded access to divorce and child custody. It became difficult to argue that a woman who had graduated from college and taught high school was unfit to vote in elections. Yet women still faced the daunting task of convincing men who held sway over politics to enfranchise women in their states. Politically, women needed to forge strategic alliances with political parties seeking to gain favor with existing constituents or from newly empowered women voters. In Colorado, the suffragists allied with the insurgent Populist Party; in California, with the Republican Party.

The victory in California led to winning suffrage campaigns in a half-dozen other states during the next three years, including presidential and municipal voting rights in Illinois, the first suffrage state east of the Mississippi River. Still, the state-by-state campaign promised only limited success and protracted struggle. Opponents defeated suffrage referenda in the northeastern states of Massachusetts, New Jersey, New York, and Pennsylvania in 1915, and suffragists saw little hope of victory in southern and border states. So, when Carrie Chapman Catt became president of NAWSA for the second time in 1915, women regrouped and changed their strategy.

Under Catt's leadership, the 1916 NAWSA convention adopted her "Winning Plan," which substituted national strategy for disjoined efforts in the states. The movement would push for state-level suffrage only to advance prospects for the Anthony Amendment; the more states they won for suffrage, the more members of Congress they could muster for their cause. NAWSA would focus on winning one state in the South, one full suffrage state in the Midwest, and one populous state in the East. The women would peacefully and respectfully but persistently lobby members of Congress and speak before congressional committees. They would work to elect representatives and senators who backed suffrage for women. Like Stanton earlier, Catt also played on racist sentiments, decrying that ignorant blacks could vote but not educated, refined women.[55]

In 1916, both Republicans and Democrats had endorsed suffrage for women in their party platforms, but only by the states. However, Republican presidential nominee Charles Evans Hughes called for adoption of the Anthony Amendment, putting pressure on his opponent, President Woodrow Wilson, who felt constrained by opposition from the solidly Democratic South. Although Wilson's victories in 1912 and 1916 appeared to set back the suffragists' cause, they achieved their most notable success in 1917 by winning voting rights for women in a New York State referendum. Given the recent defeat in New York and other large states such as Pennsylvania and New Jersey, another loss in New York might well have stalled the suffrage movement indefinitely.

In a stunning turn of events, the suffrage amendment, which had lost 42 to 58 percent in 1915, prevailed 54 to 46 percent just two years later. In 1915, no borough of New York City and only seven small counties out of fifty-seven upstate backed suffrage. Yet in 1917, every borough and a majority of upstate counties voted for suffrage. The city's vote for suffrage exceeded 60 percent. As compared to the earlier tally, the results of the 1917 referendum reflected the expansion of the traditional suffrage base. A dynamic coalition of labor, socialists, and New York City's Tammany Hall Democratic Party machine led to newly won support from immigrant and African American voters. To illustrate, the majority-foreign-born assembly districts in Manhattan according to the U.S. censuses of 1910 and 1920 voted 57 percent against suffrage in 1915 but 69 percent for suffrage in 1917.[56]

Despite this victory, by 1918, only about a third of the states had granted women full suffrage. It took America's entry into World War I and a combination of political action and protest to rescue the An-

thony Amendment from legislative limbo. In 1916, militant suffragists, led by Alice Paul and Lucy Burns, defected from NAWSA to form
the independent National Woman's Party (NWP), backed by a few
wealthy women donors. Unlike the liberal maternalists of NAWSA,
the feminists of the NWP rejected sex differences and advocated the
complete social and legal equality of men and women. The small,
lily-white, but ideologically consistent NWP pushed for suffrage
nationally through a constitutional amendment and rejected
NAWSA's conventional political tactics in favor of nonviolent civil
disobedience to humiliate President Wilson and his Democratic
Party for their failure to back the Anthony Amendment.[57]

After America's entry into World War I, many women joined the
industrial labor force to replace men serving in the military, proving
that women could shoulder traditionally male responsibilities.
NAWSA organizers, who backed the war effort, made the case to
Congress, the president, and the public that women's patriotic
wartime service merited voting rights. NAWSA leaders also drew on
support from members of Congress in states that had already enfranchised women and campaigned for new members favorable
to women's voting rights. Catt told a Senate committee in January 1918
that her intention was "to replace our opponents with men who will
give us what we want."[58]

Leaders of the NWP exploited the contradiction between a war "to
make the world safe for democracy," in Wilson's words, and the denial of democratic rights to women at home. In 1917, NWP protesters
picketed the gates of the White House, braved arrest, organized
hunger strikes in prison, and suffered forced feedings, all to drama-
tize their cause and shame the Wilson administration.

Police arrested and jailed NWP leader Lucy Burns three times for
illegal protests. To make an example of the unrepentant Burns,
prison guards at the District of Columbia Occoquan Jail in Virginia
handcuffed her above her head, looped the handcuffs to the top of
her cell door, and left her to suffer for an entire night. To show their

solidarity with Burns, suffragists from an adjacent cell voluntarily held their hands above their heads and stood fixed in that position. These were not women hardened to prison life but society ladies accustomed to deference and respect. After enduring this "Night of Terror," Burns and other women prisoners refused to eat. Worried about having to account for dead women prisoners, the warden ordered Burns transferred to another jail where a doctor forced a feeding tube through her nostril. Burns recalled, "It hurts nose and throat very much and makes nose bleed freely. Tube drawn out covered in blood."[59]

In a remarkable speech delivered on the floor of the Senate on September 30, 1918, the president openly endorsed the Anthony Amendment. It had passed the House but remained stalled in the Senate. The mistreatment of protesting women appalled Wilson, who looked ahead to a difficult midterm election, with Republicans leading his party on the suffrage question. In the longer term he wanted not to antagonize but to win over for his party the many women who were already voting and the millions more who would eventually vote. Wilson tied suffrage to the war effort, saying, "We have made partners of the women in this war.... Shall we admit them only to a partnership of suffering and sacrifice and toil and not to a partnership of privilege and right?" Never had a president intervened so directly and dramatically in congressional deliberations. Still, the suffrage amendment stalled in the Senate, with unanimous opposition from southern Democrats in defiance of their president. But prospects for the Anthony Amendment improved when Republicans regained control of both houses of Congress in the midterm elections of 1918.[60]

In February 1919, the Anthony Amendment fell short in the Senate by one vote of the needed two-thirds majority. Three months later, the House once more voted in favor, with many votes to spare. Then on June 4, 1919, the Senate finally passed the amendment, by a vote of fifty-six to twenty-five, after southern Democrats abandoned a filibuster. Senate Republicans voted thirty-six to eight for the amendment and Democrats twenty to seventeen. Twelve senators were paired for and against, and three senators did not vote. Senators representing southern and border states cast all but two of the Democratic no votes.[61]

Leaders of both the NWP and NAWSA hailed the Senate vote and looked ahead to ratification by the states. "There is no doubt of immediate ratification," Paul said. "We enter upon this final stage of the campaign joyously, knowing that women will be enfranchised citizens of this great democracy within a year." Catt echoed this optimistic view of ratification. She looked ahead to "the end of a long and arduous struggle, needlessly darkened and embittered by the stubbornness of a few at the expense of the many."[62]

The women of the NWP have become icons of popular culture, memorialized in the acclaimed docudrama *Iron-Jawed Angels* starring double Oscar-winner Hillary Swank as Alice Paul and Golden Globe–nominee Frances O'Connor as Lucy Burns. But Congress would not have passed the Susan B. Anthony Amendment in 1919 without the meticulous political work of NAWSA or the dynamics of party competition. It was NAWSA that led the campaign for state ratification, by no means a sure bet given widespread opposition in the South and border regions.

After thirty-five states ratified the amendment by March 22, 1920, it stagnated one state short of the three-quarters needed for ratification. Only one southern state (Texas) and only four border states had voted for ratification. The suffragists' last chance for ratification in time for women to vote in the presidential election of 1920 came in mid-August in the former Confederate state of Tennessee.

Suffragists and anti-suffragists from across the nation converged on Tennessee to make their case to legislators, and President Wilson intervened to urge ratification of the suffrage amendment. Then, in one of the most extraordinary reversals of fortune in American history, twenty-four-year-old representative Harry F. Burn, who had

been elected two years earlier as the youngest member of the legislature, switched his ratification vote from no to yes. Apparently, Burn
had heeded the plea of his mother, Phoebe Ensminger Burn, who
wrote to him saying, "Hurrah, and vote for suffrage! Don't keep
them in doubt. . . . Be a good boy and help Mrs. Catt put the 'rat' in
ratification."[63]

Although the Nineteenth Amendment still faced court challenges
on the ratification process, suffrage leaders hailed the victory in Tennessee, which in Paul's words, "completes the political democracy
of America and enfranchises half the people of a great nation."[64] Catt
said, "Now that it is all over the feeling of 'ceaselessness' is probably
the sensation uppermost with us all." But "women cannot stop."
NAWSA, she said, now had "a new purpose of making the vote register for an improved citizenship. The women of the national are
already lined up under a new name, The League of Women Voters."
Legal challenges to the amendment's ratification failed, and for the
first time in U.S. history, women across America who otherwise
qualified for the ballot could vote in 1920.[65]

The NWP maintained its identity after 1920, with its feminists
following a divergent path from that of the liberal maternalists in
the League of Women Voters. The NWP pressed for absolute legal
equality between men and women, whereas the league supported
special protective legislation for women. In 1923, the NWP introduced into Congress an Equal Rights Amendment (ERA), which
both conservatives and the League of Women Voters opposed.

The league, which devoted itself to backing "good government"
reforms, declined to help women become decision-makers through
efforts to recruit, train, and fund women to compete for public
office. President Catt said in 1921, we should be "working primarily
for the education of women in citizenship and the removal of
illiteracy. . . . We should drop the committee on Election Laws and
Methods." The league also backed Americanization programs
and Prohibition, social welfare and consumer rights, jury service

and equal property laws for women, and disarmament. Their work reinforced efforts to "Americanize" immigrant women and instill the virtues of respectable mothering through training in citizenship, English, morals, nutrition, cleanliness, and household budgeting.[66] In her 1924 farewell address, President Maud Wood Park of the League of Women Voters said, "The fact that we should like to see more women of the right sort in public office, does not imply, however, that the League as an organization ought to start electioneering for women." Rather, the league would "help women make the best of themselves as voters" and advance "the human welfare side of government, in which women are particularly fit to be useful."[67]

League women cut themselves off from alliances with racial or ethnic minorities and worked to maintain their Victorian respectability. We "did not want to form a woman's political party, and we are not 'feminists' in the embittered sense so often given to the word," said Illinois chapter president Mary Morrison.[68] Despite its heritage as an advocacy group for excluded women, the league backed stricter naturalization laws and educational requirements for voting. League women upheld the traditional ideal of voting as an individual decision by educated citizens, not as the mobilization of any organized bloc of voters, including women.[69]

Like the NWP, the league did nothing to combat the disenfranchisement of black women in the South. Its lily-white "Negro Problems Committee" ignored the boulder of racial disenfranchisement and bypassed the South when it opted to kick away a few pebbles through "ballot marking classes for colored women" in "the states where the colored vote is a material and accepted fact." Two years later, the chair of the committee, renamed "Inter-Racial Problems," said that she had "no report of meetings held or conferences conducted," but that she had worked to block civil rights laws, because racial issues are "best considered outside of legislative halls."[70] In the 1920s, turnout campaigns led by the League of Women Voters and other groups such as the National Association of

Manufacturers, the American Legion, and the National Civic Federation did not target typical nonvoters but focused on white, native, middle-class Americans as ideal voters, shutting out allegedly less-qualified "problem" voters.[71]

The league's post-suffrage decision-making greatly diminished its impact on the next goal for women: translating voting opportunities into the holding of political office and participation in the policy-making of Congress and state and local governments. In effect, the league became a nonpartisan advocate of what it viewed as good government measures, not an advocacy group for the enhanced role of women in the political process. During the 1920s, only one woman served in the U.S. Senate (for twenty-four hours to fill a vacancy), and no more than five served in any session of the House. Two women won governor's positions, one to replace her term-limited husband. In 1930, women held fewer than 2 percent of state legislative seats. A 1924 editorial in *Youth's Home Companion* rhetorically asked, "What would have happened if women had aspired to office? . . . It is noteworthy that they have not done that and the number who have displayed any marked political ambition is small—smaller than most persons anticipated when suffrage was conferred on them."[72]

In the United States in 2017, nearly a hundred years after suffrage, women held about 20 percent of seats in the U.S. House of Representatives and Senate, comparable to the worldwide average of representation for women in national legislatures. Unlike the United States, however, other nations have affirmatively addressed the issue of women's underrepresentation in elected office. About half of the world's nations have adopted legislative or voluntary quotas for women's parliamentary representation. Quotas apply both to candidates for office and to legislative seats reserved for women. In the 2012 elections, women won 24 percent of national legislative seats in nations with legislated quotas, 22 percent in nations with voluntary quotas, and 12 percent in nations with no quotas.[73]

As of 2017, the United States has not elected a woman president. Other nations have done somewhat better: among 146 nations studied by the World Economic Forum, 38 percent have had a woman head of state serve for one year or more. However, in 2017, only fifteen women (10%) were serving as heads of state worldwide. Thus, women of the United States, as in other democratic nations across the globe, have yet to attain full participation in political life.[74]

THE ABSENT VOTER

If the people *fail to vote,* a government will be developed
which is *not* their government.... The whole system of
American Government rests on the ballot box. *Unless*
citizens perform their duties there, such a system of
government is doomed to failure.[1]

—PRESIDENT CALVIN COOLIDGE, 1926

In the presidential election of 1888, W. W. Dudley, the treasurer of
the Republican National Committee, distributed a circular on
committee stationery that instructed party operatives in Indiana to
"divide the floaters [bought voters] into blocks of five, and put a
trusted man with necessary funds in charge," being sure to "make
him responsible that none get away and all vote our ticket."[1]

Although Dudley denied having engaged in the actual buying of
votes, this incident fueled the perception of an American politics af-
flicted by an epidemic of voter fraud. The *New York Evening Post* typically claimed in 1888, "There are thousands of voters in both parties
who wait in every important election to be paid, even to vote the
ticket of their choice. A high Democratic authority has placed this
number at one-third in each party in many sections of the state."[2]
Despite anecdotal rather than systematic and analytical evidence of
voter fraud, reformers still perceived that vote-buying and other il-

licit practices corrupted elections in late nineteenth-century America and compelled respectable citizens to impose countermeasures.

Reformers of the time found it difficult to reconcile their conflicting instincts to simultaneously expand and purify the vote. The democratic impulse led to the innovations of primary elections, the direct election of senators, votes for women, and the initiative, referendum, and recall. Yet voter turnout declined gradually in the early twentieth century, partly through the countervailing effect of reforms to protect the vote from fraud and abuse: government-issued secret ballots, personal registration requirements, literacy tests, poll taxes, at-large elections, and the disenfranchisement of aliens, felons, and Native Americans.

The problem of nonvoting was both institutional and individual as Americans turned away from politics in the early twentieth century. The irony is that Americans reduced their voting at a time of expanding government influence over people's lives, and growing affluence and educational attainment, characteristics typically associated with heightened participation in politics.

Revisions in the system of voting and elections fit within a broad context of social and political change. Highly ethnocentric notions of nation and citizenship had guided the shaping of the franchise since the early republic. These concerns expanded in the late nineteenth and early twentieth centuries when millions of largely Catholic and Jewish "new immigrants" from eastern and southern Europe poured into America's cities, became voters, and found themselves recruited by allegedly corrupt urban political machines. The same impulses that drove white, Protestant Americans to back Prohibition, immigration restriction, and campaigns against drugs, smut, and vice motivated efforts to purify politics.

These anti-pluralists sometimes joined forces on political reform with secular activists dismayed by the baleful influence of a new force in American life: the wealthy corporations, whose money greased the gears of party organizations. A *New York Times* editorial in 1905 denounced "the trusts and great corporations" that "continue without hindrance to furnish large sums of money for the use of party committees in electoral campaigns.... If the trusts can elect Congresses and Presidents with their money they can at pleasure guide the activities that make the laws or palsy the arm that enforces them."[3]

Until the 1880s, Americans routinely voted openly by voice or, more frequently over time, through preprinted party ballots, emblazoned with distinctive different colors, that they handed to election judges at the polling place. Elections turned less on persuading doubtful voters and more on drilling and mobilizing partisans who could be readily identified by the color of their ballots. Brawling, rioting, and even murderous violence marred voting at the nineteenth-century polls. "In the middle decades of the nineteenth century, eighty-nine Americans were killed at the polls during Election Day riots," writes historian Jill Lepore. On one gruesome election day in Louisville, Kentucky, in 1855, at a time of anti-immigrant agitation, rioters massacred twenty-two voters, mostly Irish and German immigrants.[4]

For reformers, party ballots and the mass mobilization of voters confirmed George Washington's warnings about divisive party politics that subverted the historic ideal of autonomous voters devoted to the common good. Reformers further objected to party ballots as a ripe source of fraud. Unscrupulous politicians could buy voters and verify that they stayed bought by casting the right color ballot. American opinion-makers had fretted about electoral fraud from the earliest days of the republic. But the campaign against fraud became urgent as the growing, heavily immigrant working class mobilized by political machines seemed to validate Alexander Hamilton's warning about the rise of purchasable votes in America's cities. As historian Melvin G. Holli explained, "The inferior moral fiber of foreign-born and lower-class electorates and their representatives, and the dereliction of upper classes was one of the most pervasive themes in the early Conferences for Good City Government" sponsored by the National Municipal League.[5]

Reformers pushed for states to adopt the secret ballot pioneered in Australia in 1856. An 1889 editorial in the *New York Times* said that the abolition of open party ballots would "make it impossible" for fraudsters "to tell whether any single vote that they had purchased or contracted for was really given in the way they wish," and "would completely destroy their base but profitable occupation."[6] The so-called Australian ballot, printed by governments, not parties, would include the names of candidates. It would be distributed only at the polling place and cast in private by each voter. By 1908, thirty-nine of forty-six states and the territory of Arizona had adopted some form of the secret ballot.[7]

The candidate-centered ballot printed a heading for each office, with candidates listed below, typically identified by party. The party-centered ballot printed a separate heading for each party, with its candidates for each office listed below. It most closely resembled the ballots previously distributed by the parties. It facilitated straight-party voting, making it difficult for voters to split their tickets. However, some states with candidate-centered ballots also included an option to vote for a straight-party ticket. By 1908, most states were using either the party-centered ballot or the candidate-centered ballot with a straight-ticket option. Although states eventually moved away from party-centered ballots, some still maintained a form of straight-ticket voting, and third parties still had to struggle for ballot spots.[8]

Reformers alone could not have engineered the turn to the Australian ballot without backing from Democrats in the South and primarily Republicans in the North. The nation's major parties had something to gain from a transition to official, secret ballots that spared them the expense of printing and distributing their own ballots and made elections more orderly and predictable than before. The Australian ballot system, moreover, placed a disparate burden on third parties and independent candidates or rogue party factions who lacked guaranteed places on official ballots. Each state adopted its own ballot access laws, which the two major parties, with their guaranteed places on the ballot, typically wrote to impose burdensome deadlines and signature requirements for third parties and independent candidates. In the presidential election of 1936, for example, five nationally organized parties—Socialist, Communist, Union, Prohibition, and Socialist-Labor—failed to get ballot positions in nine to twenty-nine states.[9]

The adoption of the Australian ballot eventually dampened the turnout of voters, a generally welcome result for purity crusaders who hoped to staunch what one reformer called "the admitted evils of 'tramp' suffrage" and a "licensed mobocracy." The secret ballot weakened the incentive for partisans to pay or compel voters to back the party ticket, when operatives could not readily verify voter compliance. Yet the secret ballot may have prompted a new kind of corruption, paying likely opposition voters not to vote, which operatives could easily verify, thereby eliminating the problem of bought voters who would not stay bought. James K. McGuire, the chairman of the Executive Committee of the New York State Democratic Party, charged in 1900 that "under the new ballot law you cannot tell how a man votes when he goes into the booth, but if he stays at home you know that you have got the worth of your money." Paying potential voters to stay home, he said, "is the only sure way to buy votes."[10]

Likely much more important than voter payoffs, whose numbers remain speculative, the lack of verification reduced the incentives for parties to mobilize the ranks of purportedly loyal voters. It made voting a dull, industrial-style event, even as other forms of diversion emerged in the early twentieth century through the radio, movies, amusement parks, and automobiles. Studies by political scientists have found that by the early twentieth century, secret ballot laws had an independent effect of depressing voter turnout, notably in states that relied on candidate-centered ballots. The lack of voter participation fell most heavily among lower-income voters, which was precisely as the reformers had intended.[11]

The adoption of secret ballots led to the innovation of voting machines to make voting more private and secure than before. Cloaked behind a curtain, voters would pull the levers for their favored candidates, with gears in the machine preventing multiple voting. The counter inside the machine tallied the votes. By 1929, about half the states had adopted machine voting.[12]

To curb further the undue influence of urban political party machines and establish a bipartisan, scientific basis for government, many municipalities adopted a city manager form of government under which an elected council appoints a city manager responsible for the day-to-day administration of the municipality. From its inception in Staunton, Virginia, in 1908, 321 cities had adopted the city manager system by 1924, limiting the influence of voters over the operations of their local governments. Municipalities with the city-manager system tend to have lower turnout than other municipalities with direct voter control over government, due to the remoteness of the city-manager form from voter control.[13]

Cities and counties shifted from district-based elections for local legislative bodies to at-large elections in which all voters in the jurisdiction selected all members. This was yet another means for restricting the power of political machines and their immigrant and minority loyalists. At-large elections submerged minorities in white-controlled electorates and favored politics driven by money rather than low-budget tactics like door-to-door canvassing. By 1960, 60 percent of cities with a population of more than ten thousand people elected members of their councils citywide, while only 23 percent elected them from districts, some of which had African American and immigrant majorities. The remaining 17 percent had mixed at-large and district systems. The consensus of statistical studies indicates that ward elections through the mid-twentieth century provided minorities better opportunities to elect candidates of their choice than citywide or at-large elections, although the effect could be minimized by the racial gerrymandering of districts.[14]

As part of these initiatives to insulate local elections from the mobilization of voters by political machines, reformers decoupled the timing of local and national elections. The reformers extended a nineteenth-century practice of holding local elections on off-years and dates prior to the November elections for national and state positions. To diminish the influence of political parties, they also adopted in many cases officially nonpartisan elections for local offices, in which candidates competed without party nominations or labels. As with other reforms, however, party machines that believed their superior organizations would most effectively mobilize voters lent support to these reforms. Today, about 80 percent of U.S. cities hold municipal elections on days other than the national election day.[15]

Although the evidence does not suggest that nonpartisan elections by themselves reduce voter turnout, scholars have established that off-cycle elections substantially reduce the participation of voters. According to political scientists Zoltan L. Hajnal and Paul G. Lewis, "The existing evidence suggests that turnout in city elections may average half that of national elections, with turnout in some cities regularly falling below one-quarter of the voting-age population." They conclude that "ultimately, important policy decisions are being made by local officials who are chosen by a relatively small and likely unrepresentative group of citizens."[16]

Off-cycle elections expand both the influence of well-organized party machines and of nonparty groups, like labor unions, chambers of commerce, trade associations, and good-government organizations with special interests in local election outcomes. At the 1908 meeting of the National Municipal Association, Robert S. Binkerd of the Buffalo Municipal League foreshadowed the rise of independent groups in local politics. He noted that with the reform of local elections, "there is need, in every community, for a non-partisan organization which shall, primary after primary and election after election, present to the press and voters the facts concerning office-holders and candidates." Of course, competing interest groups had their own conceptions of the relevant facts and different levels of resources available to influence elections.[17]

In 1955, Charles R. Adrian, a scholar of municipal politics, concluded that for low-turnout, off-cycle elections, "highly organized groups, whether of the nature of old-fashioned city machines or of special interest groups of any type, will thereby be able to control the government, for the lighter the vote the easier it is for such groups to win. They have a solid nucleus of dependable voters. A small turnout does not result in the same percentage distribution of the vote among the various segments of the population as would be found in a large turnout." A recent study found that low-turnout, off-cycle elections disproportionately reduced the turnout of minority groups. Thus, an inherently discriminatory process is built into the system for electing most local officials in the United States, largely beneath the notice of the American people.[18]

To combat manifestations of alleged fraud and corruption that could not be cured by official secret ballots—repeat voting, voter impersonation, and voting the graveyards—reformers imposed a barrier between voters and their vote: personal registration requirements. Unlike the secret ballot, personal registration laws had a long history in the United States. Massachusetts began the practice in 1800, with a few other states soon following. But personal registration requirements revived in the 1860s and became nearly universal in the early twentieth century. The registration process was often intrusive and onerous. In Ohio, for example, in addition to age, citizenship, and place and term of residence, applicants had to attest to their place of birth, their occupation, the name of their employer if they had one, their marital status, and whether they were "the head of their family."[19]

In the North, to throttle the urban machines, states targeted personal registration laws to the cities, often exempting rural areas where fraud was supposedly uncommon and voters and election officials often knew one another. A 1909 state court decision upholding a registration law aimed at New York City held that "it is a matter of common knowledge that the great centers of population offer peculiar opportunities for fraud and corruption in the conduct of elections, which can be prevented or minimized only by special regulations adapted to the conditions out of which these evils arise."[20]

In most large cities, voters had to renew their registration annually, biennially, or within four years. Few states or municipalities had registration offices open all year, and most imposed stringent registration deadlines prior to an election. States frequently revised their registration laws, sowing confusion and erecting new hurdles for voters to surmount. A 1924 compilation found that substantial percentages of otherwise eligible urban voters remained unregistered, including 47 percent in cities with annual renewal requirements and 31 percent in cities with permanent registration. It is unknown how many of those unregistered city dwellers would have voted in the absence of registration requirements.[21]

Even as states largely abandoned re-registration laws by the mid-twentieth century, voters still risked exclusion through lengthy residence requirements for registration, early deadlines before elections, and the purging of registration rolls for failure to vote, even for periods as brief as two years. Some states automatically purged nonvoters, while others provided notices to registrants before removal. In every state, purged voters could re-register with appropriate documentation. A 1963 report by the President's Commission on Registration and Voting Participation identified nonvoting, not fraud, as the major flaw in American elections. It found that restrictive registration laws disenfranchised millions of Americans. It recommended that residence requirements should not exceed six months, that registration should not end more than three or four weeks before Election Day, and that no registrant should be purged for failing to vote for any period of less than four years. The report also recommended that states should provide the option to register by mail. Most states, however, would not implement these recommendations until after enactment of the National Voter Registration Act of 1993. But the issue of restrictive registration requirements would continue to provoke litigation in federal and state courts.[22]

In the South, registration laws shifted disenfranchisement from the point of voting to the point of registration, erasing, not just restricting, the black franchise. Southern registration laws imposed poll tax and literacy test requirements and ceded discretion to all-white local officials for adding and subtracting registrants. Black leader Thomas E. Miller, a former member of Congress from South Carolina, dubbed the local registrar the "Emperor of Suffrage." L. C. Coulson, a critic of the registration restrictions in the Alabama constitution of 1901, said, "Under the law as it now stands, white men steal the vote; if we adopt the new constitution, white men will steal the voter."[23]

African Americans turned without success to the federal courts for relief from the registration discrimination in the South. In 1895, a panel of the Fourth Circuit Court of Appeals, presided over by Chief Justice Melville Weston Fuller of the U.S. Supreme Court, overturned a lower court decision that had permanently enjoined the enforcement of South Carolina's 1894 restrictive registration law. Fuller's majority opinion said that the courts should avoid entanglement in political issues and that any remedy must be found in the same southern political system that denied African American voting rights, not in the judiciary. The U.S. Supreme Court dismissed an appeal by the plaintiff as moot because the election in which he alleged a denial of his franchise had already taken place.[24]

In 1898, the U.S. Supreme Court turned away a challenge to the administration of Mississippi's registration laws. A unanimous court rejected the plaintiffs' claim that registrars used their discretion to block African Americans from registering. The court ruled that "discriminations by the general government or by the states against any citizen because of his race . . . must be the result of the constitu-tion or laws of the state, not of the administration of them." It found that Mississippi's registration laws, which included literacy and poll tax requirements and a grandfather clause, "do not on their face discriminate between the races, and it has not been shown that their actual administration was evil; only that evil was pos-sible under them." The Court found that the registration provisions and their administration law targeted not race per se but only "the alleged characteristics of the negro race," and reached both "weak and vicious white men as well as weak and vicious black men." Five years later, the Supreme Court extinguished any hope of relief from discriminatory registration laws when it rejected black plaintiffs' challenge to Alabama's registration laws and their administration.[25]

Commentary from the first decade of the twentieth century re-flected the failure of African Americans to win the restoration of their voting rights in the courts. "Under existing court decisions and present legal practice," the *Atlanta Constitution* announced in 1904, "the southern states have lawfully accomplished the disenfranchise-ment of the Negro." In a 1910 analysis in the *Harvard Law Review* entitled "Is the Fifteenth Amendment Void?" Arthur W. Machen, Jr., noted that the Supreme Court "has in no single instance held any state or federal statute or the act of any state or federal officer to be in conflict with the Amendment; and no case in that court can be found which would have been decided differently if the Amendment had never existed."[26]

Southern lawmakers exploited the institution of the primary, de-signed to expand democracy, as another means for extinguishing black voting. In the solidly Democratic South, where victory in the Democratic primary was tantamount to election, states adopted majority-vote rules that required one-on-one runoffs unless a single candidate gained a majority vote in the initial primary. This require-ment guarded against the possibility of nominating an African American because white voters split their ballots among multiple white candidates. Most southern states also restricted primaries to whites only. To avoid adverse court decisions against government-sponsored white primaries, the Democratic Party typically adopted the white primary as a party, not a state, institution.

For reformers who sought a purified American politics it was not enough to change the conduct and administration of elections. They would also purge the electorate of people they deemed unfit for the responsibility of voting, no longer women but now illiterates, felons, aliens, Native Americans, and insane or "feeble-minded" individuals.

Driven by the fear of voting by Irish and German immigrants, literacy tests originated in the North, led first by Connecticut in 1855 and then by Massachusetts in 1857. The literacy test, said an editorial in the *Connecticut Courant,* was aimed at the "miserable tribe of low, hack, partisan, demagogic, hollow, hypocritical democrats" who "would give the state into the arms of foreigners, or drunkards, ... or irresponsible grog-shop scoundrels and poor-house rum-blossoms." Other northern states, provoked by fears of immigrants and other untrustworthy voters, adopted literacy tests in the late nineteenth and early twentieth centuries.[27]

By 1924, eighteen of the forty-eight states had literacy tests in place, eight in southern states and ten in northern ones. The practical effect of literacy requirements on the opportunity to vote was substantial. According to the Illiteracy Commission of the National Education Association, there were 10 million American illiterates in 1924 and an additional 10 million semiliterate people. The army literacy tests in 1917–1918 found that 25 percent of men tested—nearly 90 percent of whom were white—were illiterate and another 5 percent were semiliterate.[28]

In the South, to disenfranchise black voters, common practice required of black applicants not just reading but interpreting documents like the state constitution or having to answer obtuse questions that no one could be expected to comprehend. In 2014, an instructor at Harvard administered the Louisiana literacy tests used for black voters through 1964 to a group of his students. The questions were so confusing and the time limit so constricting that not a single Harvard student passed the test.[29]

In the early republic, many states did not draw distinctions in their constitutions between inhabitants and citizens, and the federal government authorized suffrage for aliens who met property requirements in the Northwest Ordinance of 1789. When older states began replacing suffrage standards based on the status of property with standards based on the status of people, they backtracked on both black and alien suffrage. Still, new western states that needed population infusions authorized alien voting. In the 1840s, the territory of Wisconsin pioneered a compromise form of alien voting that granted voting rights to immigrants who declared their intent to became American citizens. In the acts establishing the Washington, Kansas, Nebraska, Nevada, Dakota, Wyoming, and Oklahoma Territories, Congress enabled these territories to institute noncitizen voting, and most did so. It did not, however, authorize such voting rights for the territories of California, New Mexico, and Utah, acquired after the Mexican War of 1845, perhaps because the treaty settling the war gave Mexicans the choice to remain citizens of Mexico or to become citizens of the United States.[30]

Opportunities for alien voting peaked again in the 1870s when most of the states incorporated into the union after 1800 and most territories permitted some form of alien suffrage. For at least some years in the nineteenth century, aliens could, in principle, vote in about forty states. The wave of nativist reaction to the new immigration of the late nineteenth and early twentieth centuries began another reversal of alien voting. In about nineteen states at the turn of the twentieth century, alien suffrage survived often in the modified Wisconsin form of requiring a declaration of citizenship intent.[31]

These provisions for limited alien voting toppled during the next two decades amid anti-immigrant sentiment. Buttressed by popular reaction and the prevailing "racial science" of the time, which found new immigrants mentally and morally inferior to older stock Americans, Congress enacted temporary immigration restriction in 1921 and a permanent law in 1924. The Johnson-Reed Act of 1924 limited European immigration to about 150,000 individuals per year with nationality quotas based on the origins of the American population in 1890 that heavily favored western and northern Europe. The act required entry visas with photographs—another facet of control—and excluded Japanese and other Asians. Four years later, according to political scientist Leon E. Aylsworth, "For the first time in over a hundred years, a national election was held in 1928 in which no alien in any state had the right to cast a vote for a candidate for any office—national, state or local." Congress repealed the quota law of 1924 in 1965, but since that time no state and only a few scattered localities have authorized alien voting.[32]

The extinguishing of noncitizen voting was coupled with restrictions on opportunities for certain aliens to obtain American citizenship and thus qualify for the ballot. Federal court decisions strictly construed an 1870 law that opened opportunities for naturalization only to those identified as "a white person" or person of "African descent." The unspecified meaning of "white" in the law left open the still unsettled question of how to distinguish "whites" from "nonwhites."

The U.S. Supreme Court interpreted the word "white" according to the supposed commonsense views of native-stock Americans, which excluded people of Asian and most Middle Eastern descent. Immigration officials struggled to decide whether Hispanics who appeared to be of mixed European and indigenous descent qualified as "white." In 1923, the Supreme Court ruled that even "a high caste Hindu, although of the Caucasian or Aryan race, is not a white person within the meaning of the naturalization laws," which "were to be interpreted in accordance with the understanding of the common man." Unlike Asians, the Court recognized that "immigrants from Eastern, Southern and Middle Europe, among them the

Slavs and the dark-eyed, swarthy people of Alpine and Mediterranean stock," merged into the white population "and lose the distinctive hallmarks of their European origin." Four years later, without a hint of irony, the Court ruled that a child born in Mississippi of Chinese ancestry could be classified as "colored" and consigned to legally segregated black schools.[33]

Through the Dawes Act of 1887, the Curtis Act of 1898, and the Burke Act of 1906, the federal government began a process of assimilating Native Americans into the mainstream of American life. These laws granted American citizenship to Indians who had accepted allotments of land from the government and agreed to live separately from their traditional tribes. The acts transferred millions of acres of land from Indians to white settlers in the process. From 1887 to 1934, lands owned by Native Americans dwindled from 138 million to 48 million acres. The Indian Citizenship Act of 1924 granted federal citizenship and, in principle, the right to vote to all American Indians. However, by 1938, seven states with substantial Indian populations still effectively prohibited them from voting. This was achieved, for example, by denying voting rights to Indians who maintained their tribal affiliations, lived on reservations, or were considered under the "guardianship" of government. Some states excluded from voting "Indians not taxed," mimicking a clause of the original Constitution that excluded such individuals from being counted in the U.S. Census.[34]

In Arizona, where nearly one-sixth of all Native Americans resided, the state supreme court ruled in 1928 that as "wards of the United States," Arizona's reservation Indians fell under the state's prohibition of suffrage to any "persons under guardianship," placing these citizens in a similar category to those classed by the state "*non-compos mentis,* and insane." The court found, "The man who for any reason is exempt from responsibility to the law for his acts, who cannot be trusted to manage his own person or property, certainly as a matter of common sense cannot be trusted to make laws for the government of others, and placing him under the guardianship of another conclusively establishes that incapacity" for suffrage.[35]

Barriers to Native American voting began to break down through statute and court rulings in the 1940s. In 1948, the Arizona Supreme Court reversed its 1928 decision and ruled that in excluding "persons under guardianship" from voting, the framers of the Arizona constitution did not intend to include Indians indiscriminately in that category. Rather, they "had in mind situations where disabilities are established on an individual rather than a tribal basis."[36] Simultaneously, a three-judge federal court ruled that under the Fourteenth and Fifteenth Amendments, New Mexico, another state with a substantial Indian population, could not indiscriminately disenfranchise "Indians not taxed."[37] However, statutory prohibitions on Indian voting were not repealed until 1950 in Idaho, 1951 in South Dakota, 1957 in Utah, and 1960 in Minnesota.[38] Even in the post-repeal era, Indian voting rights remained precarious as states used mechanisms such as at-large election systems and gerrymandered redistricting plans to limit the impact of the Indian vote, prompting litigation under the Voting Rights Act of 1965 and its amendments.[39]

In 1923, political analyst Frank Kent debunked the myth that "universal suffrage" prevailed in America. Rather, Americans "are hedged about by voting requirements, rigid in some States, lax in others, but all designed to do two things—first, promote the orderly and honest conduct of election, and, second, eliminate certain citizens who do not measure up to State standards." The laws excluded not only aliens but many classes of citizens: felons, the "feeble-minded" and insane, soldiers who lacked permanent residence, Indians on government reservations, paupers, delinquent taxpayers, and the uneducated. He noted that voting restrictions in most northern states are "a natural protective" against the "tides of immigration," which impresses on them "the desirability of keeping the vote out of the hands of the wholly illiterate and unworthy." Restrictions in southern states resulted primarily from "the dread of the negro vote." An untainted motivation to purify politics, he said, prevailed in only a few states with small black and immigrant populations. In states such as New Hampshire and Connecticut, the people "simply believe in restricting the vote to those citizens who have at least a certain degree of intelligence or some small stake in the community."[40]

Kent noted with dismay that fewer than half of American adult citizens voted in the presidential election of 1920, and accurately pointed to the collapse of turnout in America since the late nineteenth century. From 81 percent in the first post-Reconstruction election of 1880, the percentage of people eligible to vote by state laws pertaining to sex, age, and citizenship who turned out in the presidential contest had plummeted to 49 percent in 1920, with most of the decline coming after 1896. Turnout for congressional elections in midterm years declined comparably, falling from 66 percent in 1882 to 36 percent in 1922, with again most of the decline occurring after 1896.[41]

Kent claimed that the dismal turnout rates of his time could not be explained by suffrage restrictions alone, but rather that "the great bulk of those who do not vote, are not those who cannot vote, but those who will not." Kent was writing at a low ebb of turnout in the United States and in the early years of women's suffrage, when women's turnout trailed behind men's. Study of the broader chronology shows that at least in the North, Americans did not stop voting, contrary to Kent's implication and much scholarly opinion. Turnout in the North rebounded robustly in 1928 after women largely caught up with men in their political participation. Northern turnout in the presidential election hit 66 percent in 1928 and averaged 69 percent through 1964, only 15 percentage points below the 84 percent northern average in its 1880 to 1900 peak. Changes in the institutional context of voting are sufficient to explain most of this relatively modest drop in northern presidential turnout, without resort to broader cultural and political explanations.[42]

The state of North Dakota provides an instructive, controlled study on the influence of structural changes in voting access on voter turnout. Unique among the states, North Dakota never had a personal registration requirement or literacy test, and it adopted the secret ballot prior to its first participation in presidential elections. Thus, any changes in voter turnout in presidential elections from the late nineteenth century to the early to mid-twentieth century occurred independent of changes in electoral rules. Despite the state's sparse population and its late entry into the union in 1889, absent any institutional changes in registration or voting, presidential turnout in North Dakota averaged 72 percent from 1928 to 1964, essentially unchanged from the 74 percent average from 1892 to 1900.

Scrutiny of turnout in midterm congressional elections adds shading to this picture. In the North, congressional turnout rebounded only modestly, averaging 51 percent from 1930 to 1966, compared to 70 percent from 1882 to 1902. Thus, the shrinkage in northern turnout primarily impacted so-called core voters, those who habitually participated in elections, even without the allure of a presidential contest. This decline in core voting cannot be explained by institutional changes alone; it also reflects the erosion of the mass mobilization by political parties of their loyal followers, the rise of alternative means for influencing governance through organized interest groups, and the proliferation of unelected administrative agencies at every level of government. In North Dakota, despite a lack of institutional changes, core voting declined by about 10 percentage points from 1930 to 1966 as compared to the period from 1890 to 1902. The loss of core voters reduced turnout especially among minorities, young people, and the less affluent, not just in the South but also in the North.[43]

Through the mid-twentieth century, the South dragged down national turnout rates, lagging far behind the North in both presidential and congressional elections. From 1928 to 1964, southern presidential turnout averaged only 31 percent, well less than half the northern average of 69 percent. For midterm congressional contests, southern turnout during this period averaged merely 15 percent, less than a third of the northern average of 51 percent. This southern turnout decline reflected lack of general election competition in this Democratic Party–dominated region, as well as the uniquely restrictive registration and voting laws that blunted insurgent movements and disenfranchised some low-income whites and most African Americans.

With American democracy by the early twentieth century suffering from southern exclusionary tactics and absent voters, much of the outside world was moving in the other direction toward an expanded democracy. For the first time, the United States was falling behind other democratic nations in opportunities for voting. Significantly, by the early twentieth century, the United States had reverted not to a white man's republic but, with the enfranchisement of women, to a white citizen's republic. State laws and constitutions had extinguished alien voting. Native Americans were largely excluded from full political participation, and so too were African Americans in the South, where most black people still resided. In the North, literacy tests and personal registration requirements limited voting opportunities for nonwhites and less-affluent citizens generally.

Across the globe, elites in many nations could not resist pressure from below for the suffrage without unacceptable repression. Yet democracy proved to be a fragile commodity that remained precarious worldwide, even as it survived imperfectly in the United States. In the "Golden Age" of democracy after World War I, the number of functioning democracies soared from a handful to some twenty-nine nations. Then, from 1922 to 1942, the number dwindled to only twelve, almost all of them in western Europe or among English-speaking nations such as Canada, the United States, and Australia.[44]

· 6 ·

THE VOTING RIGHTS
ACT OF 1965

*Until every qualified person regardless of ... the color of
his skin has the right, unquestioned and unrestrained, to
go in and cast his ballot in every precinct in this great
land of ours, I am not going to be satisfied.*

—PRESIDENT LYNDON B. JOHNSON, 1964

Despite decades of futile effort, African Americans and other nonwhites continued to press for voting rights through the courts
and political system. Until the 1950s, however, a political solution to
black disenfranchisement seemed out of reach. Democrats in the
South continued their tenacious commitment to black disenfranchisement with minimal opposition from their party counterparts
in the North or from Republicans intent on pursuing other priorities. With the passing of the Reconstruction generation, the failure
of the Lodge Bill in 1891, and secure Democratic control of the South
and Republican dominance in the North, the Republicans' commitment to black voting rights faded away by the turn of the twentieth
century.

Republican leaders ceded control of the southern states to white
supremacists who had all but extinguished black voting. The

Republicans ended their efforts to enfranchise African Americans and establish a Republican Party in the region based on black votes. Their aim shifted to the building of a competitive, "lily white" Republican Party in the South that would break up the solidly Democratic South and unite white conservatives across America. Republican fusionists hoped to create a dominant, nationwide conservative majority of white citizens able to vanquish the liberal opposition in any region of the land. In short, by the first decades of the twentieth century, disenfranchised nonwhites lacked support for voting rights in either of the nation's major political parties. Instead, the dynamics of party competition reinforced the discriminatory status quo, leaving court action as the only recourse for the achievement of nonwhite voting rights.

Republican William McKinley assumed the presidency in 1897 after four years of Grover Cleveland's Democratic administration. Although McKinley paid lip service to discrimination against African Americans, the president and the Republicans who controlled Congress did not match words with deeds. In February 1899, Republican representative Edgar D. Crumpacker proposed without success a bill that would require the U.S. Bureau of the Census to assess the extent of racial disenfranchisement in the states. Crumpacker anticipated using this analysis to enforce section 2 of the Fourteenth Amendment by reducing representation in Congress and the Electoral College in proportion to the decline of black voter participation. Similar legislation languished in Congress for more than a decade without majority support from Republicans or endorsement by the successive Republican administrations of McKinley, Theodore Roosevelt, and William Howard Taft. Apparently emboldened by the opposition of conciliatory Booker T. Washington, President Roosevelt declared that he would veto the Crumpacker bill if enacted by Congress.[1]

A 1918 editorial in the influential black newspaper the *Chicago Defender* decried inaction on voting and civil rights by the GOP—an acronym for the Republican Party that took hold in the late nine-teenth century as representing first the "Gallant Old Party" and later "Grand Old Party." The editors charged that Republicans had forsaken their loyal black voters and shown instead "that they are in sympathy with their white brothers in the southern section of the country. This is evidenced by their refusal to enforce Section 2 [of the Fourteenth Amendment] of the Constitution," even though "the Republican party had both branches of Congress and the executive branch."[2]

Following the two administrations of Democrat Woodrow Wilson, who lacked any commitment to black rights, Republicans held the presidency and both houses of Congress from 1921 to 1931. They channeled their scant energy on racial issues into unsuccessful ef-forts to enact federal anti-lynching legislation. Black leaders blamed this failure on Republicans, who no longer represented the party of Lincoln, and began to reconsider their historic ties to the GOP.

The Republican Party by 1920 had radically shifted its racial ori-entation from the Civil War and Reconstruction years. Conservative Republicans, wary of federal activism on race and seeking an alli-ance with white southern conservatives, had become a dominant force within the party. Thus, African Americans found themselves caught in the 1920s between Democrats committed to the defense of racial privilege in the South and Republicans eager to ensure their dominance of American politics by capturing the voters of anti-pluralist southern white Democrats. The National Colored Repub-lican Conference complained in 1924, "In the party's willingness to be fair, many have no confidence, and a change is imperative." With an eye on the party's dedication to enforcing the Eighteenth Amend-ment mandating the prohibition of alcohol, the conference called for "the enforcement of the entire constitution with the same vigi-lance and interest in every portion of it."[3]

Instead, the party moved in the opposite direction in 1928 when presidential candidate Herbert Hoover initiated a new kind of "southern strategy," based on building a competitive "lily-white" Republican Party in the South. Relying on familiar charges of fraud and corruption, the party attempted to purge some of the black leadership of Republican organizations in the South. Hoover's supporters in the Resolutions Committee of the Republican National Convention quashed a proposal by black leaders that would have committed the party to enforcing the Fourteenth and Fifteenth Amendments no less than the Eighteenth. The platform devoted only thirty-five words to racial issues, repeating the party's empty promise to back anti-lynching legislation; it said nothing about voting rights but pledged the GOP to the observance and vigorous enforcement of Prohibition.[4]

To implement its southern strategy, the GOP walked a thin line between building a white-based southern party and repelling black Republican voters in the North. Still, Hoover became the first Republican candidate since Reconstruction to win the electoral votes of Florida, North Carolina, Texas, and Virginia, and he lost no northern state with a substantial black population. "We have an opportunity to put the Republican Party in a position where it can remain in power without much trouble for the next twenty years," said Senator William Borah of Idaho. "We have a chance to build up a party in the South which will always make those states fighting ground." However, the Republicans' longstanding inaction on civil rights and the Hoover campaign repulsed many black leaders. Neval Thomas, president of the District of Columbia NAACP, denounced Hoover's Republicans as just another "crowd of oppressors" who had besmirched the traditions of Lincoln's party and entered into "solemn compact with the Bourbon South in their wicked schemes against the Negro."[5]

The Great Depression and a wrenching realignment of American politics killed the dream of establishing a competitive, white-based Republican Party in the South. A two-tiered realignment of the American party system began after 1929. Between 1930 and 1932, the

Democrats benefited from a "Depression effect" that swelled the ranks of party voters throughout the United States but neither restored the Democrats to majority status nor reshuffled voter coalitions. After Franklin D. Roosevelt won the presidential election of 1932, his political leadership and New Deal reforms completed the realignment process by recruiting new voters and converting Republicans. From 1928 to 1936, the GOP's share of the two-party registration fell from 69 percent to 45 percent in five northern states with party-line registration statistics and from 64 to 35 percent in major cities. After the election of 1936, the GOP had lost 178 U.S. House seats as compared to 1928, 40 Senate seats, and 19 governor's mansions. The GOP retained a meager 89 House members and 16 senators. After losing New Jersey in 1937, the party held 7 governorships with a combined population of less than New York State.[6]

Disappointment with the conservative-led GOP and approval of Roosevelt's New Deal economic program realigned the loyalties of black voters. Beginning in the midterm elections of 1934, most blacks enduringly shifted their votes to candidates of the Democratic Party. In Chicago, Arthur Mitchell became the first black Democrat elected to Congress, defeating Oscar De Priest, the last remaining black Republican. In national politics, African Americans came to vote in line with white southern Democrats, within the dominant Roosevelt coalition that also included Jewish and immigrant voters.[7]

But participation in the Democrats' new majority coalition failed to advance voting rights for African Americans. A president loath to agitate the passions of race or upset his alliance with the southern Democrats let Jim Crow rule below the Mason-Dixon Line. In turn, white southerners who controlled most committees in Congress backed the New Deal and delivered their bloc votes to the Democratic Party. The Roosevelt reform agenda included no major legislative initiatives on behalf of minority voting rights. In a 1935 memo, Will Alexander, an administration advisor on race relations, listed nine reasons why "Negroes feel disappointed in the administration," including discrimination in federal programs and the lack of civil rights initiatives.[8]

Toward the end of Roosevelt's second term in 1939, Democratic representative Lee Geyer of California introduced legislation to ban poll taxes for voting in presidential elections. His bill won support from black advocacy groups and a new coalition group, the National Committee to Abolish the Poll Tax. Although Roosevelt had tepidly spoken out against the poll tax in 1938 and backed some state-level repeal efforts behind the scenes, he did not mention the Geyer bill during his unprecedented and successful third-term campaign in 1940, once more appeasing the powerful southern bloc of his party.

The Geyer bill passed the House in 1942 before succumbing to a southern Democratic filibuster in the Senate. Although Roosevelt claimed to have opposed the poll tax all his life, when asked about the Senate filibuster, the president dodged the question and said he could not express any opinion on the matter. The *Chicago Defender* denounced the filibuster saying, "national unity is still too weak to win this kind of battle centered around the race issue. . . . The North has let the South run hog wild since Reconstruction." Anti–poll tax legislation passed the House several more times in the 1940s, but each time it died in the Senate. As North Carolina, Louisiana, and Florida abolished poll taxes, African Americans did achieve some limited progress in the states. Yet other mechanisms, such as the literacy test, continued to disenfranchise African Americans in the South.[9]

With no solution to disenfranchisement coming from Congress, African Americans continued to press for their rights in the courts. The NAACP led this effort after its formal incorporation in 1911. Its rapid growth to six thousand members by 1914 made it the first mass-based civil rights organization since the abolitionist movement. The NAACP began its foray into voting rights litigation when it filed an amicus brief in the 1915 U.S. Supreme Court case that successfully challenged the "grandfather clause" of the Oklahoma state constitution. In a rare display of support for civil rights by the Wilson administration, Solicitor General John W. Davis argued for the United States that the grandfather clause violated the Fifteenth Amendment because its choice of the 1866 date antedated the Reconstruction Acts that first gave blacks voting rights in the state. Ironically, four decades later, Davis faced off against the NAACP as a private attorney representing one of the defendant school systems in the landmark Supreme Court school desegregation case *Brown v. Board of Education*.[10]

The Supreme Court unanimously agreed with the plaintiffs in 1915, giving African American voters their first victory under the Fifteenth Amendment, forty-five years after its ratification by the states. In a departure from previous decisions that upheld discriminatory laws not explicitly based on race, the Court found that although the grandfather clause does not expressly exclude "any person because of race," it "inherently brings that result into existence." The decision invalidated the grandfather clause not just in Oklahoma but also in Maryland, Alabama, Georgia, Louisiana, North Carolina, and Virginia. In a response that demonstrated the tenacity of white supremacists, Oklahoma promptly revised its registration laws in more subtle ways to exempt most whites, but not blacks, from its literacy test requirement. Not for another twenty-three years would the Supreme Court strike down Oklahoma's revised law and finally put the grandfather clause to rest.[11]

Beginning in the 1920s, the NAACP and the American Civil Liberties Union (ACLU), founded in 1920, challenged the white primary election in the South. Under a 1923 Texas law that authorized political parties to set the rules for participation in their primaries, the dominant Democratic Party banned African Americans and Mexican Americans from its primary elections. In 1927, the Supreme Court ventured into the "political thicket" and struck down the Texas law as a violation of the equal protection clause of the Fourteenth Amendment. It ruled that "color cannot be made the basis of a statutory classification affecting the right set up in this case." Texas quickly revised its law in a way that enabled the Democratic Party to stipulate that "all white Democrats ... and none other" shall participate in its primaries.[12]

In 1932, the Court invalidated the new law, and to evade this decision, the Democratic Party of Texas followed the model of adopting its own "white primary" rule, which the Court upheld three years later. Not until 1944 did a Supreme Court remade by Roosevelt appointees decisively prohibit the use of white primaries. In the landmark *Smith v. Allwright* case, Texas claimed that as a private "voluntary organization," the Democratic Party had the right to set its own rules, not subject to the protections of the Fourteenth or Fifteenth Amendments. The Court disagreed. In a reversal of its 1935 decision, it ruled that "a state cannot permit a private organization to practice racial discrimination."[13]

Black plaintiffs aided by the NAACP made further progress in 1949 when the Supreme Court struck down an Alabama literacy test, implemented to circumvent the demise of the white primary. The law required a citizen both to "understand and explain" an article of the U.S. Constitution. The Court ruled that the legislative history of this proposal and the discretion it granted registrars made it "merely a device" for racial discrimination, and indeed election officials did apply it differently for white and black applicants. A decade later, the Court upheld a North Carolina literacy test that included no requirement for interpretation. Such a test, it found, was "applicable to members of all races" and "was one fair way of determining whether a person is literate, not a calculated scheme" for discrimination. Thus, the literacy test ultimately survived court challenges even in the liberal court led by Chief Justice Earl Warren. Worse yet for potential black voters, local registrars continued their discriminatory administration of supposedly objective literacy tests.[14]

The poll tax likewise survived constitutional challenge. In 1937, in a case filed by a white male, a unanimous Supreme Court upheld

Georgia's requirement for paying a poll tax, with certain exceptions for age and gender, as a prerequisite for registration. The Court ruled that "to make payment of poll taxes a prerequisite of voting is not to deny any privilege or immunity protected by the Fourteenth Amendment. Privilege of voting is not derived from the United States, but is conferred by the State and, save as restrained by the Fifteenth and Nineteenth Amendments and other provisions of the Federal Constitution, the State may condition suffrage as it deems appropriate." In a reversion to nineteenth-century jurisprudence, the Court upheld the tax because it applied to all voters. Despite the poll tax's obviously discriminatory effects on African Americans, who generally had much more limited economic resources than whites, the Court found the policy did not violate the Fourteenth or Fifteenth Amendments. The poll tax remained intact in most southern states.[15]

In 1948, President Harry Truman attempted to break the political logjam over voting rights when he embraced the first comprehensive civil rights program in the history of his Democratic Party. The president endorsed the expansion of voting rights, federal protection against lynching and employment discrimination, and elimination of segregation in interstate commerce and the armed forces. According to strategist Clark M. Clifford, Truman was countering a potential challenge from the left wing of his Democratic Party and Republican plans "to woo the negroes away from the Administration's fold." The resulting "difficulty with our Southern friends . . . is the lesser of two evils." The South, even if provoked, would not bolt to the GOP and, critically, was less important to Democrats than some large northern states, where black voters held the balance of power.[16]

Democrats of the South decried Truman for breaking the sacred compact between northerners who let Jim Crow rule below the Mason-Dixon Line and white southerners who delivered bloc votes to the national Democratic Party. Georgia senator Richard Russell warned against tampering with "states' rights and white supremacy," the basis of "southern devotion to the Democratic Party." A "federal Gestapo," he said, was poised to deploy "every power of the Federal Government . . . to destroy segregation and compel intermingling and miscegenation of the races in the South." When the Democrats inserted a civil rights plank into the party's national platform, southern discontent turned into open revolt. The Southern Governors' Conference organized a third-party movement, with South Carolina governor Strom Thurmond as their presidential candidate. The press dubbed his movement the "Dixiecrats," which the governor disdained in favor of the "States' Rights Party." Although Thurmond waved the banner of states' rights, his real purpose, he admitted, was to preserve "the racial integrity and purity of the White and Negro races."[17]

Thurmond won 2.4 percent of the national popular vote and the electoral votes of South Carolina, Mississippi, Alabama, and Louisiana, the only states where Dixiecrat insurgents controlled the regular Democratic organization. The Dixiecrat revolt heightened the siege mentality of the South, making defense of the color line a patriotic duty. After 1948, moderation on race in the South was a vice that impeded success at the polls.[18]

After his victory in 1948, Truman continued the lengthy process of desegregating the armed forces, which he had begun by executive order before the election. He failed, though, to win Congress's approval for voting rights legislation. Truman could not crack the "conservative coalition" of southern Democrats and conservative Republicans that held the balance of power in Congress. Some advocates of black voting rights blamed him for not trying hard enough and putting other priorities ahead of his program for African Americans. Earl Brown, in the black newspaper *New York Amsterdam News,* condemned Truman and his allies for giving in "to the Dixiecrats, whom they had *just* beaten in an all-out fight" at the Democratic convention "and in the election." Brown said that "each major party inserts a holy sounding plank in its platform about its championing of civil rights and then does nothing about either the plank or civil rights."[19]

A confluence of events in the 1950s improved prospects for voting rights legislation. In 1954, a unanimous Supreme Court led by Chief Justice Earl Warren issued its landmark *Brown* decision on school desegregation. The Court overturned its 1896 decision in *Plessy v. Ferguson* that legalized the concept of "separate but equal" facilities for blacks and whites. With *Brown* the Court declared that separation of the races in public education was inherently unequal and violated the equal protection clause of the Fourteenth Amendment. The decision sparked a "massive resistance" movement by southern white leaders, which antagonized northern Republicans and Democrats.[20]

A burgeoning civil rights movement, led by the charismatic Reverend Martin Luther King, Jr., challenged massive resistance by mobilizing millions of everyday people to attain freedom for African Americans. In 1955–1956, King and NAACP activist Rosa Parks organized the Montgomery Bus Boycott, which sparked protests for civil rights across America and pressured Republican president Dwight Eisenhower and the Democratic Congress to sponsor civil rights initiatives.

Senate majority leader Lyndon B. Johnson of Texas emerged as the leading figure in Congress after Democrats recaptured control over both chambers in the midterm elections of 1954. Johnson was a master of the legislative process, but he also had ambitions to run for the Democratic presidential nomination. He understood that support for at least moderate civil rights legislation would make him a national candidate, not just a favorite son of the South.

In 1957, the administration submitted to Congress an omnibus voting rights bill drafted by Eisenhower's attorney general, Herbert Brownell, and backed by the president. Johnson maneuvered the bill through opposition from his fellow southern Democrats by eliminating its most sweeping provision to give the federal government broad authority to enforce the Fourteenth and Fifteenth

Amendments. The successful bill was the first national voting rights legislation since Reconstruction, and even in its watered-down version had important implications for black suffrage. It established the Civil Rights Division of the U.S. Department of Justice and the independent U.S. Commission on Civil Rights, and it authorized the Justice Department to initiate civil suits to prevent infringements of the right to vote.[21]

During the Eisenhower years, the Civil Rights Division cautiously enforced the act, filing fewer than ten voting rights lawsuits. Enforcement stepped up during the Kennedy administration, aided by amendments passed in 1960 that made for easier enforcement of the 1957 act. Although John F. Kennedy's Civil Rights Division filed more than fifty voting rights suits, this case-by-case approach did not put much of a dent in the disenfranchisement of black people in the Deep South. In Mississippi, Alabama, Georgia, and Louisiana (where more than 90 percent of the litigation had taken place), black registration rates on average increased by only 2.6 percentage points from 1956 to 1964. Litigation was costly and slow. The average elapsed time between the filing of a complaint and the beginning of trial was 16.3 months. An average of 17.8 months elapsed between the commencement of trial and the entry of judgment. Appeals from an adverse decision took approximately one year, and in most cases either the government or the defendant appealed. Lawsuits faced resistance from frequently hostile southern judges, and the discretion vested in the local registrar made it difficult to end discrimination even after winning judicial relief. The Roman sage Cicero famously said, "The foundation of justice is good faith." Of that, there was precious little among the white Democrats who controlled southern governments.[22]

In Dallas County, Alabama, for example, two-thirds of the county's black population lived in poverty in 1960. Only 156 of 15,115 African Americans of voting age had surmounted obstacles to registering for the vote, compared to 9,195 of 14,400 voting-age whites.

In April 1961, John Doar, Kennedy's new head of the Civil Rights Division and later the chief attorney for the U.S. House Judiciary Committee's impeachment investigation of Richard Nixon, filed his first voting rights suit in Dallas County. Predictably, trial occurred more than a year later in May 1962. The county registrar delayed the lawsuit by resigning, and after an appeal, the circuit court issued an injunction in September 1963, thirty months after the initial filing. But local police continued to harass and arrest blacks who attempted to register, forcing the Department of Justice to file yet another lawsuit in that county.[23]

Dallas County sheriff Jim Clark retaliated by breaking into the Selma headquarters of the Student Non-Violent Coordinating Committee and arresting several members for "illegal circulation of literature and promoting a boycott." Police continued to arrest many black people seeking to register in Selma or protesting the denial of their voting rights. Eventually, on February 4, 1965—nearly four years after Doar's first lawsuit and just three days after police arrested Reverend King and other demonstrators in Selma—a federal judge issued a final ruling that eliminated most formal barriers to black registration but left in place local registrars and their protectors in the sheriff's office. Despite the years of futility in Dallas County and elsewhere, the work of the Civil Rights Division established an important factual record of voter discrimination, buttressed by hearings held across the South by the Commission on Civil Rights and reminiscent of investigations in the South conducted during Reconstruction.[24]

In 1963, the one hundredth anniversary of the Emancipation Proclamation, black organizations began the most widespread civil rights demonstrations in the nation's history. Led by King, the movement turned massive resistance against itself by provoking violent responses to peaceful demonstrations in southern cities. A protest march in Birmingham, Alabama, generated national outrage as television viewers watched policemen turn dogs and high-pressure hoses on nonviolent demonstrators. This was exactly the response that King and other civil rights leaders had expected of the notorious Bull Connor, who headed the police forces in Birmingham. The demonstrators put themselves at great personal risk to sear into the American conscience the need to secure justice for black Americans.[25]

The Birmingham incident, which sparked sympathy demonstrations nationwide, moved President Kennedy for the first time to make civil rights a national priority and to draft new legislation. In a radio and television address to the nation, Kennedy became the first president of the twentieth century to make a moral commitment to ending racial discrimination. As was his style, Kennedy tied this domestic issue to America's quest for democracy and freedom worldwide. He said, "We preach freedom around the world, and we mean it, and we wish to cherish our freedom here at home, but are we to say to the world, and much more importantly, to each other that this is the land of the free except for the Negroes; that we have no second-class citizens except Negroes; that we have no class or caste systems, no ghettoes, no master race except with respect to Negroes?"[26]

Support for civil rights did not help Kennedy politically. A plurality of poll respondents in the fall of 1963 thought he was moving too fast on civil rights. Kennedy's approval rating fell about 10 points between the spring and fall of 1963. Not until after Kennedy's assassination did President Johnson and Republican Senate minority leader Everett Dirksen overcome a southern Democratic filibuster to enact the Civil Rights Act of 1964. The act banned discrimination by race or sex in employment and prohibited segregation in public accommodations and facilities.[27]

Only six Republicans joined southern Democrats in voting against the Civil Rights Act, but one of them was Barry Goldwater, the conservative senator from Arizona who ran as the party's presidential candidate in 1964. Goldwater's negative vote portended a sea change in American voting. With backing from the Republican National Committee, Goldwater launched a new "southern strategy" aimed at reanimating the dream of uniting northern and southern white conservative voters while conceding the black vote to Democrats. The GOP, Goldwater had earlier confided to party leaders, could not "out-promise the Democrats" in competition for black votes, "and that's what it takes when you appeal to people as groups." The party must "go hunting where the ducks are," he advised. With his backing, the national party urged southern voters to replace Democrats with more conservative Republicans, scrapped its minority division, and launched an organizing drive among white southerners, ironically called "Operation Dixie." Strom Thurmond, the former Dixiecrat, renounced his Democratic affiliation and joined the Republican Party in 1964 to support Goldwater.[28]

Mindful of the close race that had occurred in 1960, the GOP rolled out a "ballot security" plan in 1964, dubbed "Operation Eagle Eye" after a similar effort in Arizona. The party planned to station 100,000 "eagle eyes" at polling places to discourage fraudulent voters. With Eagle Eye targeting heavily Democratic minority neighborhoods in thirty-six cities, critics scorned it as a thinly disguised effort to reduce turnout by Democrats. In Houston, handbills circulated in heavily black neighborhoods warning that anyone with outstanding parking tickets or convictions for traffic offenses were subject to arrest if they tried to vote in the election. Neither proponents nor critics of the operation, however, could show any demonstrable effects on turnout. Allegations about the participation of former state party chair William Rehnquist in Arizona's Eagle Eye program resurfaced at his hearings to become Supreme Court justice in 1971 and chief justice in 1986, but they did not derail his confirmations for either position by wide margins in the Senate.[29]

President Johnson decisively defeated Goldwater in the general election. He won a record 61 percent of the popular vote and 90 percent of the Electoral College. His Democrats gained better than two-thirds majorities in both houses of Congress. But Goldwater swept all five Deep South states, four of which had not voted Republican since Reconstruction. He captured three-quarters of the Deep South counties, compared to the just one in five won by Eisenhower in his landslide victory of 1956. Four months before the election, when he signed the Civil Rights Act, Johnson mused to his aide Bill Moyers, "I think we have just delivered the South to the Republican Party." Johnson's prophesy slowly unfolded through the remainder of the century. The Republican Party's executive director John Grenier brushed aside criticism that his party was exploiting southern race prejudice. "History will not be concerned with motives of the Southern vote," he said, but only with the fact of its conversion to the GOP. Johnson and Grenier had each in their own ways anticipated the white South's conversion from solidly Democratic to predominantly Republican.[30]

By the time of Johnson's victory, the U.S. Supreme Court had triggered a revolution in how voters selected members of Congress and state and local legislatures, resolving the vexed question of geographic- versus population-based representation. In the 1962 case of *Baker v. Carr,* the Court rejected claims that redistricting was a strictly "political question" and authorized judicial review of redistricting plans. Plaintiff Charles Baker's heavily urban state representative district in Tennessee had ten times the population of some rural districts in the state, a common phenomenon across the nation. The Court found that "examples could be endlessly multiplied" of "geographic inequality in relation to the population standard."[31]

Two years later, in follow-up cases, the Supreme Court elucidated the standard of equal population for judging the constitutionality of legislative districts. In the Georgia case of *Wesberry v. Sanders,* the Court ruled that congressional districts must be drawn with roughly equal population. With its ruling that under the Constitution, "one man's vote in a Congressional election is to be worth as much as another's," the Court established for the first time in American history the principle of "one person, one vote." In the Alabama case of *Reynolds v. Sims*, the Court extended this principle to state legislative districts. In rejecting any basis for apportionment other than population, Chief Justice Warren wrote that "legislators represent people, not trees or acres. Legislators are elected by voters, not farms or cities or economic interests." In later decisions, the Court decided that congressional districts must be as close as mathematically possible to equal population, and that state and local districts are presumptively constitutional if the deviation between the most and least populous district is 10 percent or less. Otherwise the jurisdiction must prove that a compelling interest justifies the deviation.[32]

In 1967, Congress acted to effectuate these one-person, one-vote rulings by requiring that states elect members of Congress through single-member districts. Its object was to preclude states, especially in the South, from evading the Court's decisions by reverting to at-large state elections for Congress or, more plausibly, submerging minorities in multimember congressional districts controlled by white majorities.

The states responded by redrawing the nation's political map as they reapportioned congressional, state, and local legislative seats so that no person's vote would be substantially weighted more than another's. This reapportionment revolution substantially expanded the voting power of African Americans and other minorities, who were previously heavily concentrated in malapportioned urban areas. Now urban minority votes carried the same weight as the votes of white people, who predominated in rural districts. However, equal population requirements did not end the gerrymandering of legislative districts. Resourceful politicians found ways to protect themselves as incumbents and to favor their political party in redistricting within the constraints of one person, one vote.[33]

In the short term, Johnson's landslide victory in 1964 opened the way for him to extend the liberal state through his "Great Society" program. Among other initiatives, Johnson privately instructed his attorney general, Nicholas Katzenbach, to draft "the goddamndest, toughest voting rights act that you can." He still hesitated to put the power of the presidency behind the bill, though, for fear of jeopardizing other Great Society priorities, such as Medicaid and Medicare, which needed southern Democratic support.[34]

Jimmie Lee Jackson, the civil rights worker murdered after the February 1965 voting rights march in Alabama, did not die in vain. After hearing about the killing of this young voting rights activist, civil rights leaders, who had witnessed many deaths of workers in their cause, considered dumping Jackson's body on the doorstep of Alabama's segregationist governor George Wallace. Instead, King organized a march for African American voting rights from the town of Selma to the city of Montgomery, Alabama. "We are going to march the length of Alabama until we can vote," King said. Jackson "died that we can vote and we will vote."[35]

On March 7, 1965, voting rights marchers began their crossing of the Edmund Pettus Bridge, which spans the Alabama River in Selma and was named for a Confederate general. State troopers attacked the marchers on the bridge with nightsticks, tear gas, and police dogs, while television cameras carried these brutal images into America's living rooms. National outrage over the violence on this "Bloody Sunday" provided the momentum needed for adoption that summer of the landmark Voting Rights Act of 1965. On March 15, 1965, just a week after Bloody Sunday, President Johnson in a televised address to a joint session of Congress called for adoption of his administration's voting rights bill. "It is wrong—deadly wrong—to deny any of your fellow Americans the right to vote in this country," he said. "What happened in Selma is part of a far larger movement which reaches into every section and State of America. It is the effort of American Negroes to secure for themselves the full blessings of American life."[36]

The counter-claims made by southern opponents of voting rights, which focused on states' rights, federal tyranny, black inferiority, and the specter of voter fraud, showed how little had changed since Reconstruction. Senator John Stennis of Mississippi said, "We are paving the way for the destruction of self-government by the mad, emotional rush to destroy standards, whether literacy or any other, that the experience of the American people has proved not only wise, but essential in protecting the ballot box." Senator Strom Thurmond of South Carolina argued that "the Constitution gives no one the right to vote," and that restrictions imposed by the states do not apply "unequally to any one race or sex." The bill, he said, "is unjustly discriminatory to the States." Senator Spessard Holland of Florida warned that the act would result in violence directed against "the people whom it is most expected to help." Senator Lister Hill of Alabama charged that the bill's proponents were "usurping the rights of the States . . . to set voter qualifications which were clearly reserved to the States respectively." Senator John Tower of Texas said that repeal of the poll tax in Texas would allow "unscrupulous political bosses to bloc-vote certain people," defeating the purpose of "curing voter fraud." Leander Perez, the influential political boss of Plaquemines Parish in Louisiana, gave the Senate a taste of old-school racism, saying that it "doesn't understand Negroes, their thinking, their mentality. . . . They are of immoral character, they are a low type of citizenship."[37]

Senator James Eastland of Mississippi prophesied a coming apocalypse if Congress were to enact the voting rights bill: "You will unleash a chain reaction which will finally culminate in the establishment of an all-powerful, un-checked, unanswerable, super-socialist state. . . . When that occurs, Mr. President, the dark night of despotism will descend like a pall upon this great Nation and the rule of tyranny will pervade this land."[38]

As northern Democrats joined with Republicans to overcome southern Democratic opposition and pass the Voting Rights Act, it became clear that this time the opponents of voting rights were not going to prevail in Congress. In the House, the bill's backers defeated a weakened alternative promoted by the Judiciary Committee's ranking Republican, William McCulloch of Ohio, and Republican minority leader Gerald Ford of Michigan. In the Senate, the Johnson administration, working again with Minority Leader Dirksen, surmounted a filibuster by southern Democrats to secure final passage. Thus, African Americans gained the vote in most states of the new republic in the eighteenth century, then broadly lost it by the mid-nineteenth century. They regained voting rights in the post–Civil War Reconstruction, only to lose them again in the redemption of white supremacy, and ultimately regained the vote with passage of the Voting Rights Act of 1965. The act put a coda on the twentieth century's version of a white citizen's democracy in the United States, although it did not immediately or fully enfranchise nonwhites across the land. Struggles over the judicial interpretation and enforcement of the Voting Rights Act have continued through our own time.

The comprehensive and complex Voting Rights Act, which contains some 5,500 words and 19 sections, would be enforced through both direct administrative action by the U.S. Department of Justice and lawsuits that could be filed by both the Justice Department and private parties. The act banned the use of literacy tests in jurisdictions in which less than 50 percent of voting-age residents were registered as of November 1, 1964, or had voted in the 1964 presidential election. It made it a federal crime for any person or conspiracy of people, whether acting under color of law or not, to intimidate, threaten, or coerce anyone for attempting to vote. It declared that individuals could not be denied the right to vote for a lack of English proficiency if they had completed at least a sixth-grade education. It authorized the courts nationwide to suspend the use of any discriminatory test or device used by a jurisdiction as a prerequisite for voting and to appoint federal election examiners to register voters and monitor elections.[39]

The act did not explicitly outlaw the poll tax, which the Twenty-Fourth Amendment to the U.S. Constitution had banned in 1964 for federal elections, and so five southern states continued to require poll taxes for participation in state and local elections. The act noted the finding of Congress that poll taxes abridged the right to vote and authorized the attorney general to file suit against these lingering states. In 1966, the U.S. Supreme Court reversed its 1937 precedent, ruling six to three that Virginia's poll tax violated the Fourteenth Amendment. The Court held that "a State violates the Equal Protection Clause of the Fourteenth Amendment whenever it makes the affluence of the voter or payment of any fee an electoral standard. Voter qualifications have no relation to wealth nor to paying or not paying this or any other tax."[40]

The act included other broader and more enduring provisions. Section 2 stipulated that "no voting qualification or prerequisite to voting, or standard, practice, or procedure shall be imposed or applied by any State or political subdivision to deny or abridge the right of any citizen of the United States to vote on account of race or color." Beyond prohibiting practices that deny the vote to minorities, Congress designed section 2 to assure that minorities can make their vote count by having a reasonable opportunity to participate fully in the political process and elect candidates of their choice.

Sections 4 and 5 singled out for special treatment certain "covered" jurisdictions that employed discriminatory tests or devices and had low rates of voter registration or turnout. Covered jurisdictions under the formula spelled out in section 4 included Alabama, Georgia, Louisiana, Mississippi, South Carolina, Virginia, and forty counties in North Carolina. The attorney general could appoint registration examiners for such "covered" jurisdictions, which under the enforcement provisions of section 5 had to submit any change in voting laws or regulations to the Department of Justice for pre-clearance. The department had the authority to block any such change that had the purpose or effect of discriminating against minorities, with effect defined by the federal courts as a retrogression or diminution of the opportunity for minorities to participate in the political process and elect candidates of their choice. Alternatively, covered jurisdictions could seek to gain prior approval for voting changes from the federal district court of the District of Columbia, with the burden of proof placed on the state or locality. Jurisdictions could also seek a permanent "bail-out" from preclearance requirements by demonstrating an extended lack of discrimination. States that were not included under the coverage formula for section 5 could still be "bailed-in" to the preclearance process if found by the courts to have intentionally discriminated against minorities seeking to exercise their voting rights.

Echoing familiar arguments that its provisions exceeded the constitutional authority of Congress and encroached on matters reserved to the states, South Carolina led a coalition of several other southern states in promptly challenging the constitutionality of the Voting Rights Act. Such claims no longer had traction in the Supreme Court, however. After breaking with usual practice by assuming original jurisdiction over the case, a majority opinion written by Chief Justice Warren found that the act "reflects Congress' firm intention to rid the country of racial discrimination in voting" and falls within the scope of its authority to enforce the Fifteenth Amendment. "As against the reserved powers of the States, Congress may use any rational means to effectuate the constitutional prohibition of racial discrimination in voting," Warren ruled. Putting a rhetorical flourish on his opinion, Warren said, "After enduring nearly a century of widespread resistance to the Fifteenth Amendment, Congress has marshalled an array of potent weapons against the evil, with authority in the Attorney General to employ them effectively.... We may finally look forward to the day when truly '[t]he right of citizens of the United States to vote shall not be denied or abridged by the United States or by any State on account of race, color, or previous condition of servitude.'"[41]

Congress has significantly amended the Voting Rights Act five times to extend temporary provisions and to expand its scope and impact. Congress expanded the act's coverage formula in 1970 and banned literacy tests nationwide. In 1975, it added English-only ballots to the list of discriminatory tests and devices in jurisdictions that had at least a 5 percent single-language minority. The 1975 amendments included language minorities, defined as "persons who are American Indian, Asian American, Alaskan Natives or of Spanish heritage," within the groups of people covered by protections of the act. Congress added a bilingual election requirement in section 203, which requires election officials in jurisdictions with large numbers of English-illiterate language minorities to provide ballots and voting information in the language of the minority group. The 1970 and 1975 amendments added to the covered jurisdictions under section 5 the states of Texas, Alaska, and Arizona; several counties in California, Florida, New York, and South Dakota; and two townships in Michigan.[42]

The 1970 amendment also overturned the traditional voting age of twenty-one that prevailed in nearly every state. It guaranteed the right to vote in all elections for citizens who had reached the age of eighteen. Later that year, however, the Supreme Court ruled that Congress could set by law voting age qualifications for federal but not for state and local elections. Congress responded the following year by enacting the Twenty-Sixth Amendment to the Constitution, forbidding states from denying or abridging the right to vote of citizens "who are eighteen years of age or older." The states quickly ratified the voting age amendment, which, like the Fifteenth and Nineteenth Amendments, was framed negatively in terms of what states could not do. In 1972, eighteen-year-olds voted nationwide for the first time in a presidential election.

In 1982, the U.S. Supreme Court in *City of Mobile v. Bolden* limited the scope of the Fourteenth Amendment and the Voting Rights Act. It ruled that to prove a violation of the amendment's equal protection clause or section 2 of the Voting Rights Act, plaintiffs had to prove that voting laws and regulations not only had the effect of discriminating against minorities but were adopted or maintained with the intent to do so. In response, Congress amended section 2 in 1982 to ban any voting practice that had a discriminatory effect, whether or not it was enacted or maintained for a discriminatory purpose. It was only after the 1982 amendments that section 2 fully protected minorities from discriminatory practices for registration or voting. In 1992 and 2006, Congress extended provisions of the act. The 2006 amendments also strengthened the preclearance provisions of section 5. A substantial bipartisan majority in Congress backed each of these amendments.[43]

The Voting Rights Act immediately opened the door to registration and voting by black people in the South. By July 1967, the Justice Department had assigned federal registrars to twelve counties in Alabama, three in Georgia, nine in Louisiana, and thirty-four in Mississippi. The percentage of registered blacks in these states more than doubled from 21.1 percent in 1964 to 48.5 percent in 1967. Local officials who were unwilling to risk usurpation of their functions by federal officials registered most of the new African American voters. This experience shattered the myth that federal assumption of traditionally local functions would dissuade local officials from fulfilling their responsibilities. Federal oversight was working to combat many decades of efforts to disenfranchise African Americans in the South.[44]

Across the decades, section 2 litigation and section 5 objections have targeted methods of elections, annexations that diluted minority voting strength, the elimination or moving of polling places, qualifications for registration or voting, changes in the composition of legislative bodies, redistricting plans, and majority vote requirements. Most enforcement efforts have focused on "dilution" of minority voting strength through at-large elections and redistricting plans that "cracked" or "packed" minority voters. "Cracking" is the fissuring of minority communities so that they are submerged in white-dominated districts. "Packing" is the concentration of minority voters in one or a few districts well beyond what is needed to elect candidates of their choice. This results in "wasted" minority votes that could expand minority opportunities in other districts. At-large elections in which all candidates for office are elected jurisdiction-wide have a discriminatory effect if they enable a white voting majority to elect all or most candidates, overriding the preferences of minority voters. Through 2000, the Department of Justice interposed more than a thousand objections, more than 95 percent in southern states. The department issued more than half of these objections against at-large elections or redistricting plans.[45]

Section 2 litigation challenged discriminatory practices across the nation. The following examples of section 2 litigation against at-large elections and discriminatory redistricting plans come from my personal experience as an expert witness. The cases involve the voting rights of the nation's two largest minority groups, African Americans and Hispanics, and arise in different regions of the country.

In 1978, the U.S. Department of Justice returned to Dallas County, Alabama, whose county seat of Selma was the birthplace of the Voting Rights Act, to challenge the county's at-large system for electing its county commission. African Americans and whites were about equal in voting-age population in Dallas County according to the 1980 census, but whites still led in registered voters as African Americans fought against a century of discrimination. Thirteen years after King's march across the Pettus Bridge, Dallas County had not elected a single African American to its commission, which consisted of four members plus an ex-officio chairman empowered to break ties, all elected at-large by all county voters. Under this system, the white voting bloc majority consistently voted against any African American candidate for a commission position, shutting out black people from participation in their county government.

The city of Selma, the site of the Dallas County trial in the 1980s, was little changed from the Jim Crow era. White people held all the prestigious positions and all public offices. Black people cleaned the streets, waited tables, and scrubbed hotel rooms. They lived in an isolated enclave with unpaved roads and aging, dilapidated homes. Yet despite repeated defeats, blacks continued to mount candidates for public office in the city and county. They pressed for black representation on the board of registrars and for the appointment of black poll officials and deputy registrars. Four local African Americans—Samson Crum, Sr., Edwin Moss, Frederick D. Reese, and Clarence Williams—risked reprisals to join in the government's suit as plaintiffs against Dallas County.[46]

The Dallas County litigation dragged on for ten years, delayed by the *Bolden* decision on intent, the 1982 voting rights amendment, and adverse decisions from conservative white judge W. Brevard Hand, who had gained notoriety for his ruling that banned forty-four public school textbooks in Alabama because they allegedly promoted the "religion" of secular humanism. The Eleventh Circuit Court of Appeals unanimously reversed this decision.

Judge Hand's conduct during the trial was as surreal as his rulings. He roamed through his antiquated courtroom, sometimes sitting on the radiator rather than the bench. He ruffled his hand through the hair of the Justice Department's attorney, Gerald Hebert. When one of the department's shorter experts appeared to testify, Judge Hand asked if he wanted some telephone books to sit on. When I appeared to testify for the Justice Department for a second time, he said, "Oh no, not Dr. Lichtman again. You're just going to say whatever Mr. Hebert wants you to say." During one of the trials, the judge graciously invited Hebert and myself to play golf with him at his private club. When we asked if the club had any black members and he failed to respond, we politely declined his invitation. Instead, we played at the public course, which was next to the city dump, where they happened to be burning garbage that day. The smoke was so thick that we could barely see the fairway in front of us, but with our duffer golf skills it did not make much difference. After the case closed, Judge Hand sent us framed, signed photographs of himself.

After several trips to the Eleventh Circuit, in 1988, an exasperated appeals court ordered the implementation of what they termed the "Lichtman Plan," a plan that I had drafted to establish single-member districts for electing each of the five members of the Dallas County Commission. The plan included two clear majority-black voting districts, two clear white-majority voting districts, and one "swing" district. One white commissioner said derisively that if the court implemented this plan, "we might as well change the name of Dallas County to 'Lichtman County,' Alabama." The plan was implemented, and the name of the county remained the same, but in the November 1988 election, Dallas County elected three black and two white commissioners, reflecting the new black voting majority in the county. Three decades later, in a special election held in 2017, the black voters of Dallas County were instrumental in electing Doug Jones as the first Democratic senator in Alabama since 1992.[47]

This 1988 election, twenty-three years after the Pettus march, ended the all-white government that had prevailed in Dallas County for nearly ninety years. The Dallas County case exploded the theory that discrimination applied only to individuals. If so, there would have been no remedy for the exclusion of blacks from Dallas County governance, since, as individuals, blacks could register and vote. As a group, however, the ground rules of county politics barred them from effective participation in the selection of public officials. In the late twentieth century, section 2 litigation and section 5 objections eliminated many discriminatory at-large election systems across the nation.

In 1988, Latino plaintiffs and the U.S. Department of Justice filed suit against the districts drawn for supervisors of Los Angeles

County, the nation's most populous, with 8.7 million people and a budget of some $10 billion in 1990. No Hispanics in modern history had been elected to even one of the powerful supervisor positions that California politicians prized more than a seat in Congress. The suit charged that the existing board of supervisors had intentionally fragmented or cracked Hispanic communities to forestall the creation of a Hispanic-majority district and preserve the seats of incumbent white supervisors.

During a three-month trial, expert testimony established that bloc voting underlay the board's intentional refusal to create a Hispanic opportunity district; Hispanic candidates in Los Angeles County cohesively backed Hispanic candidates who were defeated by white bloc voting in white-majority districts. Federal District Court judge David V. Kenyon, a Republican appointed by President Jimmy Carter, ruled that the districting plan had both the intent and effect of discriminating against Hispanic voters.

He found that "Hispanics are politically cohesive and that voting behavior is polarized between Hispanics and non-Hispanics." The judge held that given such polarization, "the Supervisors appear to have acted primarily on the political instinct of self-preservation.... However, the Supervisors also intended what they know to be the likely result of their actions and a prerequisite to self-preservation—the continued fragmentation of the Hispanic core and the dilution of Hispanic voting strength." Judge Kenyon presciently rejected the claim of the attorney for the board's chair that "it was the Republican protecting himself or protecting his philosophical concerns and those of the ones who elected him from a change to a Democratic seat.... It was not because of a desire on anyone's part to dilute or diffuse or to keep the Hispanic community powerless." Kenyon ruled that "it is undeniable, however, that the Los Angeles County Board of Supervisors knew that by adopting the 1981 redistricting plan, they were further impairing the ability of Hispanics to gain representation on the Board." Self-preservation or partisan benefit could not justify racial discrimination.[48]

The Court of Appeals for the Ninth Circuit upheld the finding of intentional discrimination and ordered the imposition of a new plan with a majority-Hispanic district.[49] On January 7, 1991, the U.S. Supreme Court denied an appeal for certiorari (review of a lower court's decision) and let stand the circuit court's holdings. In a special election held in a court-ordered, majority-Hispanic district in February 1991, Los Angeles city councilwoman Gloria Molina became the first Hispanic elected to the County Board of Supervisors in one hundred years and the first woman to serve on the board.[50] The case set a precedent for the empowerment of the rapidly growing Hispanic electorate across the nation. According to exit polls, from 1992 to 1996 the Hispanic component of the presidential electorate rose from 2 to 5 percent, and then rose again to 11 percent in 2016.

In 2001, a three-judge federal court in New Jersey held an important trial on the packing of minority districts. Following the 2000 census, New Jersey's independent Apportionment Commission adopted a redistricting plan for state legislative seats. The "Bartels Plan," named after its principal author, Princeton political science professor Larry Bartels, the tie-breaking member of the commission, reduced the minority population (black and Hispanic) in several districts and increased the minority population in neighboring districts. A coalition of Republicans and civil rights organizations challenged the plan, contending that it would dilute the minority vote by spreading minority voters too thinly across districts. The seemingly odd coalition came together because many within the civil rights community had yet to realize that packed districts often created wasted minority votes, fenced in minorities within a few districts, and limited the ability of minority voters to expand the power of their votes in a larger number of districts. They joined forces with Republicans who recognized that excess Democratic votes in packed minority districts improved GOP prospects in all other districts.

The court cited testimony on behalf of the Bartels Plan that (1) packed districts were not necessary in New Jersey because minority voters could elect candidates of their choice in coalition with whites, and (2) that more dispersed districts would expand the opportunity for minorities to elect candidates of their choice to the state legislature. The court ruled that "drawing all the threads of the evidence together, we are satisfied that the Bartels plan is designed not to prevent or interfere with the election of minority representatives but rather will enhance and expand the opportunity for African Americans and Hispanics to participate in a meaningful way in the political process." The results of the subsequent election affirmed the court's position; no incumbent minority legislator lost his or her seat, and minorities increased their representation in the state legislature.[51]

Despite enactment of the Voting Rights Act and bolstered turnout in the South, nationwide voter participation declined after 1968 and remained at low levels through the 1970s and 1980s. Congress responded with legislation designed to expand access to voting and registration. In 1984, it passed the Voting Accessibility for the Elderly and Handicapped Act, which requires states to provide "a reasonable number of accessible permanent registration facilities" for elderly and handicapped voters. Two years later Congress enacted the Uniformed and Overseas Citizens Absentee Voting Act, which requires states to authorize overseas citizens and members of the military and their families to register and vote absentee in federal elections. The later Americans with Disabilities Act of 1990 expands the mandate of earlier legislation by requiring "public entities [to] ensure that people with disabilities can access and use their voting facilities." However, a still largely unexplored realm of voting rights pertains to an unspecified number of people with mental disabilities who are denied voting rights by various laws that still exist in many states. This issue has gained attention in recent years as professionals have rethought their views on mental health.[52]

Beginning in 1988, voting rights advocates introduced broader legislation to ease access to registration, eventually focusing on a bill dubbed "Motor Voter" that would obligate state governments to accept registration by mail for federal elections and to offer opportunities for registration upon application for a driver's license or public assistance. It would require states to accept a federal form for registration for federal elections that required an affirmation of U.S. citizenship, under penalty of perjury, but not documentary proof. Republican senator Mitch McConnell of Kentucky led the opposition to motor voter. He disparaged concern about low voter turnout, saying, "relatively low voter turnout is a sign of a relatively content democracy," and warned of massive voter fraud that would follow in the wake of motor voter legislation. "Perhaps the most disturbing aspect of the motor-voter bill," he said, "is its potential to foster election fraud and thus debase the entire political process in this country.... That is why the motor-voter bill is acquiring a new nickname: auto-fraud."[53]

Congress enacted the motor voter bill in 1991 after overcoming a filibuster in the Senate, but President George H. W. Bush vetoed the legislation, echoing McConnell's concerns about voter fraud. Bush wrote that "the bill would increase substantially the risk of voting fraud. It would not, however, provide sufficient authority for federal law enforcement officials to respond to any resulting increases in election crime and public corruption." In 1993, Congress again passed and President Bill Clinton signed the legislation that became the National Voter Registration Act of 1993, known as the "Motor Voter Act." It expanded registration opportunities but produced no discernable increase in voter fraud. Scholars, however, disagree on the law's impact on voter turnout.[54]

For minorities, the removal of barriers to minority registration and voting, section 5 objections, and litigation under section 2 of the Voting Rights Act all led to meaningful participation in policymaking through the holding of public office. African Americans' representation in Congress rose from five in 1965 to thirty-nine in 2000, and Hispanic representation from near zero to twenty. African American representation in state legislatures rose from fewer than two hundred members in 1965 to nearly six hundred in 2000, and Hispanic representation from fewer than fifty to more than two hundred. The number of African Americans holding elected office at all levels of government rose from fewer than a thousand in 1965 to more than nine thousand in 2000, and the number of Hispanics from an unknown but likely small number in 1965 to about four thousand in 2000.[55]

The Voting Rights Act and its enforcement contributed to the realization of President Johnson's prediction that the South would turn from voting Democratic to voting Republican. In a role reversal of the post-Reconstruction era, the white South became a solidly Republican voting bloc, leaving Democrats dependent on black and Hispanic voters. This realignment culminated in the midterm elections of 1994, when the GOP picked up more than fifty House and nine Senate seats and won control of both chambers of Congress for the first time since 1954. Republicans gained a net of some five hundred state legislative seats and ten governorships.[56]

The GOP achieved its first post-Reconstruction majority of southern U.S. House and Senate seats in 1994. The rise of southern Republicanism reflected class as well as racial polarities. In 2000, the American National Election Study found that 70 percent of white Protestant southerners in the top one-third of earners identified as Republicans, compared to 38 percent in the bottom one-third.[57]

Realignment in the South in the late twentieth and early twenty-first centuries polarized American politics by pushing Democrats to the left and Republicans to the right. Moderate southern Democrats were replaced in the U.S. Senate by extremely conservative Republicans, like Jeff Sessions of Alabama and George Allen of Virginia, and in the U.S. House by either conservative Republicans or liberal black and Hispanic Democrats. In 2016, only two House Democrats voted more conservatively than the most liberal House Republican. On the liberal scorecard of Americans for Democratic Action, House Democrats averaged 91.1 percent, compared to 2.3 percent for their Republican counterparts. Similarly, in the Senate, only two Democrats voted more conservatively than the most liberal Senate Republican. Senate Democrats averaged 88.8 percent in Americans for Democratic Action scores, compared to 6.7 percent for Republicans.[58]

The confirmation of this southern realignment in voting came with the contested presidential election of 2000, the first contest since 1888 in which the popular and Electoral College votes diverged. Its outcome ultimately turned on disparities in the counting of ballots cast by black voters as compared to other voters in the pivotal state of Florida. With George W. Bush's narrow 537-vote victory in Florida, the Republican candidate prevailed in every southern and border state.[59]

The questions of minority voting rights and representation, which the Voting Rights Act had seemingly settled in the United States, arose again during the new voting war of the twenty-first century. The war began with skirmishes after the contested presidential election of 2000. It escalated into full-scale battles after the election of Barack Obama in 2008. Democrats and Republicans have changed sides since the nineteenth century, and maneuvers to restrict the vote are subtler and more refined than ever before, but the partisan spoils of war have changed little. In a nation with no constitutional guarantee of the vote, this fundamental right of democratic government remains bitterly contested, with old arguments about voter fraud used to justify new restrictions on the franchise.

7

THE NEW WARS OVER
THE VOTE

In the years since the Florida debacle of 2000 we have
witnessed a partisan war over election rules. . . . Florida
mainly taught political operatives the benefits of
manipulating the rules, controlling election machinery,
and litigating early and often. Election law has become
part of a political strategy.

—RICHARD L. HASEN, 2012

The results that poured in on election night November 7, 2000,
showed that George W. Bush was poised to become the first Republican presidential candidate in U.S. history to sweep every
southern and border state—except perhaps for one crucial state. At
7:50 P.M., NBC called Florida for Al Gore, which virtually guaranteed
him an Electoral College majority. Other major news networks followed NBC's lead. As election night dragged on, however, the results from Florida looked less certain, prompting the news outlets
to recant their call. At 2:16 A.M., Fox News Channel declared Bush
the winner in Florida and the next president of the United States;
other outlets followed in lockstep. Vice President Gore then conceded the election. By 4:00 A.M. the media for a second time recanted

their call after Bush's lead diminished; by then, Gore had retracted his concession, a first in American history. The recount battle in Florida would soon begin, marking the beginning of what constitutional scholar Richard L. Hasen has called the "voting wars" in the United States.[1]

As dawn broke in Florida, less than two thousand votes separated the candidates, a difference of fewer than 0.1 percent of some 6 million votes cast. Under Florida law, a margin of 0.5 percent or less triggers an automatic recount. The following day, November 9, the Gore campaign made a crucial mistake. It requested a hand count of presidential ballots not statewide but in four Florida counties only. The Gore campaign sought the recount because election officials in Florida had rejected many thousands of ballots cast by punch-card voting machines that did not seem to properly record a discernable vote—the so-called undercounted votes. Jeb Bush, Florida's then-governor and the candidate's brother, recused himself from the recount process, but Secretary of State Katherine Harris did not, even though she had worked as the co-chair of Bush's Florida campaign.[2]

With both sides pursuing litigation in state and federal court to extend or halt the recount, Bush rejected Gore's new proposal for a statewide recount. Secretary Harris had announced that she would certify the results of the election on November 18, regardless of the progress of the recount. But a state court ruling allowed the hand recount to continue, and the Eleventh Circuit Court of Appeals rejected a motion by the Bush team to stop this recount on constitutional grounds. On November 20, nearly two weeks after election day, the Florida Supreme Court heard arguments on whether Harris should consider hand-recounted ballots before certifying the election results, with Bush still ahead. The court unanimously ruled that state election officials must include the results of manual recounts in Florida's presidential tally, with a court-ordered deadline of November 26 or early on November 27.[3]

In majority-Democratic Miami-Dade County, Florida's largest jurisdiction, a partial recount of slightly more than one-fifth of disputed ballots netted Gore 157 votes. With Bush clinging to a precarious lead of just a few hundred votes, it became clear that a full recount might add enough votes to Gore's tally to swing Florida and the presidency to him. On November 22, the Bush team executed a brilliant maneuver to halt the Miami-Dade recount. The Bush campaign decided to stop cold the recount in Dade County. Its high command in Austin, Texas, worked with leaders of the county's conservative Cuban American community to muster 150 demonstrators, including 40 to 60 out-of-state Republicans, to protest the Dade County recount. Al Gore's supporters were nowhere to be found. Conservatives owned the streets. Led by activists flown into the state, including Ken Mehlman, national field director of the Bush campaign, and employees of national GOP senators and representatives, demonstrators stormed the county's election office, disrupted the ballot counting, and influenced an intimidated canvassing board to halt the recount. What later become known as the "Brooks Brothers riot," after the imported participants' corporate, upscale attire, had worked to perfection.[4]

The Bush lawyers simultaneously pursued a legal strategy to halt the recount. They filed a certiorari petition, which asked the U.S. Supreme Court to reverse the decision of the court of appeals that had denied their motion to stop the recount. On November 26, despite ongoing litigation, Secretary Harris certified George Bush the winner in Florida by 537 votes. Governor Jeb Bush signed the Certificate of Ascertainment designating twenty-five Florida electors pledged to George W. Bush and sent the document to the National Archives as required.

Gore's lawyers then filed an election contest action under Florida Election Code, challenging the vote counts in Palm Beach, Miami-Dade, and Nassau Counties. State judge N. Sanders Sauls rejected Gore's claims, but on appeal, the Florida Supreme Court in a four-to-three ruling on December 8 reversed his decision and ordered a manual recount of undervotes that covered most counties in the state. Crucially, the court's ruling did not include overvotes, where a ballot contained more than one mark for president, even if one of the two marks was a write-in for the same candidate.

On December 9, Florida began its statewide manual recount of the undervoted ballots, while the Florida Supreme Court and Eleventh Circuit Court denied the Bush team its stay to stop the recount. However, a divided U.S. Supreme Court issued a stay, halting the recount. Then on December 12, the U.S. Supreme Court issued its ruling in *Bush v. Gore*. By a five-to-four decision along ideological lines, the Court overturned the Florida Supreme Court ruling and stopped the manual recount of undervoted ballots. The U.S. Supreme Court ruled, "Because it is evident that any recount seeking to meet the Dec. 12 date will be unconstitutional . . . we reverse the judgment of the Supreme Court of Florida ordering the recount to proceed." The decision continued, "It is obvious that the recount cannot be conducted in compliance with the requirements of equal protection and due process without substantial additional work." With the recount frozen and Bush ahead by 537 votes, he officially won the state of Florida and became president of the United States by a one-vote majority in the Electoral College.[5]

The backstory in Florida struck a familiar theme: the suppression of African American votes. Studies showed that election officials had eliminated allegedly disenfranchised felons from the voter rolls with a flawed list that overcounted African Americans, who voted 93 percent Democratic, and undercounted Hispanics, who usually voted Republican in Florida. Florida officials had also rejected as invalid some 180,000 ballots—3 percent of votes cast—either because a presidential vote could not be discerned or the ballot appeared to register more than one vote. Analysis showed that election officials discarded as invalid more than one out of every ten ballots cast by African Americans, compared to less than one out of every fifty ballots cast by whites, who voted 57 percent for Bush. Two-thirds of the allegedly invalid ballots cast by black voters were not undervotes, where a vote could not be accurately determined, but uncounted overvotes, where more than one candidate seemingly was marked on the ballot. Officials rejected overvotes even if a voter punched in Al Gore and then wrote in Al Gore to assure that there would be no mistaking their intent. A study of overvotes by University of Michigan political science professor Walter R. Mebane, Jr., "estimated the number of true votes that were not counted because they were recorded as overvotes." He found that Gore lost 46,465 votes, compared to just 10,939 for Bush.[6]

Racial disparities in rejected ballots persisted when controlling for education, income, poverty, literacy, ballot design, and voter technology. If ballots cast by blacks had been rejected at the same rate as ballots cast by whites, more than fifty thousand additional black votes would have been counted in Florida and Gore would have easily won Florida's election and the presidency.[7]

The postelection mess reflected the legacy of a fragmented, eighteenth-century political system that deferred to the states, and then to more than ten thousand localities, the conduct of elections. Each of Florida's sixty-seven counties in effect administered its own election, deciding the design of ballots, the technology for casting votes, the training of poll workers, and the procedures for manual recounts. As a result, voters across Florida's counties did not have an equal opportunity to have their votes counted in the election. Differences in voter technology and procedures partially but by no means fully accounted for racial disparities in rejected ballots. African Americans were more likely than members of other racial groups to reside in counties using defective punch-card technology. However, vast racial disparities persisted within counties using the same voting machines. Technology alone is not the answer to racial disparities in ballot rejection.

Florida's counties used five distinct voting technologies implemented by twelve different kinds of machines made by seven different manufacturers. Among the sixty-seven counties, twenty-six used optical scanning machines tabulated by precinct, and fifteen used such machines tabulated centrally. Twenty-four counties used punch-card machines; one county used paper ballots, counted by hand; and another used old-fashioned lever machines. The punch-card counties accounted for 60 percent of all votes cast but 89 percent of undervotes and 78 percent of overvotes.[8]

Ballot design, with two major party candidates and eight minor party and independent candidates competing for president along with candidates for state and local offices, daunted county officials. These challenges produced a perfect storm in Palm Beach County. Election officials designed the so-called butterfly ballot, which put the presidential candidates on two separate pages, with the punch holes between the pages, hence the butterfly design of two wings and a spine between them.

Instead of having Bush and Gore as their first two choices, voters, many of them elderly retirees and loyal Democratic voters, confronted a confusing ballot with the punch-card hole for Reform Party candidate Pat Buchanan placed between Bush on top and Gore in the third position. Only by looking at the second page and figuring out the correspondence between names and punch holes could voters discern that punching the second hole was a vote for Buchanan, not Gore. Many voters who clearly intended to vote for Gore voted instead for Buchanan or for both Gore and Buchanan, thereby invalidating their ballots. A postelection analysis by the *Palm Beach Post* found that the "visually challenging ballot design" in Palm Beach County "turned an estimated 2,800 would-be Al Gore voters into Pat Buchanan voters," more than enough to reverse the statewide election results in Gore's favor.[9]

The conclusion is inescapable that Florida's 2000 presidential election certified the wrong winner and elected the wrong president. Yet the vast racial disparities in rejected ballots, which cost Gore more than fifty thousand votes, remains the great underreported scandal of the twenty-first century. It was only lightly covered in the press, and even civil rights groups like the Urban League and the NAACP failed to publicize the scandal or investigate its cause, beyond citing outmoded voting technology. It was the same old story of blacks in the South denied their full voting rights. Imagine the unending cries of voter fraud that would have issued from conservative pundits and media if Florida officials had rejected more than one out of ten ballots cast by whites, compared to just one out of fifty ballots cast by African Americans.

In the wake of the fiasco in Florida, Congress enacted with overwhelming bipartisan support the Help America Vote Act (HAVA) of 2002. The act established an Election Assistance Commission to provide the states with voluntary guidelines on voting technology and administration. HAVA requires any first-time voter who registers by mail to show current and valid photo or non-photo identification at the polls. It authorizes voters identified by local officials as ineligible, for example because officials could not find them on registration rolls, to cast provisional ballots. Election officials must count the ballots of people later determined as eligible. In the 2016 election, voters cast nearly 2.5 million provisional ballots, 62 percent of which were fully counted and 9 percent partially counted, saving some 1.8 million votes.[10]

The act provided federal funds to states for upgrading voting machines, registration databases, voter education, poll worker training, and disabled access. In the decade following HAVA's enactment, more than three-quarters of the jurisdictions across the nation replaced the voting equipment they had used in 2000. Still, the act's voluntary guidelines did not impose order or consistency on local jurisdictions, and the initial HAVA funding for the states has faded away. It also did not impact the partisan administration of elections by Republican and Democratic officials in state and local governments, a problem that was so prominently on display in the Florida recount.[11]

At the state level, other reforms supplemented HAVA. By 2017, reforms to expand access to the vote included early voting prior to election day (33 states), voter registration during the early voting period or on election day (16 states), online registration (38 states), absentee voting without an excuse (27 states), preregistration by individuals aged sixteen or seventeen (18 states), and all-mail elections (3 states).

As in the post–Civil War Reconstruction era, with the voting rights revolution came the reaction. In a book published in 1967, a year before his assassination, Reverend Martin Luther King warned, "For the Negro, there is a credibility gap he cannot overlook. . . . Each step forward accents an ever-present tendency to backlash." In our time, it is white Republicans, not white Democrats, who have made voting more difficult, especially for minorities burdened by a history of discrimination and disparities in income, education, housing, health, and access to vehicles and computers. Once again, patterns of racially polarized voting established the political motivations for restricting minority voting. In a reversal of nineteenth-century voting patterns, Republicans are now dependent on older and white voters and Democrats on younger and minority voters. Despite some variations, these voting patterns are remarkably similar in states and localities in all regions of the nation. Thus, it is today's Republicans, like yesterday's southern Democrats, who have taken the lead in enacting measures to restrict voting, especially by minorities and young people.[12]

The reaction against expanded voting opportunities began through laws requiring some form of identification for voting at the polls, which could include photo identifications, such as driver's licenses and passports, or non-photo IDs, such as utility bills or bank statements. From 2001 to 2004, seven states passed voter identification laws, most with governments controlled by Republicans. Then in 2005, Indiana raised the stakes by enacting a strict law requiring government-issued photo-only identification as a prerequisite for voting. With limited exceptions, a voter could not cast a ballot at the polls without presenting such ID. Non-photo identification or photo identification from nongovernmental sources such as private employers did not count. Upon personal application to a Bureau of Motor Vehicles office, voters could obtain a free photo ID card, provided they presented documentary proof of residence and U.S. citizenship. Voters lacking such identification could cast a provisional ballot, which would count only if the voter presented an authorized identification to election officials within ten days after the election. Voters could also sign an affidavit affirming that they could not obtain a photo ID because they are indigent or have legitimate religious objections to being photographed. This was the first state law in U.S. history that barred eligible registered voters from casting a ballot unless they could meet photo identification requirements.[13]

Plaintiffs led by William Crawford, a Democratic member of the Indiana House of Representatives, challenged Indiana's law prior to its implementation. They did not present evidence that the law discriminated against minorities in violation of the Voting Rights Act or the Fourteenth Amendment. Nor did they present evidence showing that Indiana citizens could not meet the photo identification requirements. Rather, plaintiffs claimed that on its face, the law violated the fundamental right to vote and the free speech clause of the First Amendment.

Given the lack of an explicit right to vote in the Constitution, the Seventh Circuit Court of Appeals and the U.S. Supreme Court declined to subject the law to the strict review required for constitutional rights. In upholding the law, both courts applied a more lenient test that balanced the rights of voters against the interests of the state. The Supreme Court opinion, written by the generally liberal justice John Paul Stevens, upheld the law even in the absence of a showing by the state of instances of the voter fraud that the law was allegedly designed to punish and deter. Stevens wrote, "Because Indiana's cards are free, the inconvenience of going to the Bureau of Motor Vehicles, gathering required documents, and posing for a photograph does not qualify as a substantial burden on most voters' right to vote, or represent a significant increase over the usual burdens of voting." He reasoned that "while the record contains no evidence that the fraud SEA 483 addresses—in-person voter impersonation at polling places—has actually occurred in Indiana, such fraud has occurred in other parts of the country, and Indiana's own experience with voter fraud in a 2003 mayoral primary demonstrates a real risk that voter fraud could affect a close election's outcome." The state, he added, also had an interest in efforts "to improve and modernize election procedures criticized as antiquated and inefficient," and "in protecting public confidence in elections."[14]

The enactment of voter photo ID laws in Republican states accelerated after the *Crawford* decision and the election of America's first African American president, Barack Obama, in 2008. According to exit polls, Obama garnered 95 percent of the black vote nationwide and 67 percent of the Hispanic vote, compared to only 43 percent of the white vote. Blacks and Hispanics accounted for 22 percent of the 2008 presidential electorate, compared to just 15 percent in 1996. Obama won 66 percent of voters aged eighteen to twenty-nine, compared to 49 percent of voters over forty-four.

From the advent of the Obama administration through 2016, eleven states adopted strict photo identification laws. Nine had Republican-controlled legislatures and governors. In Arkansas, Republican legislators overrode the veto of a Democratic governor, and in Mississippi voters enacted the law in a statewide referendum. Most of these states departed from the Indiana precedent by prohibiting the use of various forms of government-issued IDs, such as employee or public college IDs, acceptable in Indiana. Most did not provide for an affidavit alternative to the ID requirement.[15]

Advocates justified adoption of voter photo ID laws by raising once again the specter of voter fraud, in this case voter impersonation at the polls. However, in the modern era, studies have debunked the notion of widespread voter fraud corrupting American elections. A nationwide 2011 study conducted by the Republican National

Lawyers Association and designed to root out as much voter fraud as possible found only 5 cases nationwide of prosecutions or convictions for voter impersonation since 1997, and fewer than 350 cases of voter fraud of any kind out of many hundreds of millions of ballots cast in primary and general elections across the United States. A more inclusive study by News21, a national reporting project of eleven universities, that considered reported allegations of voter fraud, whether prosecuted or not, uncovered only 2,068 alleged fraud cases and just 10 allegations of voter impersonation from 2000 to mid-2012.[16]

Concerted efforts by Republican officials in several states to uncover voter fraud have similarly come up short. Like in Indiana, officials defending photo voter ID laws in Wisconsin and Pennsylvania admitted they could not cite any examples of illegal voter impersonation. Ironically, during the 2016 campaign, candidate Donald Trump charged that Philadelphia was a hotbed of voter fraud. In North Carolina, during debates over the adoption of a voter photo ID law, the state board of elections reported that its study of voter fraud had uncovered only two cases of voter impersonation that "merited a referral to the district attorney's office," out of more than 15 million ballots cast from 2000 to 2012.[17]

The lack of evidence for voter impersonation or other fraud is not a matter of the difficulty of detection. Three recent political science studies of voter impersonation have relied on methods that do not turn on allegations or prosecutions, thus responding to the claim that such fraud is hard to detect or verify. These studies, which are based respectively on anomalies in voter turnout records, survey methods designed to detect illicit behavior, and the matching of individual voter files with death certificates (to test allegations of voting the graveyards) confirmed that voter impersonation fraud was virtually nonexistent in American elections.[18]

Comprehensive postelection investigations have likewise demonstrated a lack of voter impersonation or voter fraud in general. One such investigation took place in the state of Maryland, which has no voter identification requirements and no signature requirement at the polls. In 1994, Republican gubernatorial candidate Ellen Sauerbrey alleged that fraudulent votes accounted for the 5,993-vote victory of Democrat Parris Glendening. As the state of Maryland's consultant on voting rights, I was asked by Attorney General Joseph Curran to determine whether there was any truth to Sauerbrey's claims. If there was voter fraud in Maryland, Curran said he wanted to know about it. Although investigation uncovered some unintentional errors by election officials, there was not a single fraudulent vote among the more than 1.4 million ballots cast in the election.

After the presentation by plaintiffs in state district court likewise failed to uncover a single illegal voter, the trial judge, Raymond G. Thieme, who disclosed that he voted for Sauerbrey, dismissed her lawsuit. Her lawyers did not appeal Thieme's decision. Subsequent investigations by the state prosecutor, the U.S. attorney, and the FBI found no voter fraud, only a "few irregularities" that were "the result of faulty voting machines that didn't record votes, election judges' failure to check off voters and people voting in the wrong precinct because they failed to change their addresses."[19]

In Wisconsin, after John Kerry defeated George W. Bush in the state's 2004 presidential election, Republicans charged that Democrats had benefited from widespread voter fraud. Immediately after the election, Republican assembly speaker John Gard charged that Milwaukee mayor Tom Barrett "has got to be embarrassed about what happened in Milwaukee. You've got thousands of addresses they know don't exist." The speaker said that "Democrats and Republicans alike should be concerned about the incredible problems we had across this state."[20] After investigating these allegations in Wisconsin, which had no voter ID law at the time, prosecutors charged only 14 out of 3 million voters in the election with voter fraud. None of the charges involved voter impersonation. Ten of the fourteen cases alleged illegal voting by felons, and the remaining four alleged double voting. None of the double-voting cases resulted in a conviction.[21]

At any given moment, there are deceased people whose names have not yet been removed from state registration rolls. However, studies refute the claim by President Donald Trump and others that fraudsters have voted in the name of the dead. In the Maryland election dispute of 1994, we found that all of Sauerbrey's alleged dead voters were the result of clerical errors or mismatches between live voters and dead people. We knew that Sauerbrey's allegations had fallen apart when alleged dead voters arose from the grave to walk and talk, including some who said they voted for Sauerbrey.[22]

In a 2012 letter to the U.S. Department of Justice, Republican attorney general Alan Wilson of South Carolina claimed that 953 ballots were allegedly cast by voters listed as dead in prior elections during the previous six years. The South Carolina State Election Commission informed Wilson that it had the resources to investigate 207 cases of alleged dead voters from the most recent 2010 election. The commission found that 106 cases were attributable to clerical errors; 56 cases were the result of erroneous data-matching of voters to dead people; 32 cases were "voter participation errors," including stray marks on lists erroneously indicating that the individuals in question had voted; 3 cases involved absentee ballots filed by voters who later died before Election Day; and 10 cases contained "insufficient information in the record to make a determination." Not a single case involved a verified example of anyone voting in the name of a deceased person.[23]

Given the spate of post-2008 voter photo ID laws enacted almost exclusively by Republican-controlled state governments, Justice Stevens, who wrote the Supreme Court's opinion in the *Crawford* case, has since lamented that although the plaintiff's case was evidentially weak, "we ended up with a fairly unfortunate decision." He noted that the Court simply did not have before it enough information about the law's impact, and that if he had applied what he independently knew about photo voter ID laws, he might have reached a different decision. Judge Richard A. Posner, one of the nation's most respected conservative jurists, who wrote the Seventh Circuit opinion in *Crawford,* said in 2013, "I plead guilty to having written the majority opinion" in the *Crawford* case, adding that photo voter ID law is "a type of law now widely regarded as a means of voter suppression rather than of fraud prevention." He explained, "There's always been strong competition between the parties, but it hadn't reached the peak of ferocity that it's since achieved. . . . One wasn't alert to this kind of trickery, even though it's age old in the democratic process."[24]

In his dissenting opinion regarding the Seventh Circuit's five-to-five vote against holding a full court review of the challenge to Wisconsin's voter photo ID law, Judge Posner wrote that "there is only one motivation for imposing burdens on voting that are ostensibly designed to discourage voter-impersonation fraud, if there is no actual danger of such fraud, and that is to discourage voting by persons likely to vote against the party responsible for imposing the burdens." He added, "It is conservatives who support them [photo voter ID laws] and liberals who oppose them. Unless conservatives and liberals are masochists, promoting laws that hurt them, these laws must suppress minority voting and the question then becomes whether there are offsetting social benefits—the evidence is that there are not."[25]

States did not limit restrictive measures to voter photo ID laws but also enacted other legislation that restricted access to registration and voting. These measures, primarily but not exclusively enacted in Republican-controlled states, included reduced early voting, limitations on registration opportunities, and tightened laws that barred voting by former felons.

In 2013, after Republicans gained unified control over North Carolina's state government, they enacted along party lines omnibus legislation that bundled together most of these new restrictions. The full legislation, known as the Voter Information Verification Act (VIVA), imposed collectively the most restrictive voter photo identification requirements in the nation, with several other limitations on voting and registration. After the adoption of VIVA, an analysis for the civil rights research group Institute of Southern Studies concluded, "number of states with voting laws that are more restrictive than North Carolina's: 0."[26]

North Carolina adopted its voter restrictions at a time of extreme partisanship and voting that fell along racial lines. According to a 2014 study by the Pew Research Center, in the two decades since the epic Republican victories in 1994, "the partisan divide among the American people [has] widened considerably." Pew found that "the median Republican is now more conservative than 94% of Democrats, compared with 70% twenty years ago. And the median Democrat is more liberal than 92% of Republicans, up from 64%." Partisan antipathy has similarly soared. The share of Republicans with "very unfavorable" opinions of Democrats rose from 17 to 43 percent, and the share of Democrats with very unfavorable opinions of Republicans from 16 to 38 percent. Political activity is highest among the most extreme conservatives and liberals. In Congress, as already noted, political polarization has come close to reaching the mathematical maximum in voting in both the U.S. House and Senate.[27]

Political views are highly correlated with race. Pew Research found that in 2014 party affiliation, Republicans led Democrats by 49 to 40 percent among whites but trailed Democrats by 80 to 11 percent among blacks, 65 to 23 percent among Asians, and 56 to 26 percent among Hispanics.[28] Voting closely tracks these partisan affiliations. Presidential exit polls for 2012 showed that Republican Mitt Romney won 59 percent of the white vote but only 6 percent of the African American vote, 26 percent of the Asian American vote, and 27 percent of the Hispanic vote. In 2016, even without an African American Democrat on the ballot, Republican Donald Trump won

57 percent of the white vote but only 8 percent of the African American vote, 27 percent of the Asian American vote, and 28 percent of the Hispanic vote.

Republicans in North Carolina enacted VIVA shortly after the 2012 presidential election, in response to the growing presence of minorities, especially overwhelming Democratic African Americans, in North Carolina's electorate. From 2004 until passage of VIVA in July 2013, African Americans in North Carolina had increased their share of registered voters from 19.4 to 22.5 percent; members of all minority groups combined increased from 22.1 to 29.0 percent. Voting in North Carolina was even more polarized than nationally. Exit polling data for presidential and other statewide elections from 2004 through 2012 shows that African Americans supported Democratic candidates at near unanimous levels, whereas two-thirds of whites on average backed Republicans. The racial disparity in party voting far exceeded other differences in sex, age, education, and income. In 2008, Democrats had won North Carolina's presidential election for the first time since 1976, and in 2012 Democrats came within two percentage points of a second consecutive victory. Republicans in North Carolina could not reverse demography and expand the white share of the state's electorate, but they could attempt to constrain the minority vote.[29]

VIVA sparked a legal challenge by the NAACP and the U.S. Department of Justice. Rosanell Eaton, a black woman who grew up in Jim Crow North Carolina during the 1920s and 1930s, joined the litigation as a private plaintiff. Eaton had attended segregated schools, drank from colored-only fountains, and one morning woke up to find charred crosses on her front lawn. In 1942, Eaton rode for two miles on a mule-drawn wagon to register to vote at the Franklin County courthouse. Three white male officials confronted her. They ordered her to stand up straight, keep her arms at her side, and recite from memory the preamble to the Constitution. She did so word for word and then passed a written literacy test, becoming one of the few African Americans of her era to vote in North Carolina. She later marched with Martin Luther King and helped several thousand African Americans in North Carolina to register to vote. "I am where I am today," said President Barack Obama in 2015, "only because men and women like Rosanell Eaton refused to accept anything less than a full measure of equality."[30]

More than seventy years after her initial registration, a ninety-three-year-old Eaton had a much harder time qualifying to vote under North Carolina's new law, which required voters to show specific forms of photo identification at the polls. She had a driver's license, but the name on her voter-registration card (Rosanell Eaton) did not match the name on her license (Rosa Johnson Eaton). To gain new identification she made eleven trips to different agencies—four trips to the Department of Motor Vehicles, four trips to two different Social Security offices, and three trips to different banks—totaling more than two hundred miles and twenty hours. "You know, all of this is coming back around before I could get in the ground," she said. "I was hoping I would be dead before I'd have to see all this again." So, Eaton joined the lawsuit.[31] North Carolina NAACP v. McCrory produced three years of litigation through a federal district court, to the Fourth Circuit Court of Appeals and ultimately to the U.S. Supreme Court. The North Carolina case is a microcosm of the post-2000 American "voting wars."[32]

The process for enacting VIVA had turned on the U.S. Supreme Court decision in Shelby County v. Holder on June 25, 2013. This ruling relieved North Carolina and all states from preclearing new voter laws or regulations under section 5 of the Voting Rights Act. In the most significant victory for opponents of the Voting Rights Act, an ideologically riven five-to-four Supreme Court ruling struck down as unconstitutional the coverage formula of section 4. The decision, in effect, nullified section 5 preclearance because it eliminated the legal foundation for requiring states or localities to gain approval for new voting laws. The Court held that section 4 trampled on the "equal sovereignty of the states" because the differential treatment of the states is "based on 40-year-old facts having no logical relationship to the present day." It said that there was little difference in the twenty-first century between covered and noncovered jurisdictions, and that "regardless of how to look at the record no one can fairly say that it shows anything approaching the 'pervasive,' 'flagrant,' 'widespread,' and 'rampant' discrimination that faced Congress in 1965, and that clearly distinguished the covered jurisdictions from the rest of the nation."[33]

The Court majority failed to consider the subtler but still effective discrimination of the new voting wars. Just a year earlier, for example, three-judge panels of the District Court of the District of Columbia had ruled unanimously that Texas's voter photo ID law had the effect of discriminating against minorities and that Texas's redistricting plans for Congress and the state senate had intentionally discriminated against minorities. In a comprehensive study of voting rights violations, historian J. Morgan Kousser refuted the Court's claim of minimal recent voting rights violations in covered jurisdictions. Dallas minister Peter Johnson, a civil rights activist since the 1960s, said, "There's nobody that's going to shoot at you if you register to vote today. They aren't going to bomb your church. They aren't going to get you fired from your job. You don't have those kinds of overt, mean-spirited behaviors today that we experienced years ago. . . . They pat you on the back, but there's a knife in that pat."[34]

The Republican sponsors of VIVA introduced the bill as HB 589 at the beginning of the 2013 assembly session, before the *Shelby* decision. In April, the North Carolina House of Representatives passed a version of HB 589 that included voter photo identification requirements, with no other provisions.[35] This bill closely followed the legislation in Indiana by authorizing for voting all forms of government-issued photo identification, including expired IDs. The sponsors of this bill lauded their transparent process and extensive vetting, which included public hearings, testimony from interest groups and authorities in the field, several committee hearings, and two days of debate in the house of representatives. Republican representative Tom Murry, one of the bill's primary sponsors, said, "The historic vote was the result of a 10-month process that included multiple public hearings, hours of testimony by experts and members of the public, and in-depth analysis of voter ID systems in numerous other states." Representative David Lewis, chairman of the House Elections Committee, noted, "This has been a fair and open and transparent process, as we committed it would be."[36]

With North Carolina still under preclearance requirements, sponsors of HB 589 insisted that the relatively lenient voter photo ID bill balanced concerns for ballot integrity with voter access to the ballot. Then Republican speaker of the house and later U.S. senator Thom Tillis said, "We have arrived at a bill that we believe will stand up in a court of law, address legitimate concerns about voting access, and move North Carolina to a photo identification voting system."[37]

The general assembly radically changed course on HB 589 after the June 25 *Shelby* ruling. Following house passage, the bill sat in the senate for months with no committee or floor action. The *Shelby* decision, however, prompted the senate leadership to revamp HB 589 into legislation that little resembled the pre-*Shelby* version. On the day of the *Shelby* ruling, Republican Tom Apodaca, the chairman of the Senate Rules Committee, said, "I guess we're safe in saying this decision was what we were expecting." He added, "So, now we can go with the full bill." The *Shelby* decision, Apodaca suggested, eliminated "legal headaches" in adopting the many revised and new provisions of the "full bill." The ruling, he argued, "should speed things along greatly."[38]

The so-called full bill both added to and subtracted from the pre-*Shelby* version of HB 589. It added provisions that cut the number of early voting days from seventeen to ten and eliminated the option to register during this period. It prohibited the prior practice of partially counting provisional ballots cast in the incorrect precinct for countywide or statewide elections and ended the preregistration of sixteen- and seventeen-year-olds. Simultaneously, the "full bill" subtracted from HB 589 many forms of previously acceptable photo identification, including student IDs, government employee IDs, public assistance IDs, and expired IDs with an exception for registrants aged seventy or more.

As was required by federal court decisions, VIVA authorized voters to apply for a free state-issued photo ID. But applicants had to visit a Department of Motor Vehicles office in person and provide proof of voter registration, age, and identity; a valid Social Security number; and proof of citizenship and residency, documentation that often eluded poor and minority people and elderly African Americans like Rosanell Eaton, born in the Jim Crow era. Applicants had to attest that they did not already possess an authorized photo ID, which presumed knowledge of specific forms of ID included and excluded under VIVA.[39]

The senate and house passed the post-*Shelby* version of HB 589 on July 25, 2013, two days after it emerged from the Senate Rules Committee and just one day before the end of the legislative session, foreclosing any further opportunity for debate or analysis.[40] The leadership rushed the bill to passage without extended public hearings, testimony by authorities or interest groups, or extensive and open legislative debate. The lack of process given to the full bill departed from the robust scrutiny accorded the pre-*Shelby* version.[41]

In the post-*Shelby* bill, the legislature eliminated forms of photo identification that were relatively more accessible to minorities and retained forms of identification that were relatively less accessible to minorities. Analyses presented to the federal courts demonstrated that, as compared to whites, African Americans, by far the largest minority group in the state, were significantly less likely to possess unexpired forms of the two most commonly available categories of photo IDs under VIVA: valid Department of Motor Vehicles (DMV) operators' and nonoperators' IDs, and U.S. passports. In contrast, analysis showed that African Americans had greater access than whites to higher education IDs, government employment IDs, and public assistance IDs that the "full bill" had eliminated. In North Carolina, 7.3 percent of voting-age blacks were enrolled in public institutions of higher education, compared to 5.7 percent of whites; 10.9 percent of African Americans held government jobs, compared to 9.0 percent of whites; and 27.1 percent of African American households received food stamps / SNAP public assistance, compared to 8.1 percent of white households.

The challenged provisions of VIVA added to the full bill after *Shelby* similarly discriminated against black voters. African Americans were much more likely than whites in North Carolina to use early voting, which VIVA restricted, and to register during early voting, which VIVA eliminated. In the presidential election of 2012, African Americans accounted for 28.8 percent of early voters, compared to 15.5 percent of other voters, whereas whites accounted for 65.4 percent of early voters, compared to 78.0 percent of other voters. African Americans accounted for 33.7 percent of people registering during the early voting period, compared to 22.3 percent of all registered voters. Whites accounted for 53.7 percent of registrations during the early voting period, compared to 71.6 percent of all registered voters.

African Americans disproportionately cast partially counted provisional ballots and registered as sixteen- or seventeen-year-olds. In 2012, African Americans accounted for 35.0 percent of voters with partially counted provisional ballots, compared to 23.0 percent of other voters, whereas whites accounted for 51.9 percent of voters with partially counted provisional ballots, compared to 70.9 percent of other voters. In March 2013, African Americans comprised 26.2 percent of registered voters who had initially preregistered as sixteen- or seventeen-year-olds, compared to 22.4 percent of all registered voters. Whites comprised 61.9 percent of preregistered voters, compared to 70.7 percent of all registered voters. A recent study by

two political scientists "consistently found" that registering potential voters while still in high school "is a viable electoral reform for
increasing youth turnout, increasing voting by somewhere between
2 to 8 percentage points."[42]

The rationales offered by backers of the post-*Shelby* bill confirmed
the discriminatory intent of the North Carolina legislature and governor. Backers claimed that the photo ID provisions brought North
Carolina into line with other states. Senator Robert A. Rucho,
chairman of the Joint Legislative Elections Oversight Committee,
said, "There are 30 states which currently have a voter ID in place, and
33 states have passed, uh, ID—voter ID laws." Yet of the states that
Rucho cited, most accepted non-photo forms of identification or
had nonstrict laws, which enabled voters to cast a regular ballot
through alternative means of identification, such as signing a
declaration of identity. Even among states with strict photo ID laws,
North Carolina became the only one that prohibited government-
issued employee, student, public assistance, and expired IDs.

Citing poll data, backers claimed that the people of North Carolina overwhelmingly supported VIVA's photo identification requirement and electoral restrictions. However, the cited polls refer
to support for "some form of government-issued ID," which would
include many forms of identification eliminated in the post-*Shelby*
bill. In addition, a poll conducted in North Carolina by SurveyUSA
in April 2013 found that 74 percent of North Carolina's registered
voters agreed that "legislators should show evidence of significant
problems, such as real voter fraud, before they pass laws that make
voting more difficult." The polls further demonstrated that North
Carolina residents rejected the full VIVA bill. An August 2013 survey
by Public Policy Polling found that 39 percent of respondents supported VIVA in its entirety, with 50 percent opposed and 11 percent
uncertain. An August 2013 Elon University poll found that only
30 percent of North Carolina residents supported reducing early
voting by a week, with 59 percent opposed. These results show that

contrary to claims by VIVA backers, the people of North Carolina did not support the panoply of voting restrictions incorporated in the legislation.[43]

After the state Board of Elections study showed the absence of voter impersonation in the state, VIVA's sponsors pivoted to the vague notion of increasing voter confidence in the integrity of the ballot as justification for the photo ID requirement. The Supreme Court had cited voter confidence as a legitimate state concern in the *Crawford* case, but in that litigation, plaintiffs had not attempted to show either a discriminatory effect of the Indiana law or a discriminatory purpose in its enactment. "There is some evidence of voter fraud, but that's not the primary reason for doing this," said Speaker Tillis. "We call this restoring confidence in government."[44] Just a few months earlier, backers of the photo identification law had with equal conviction affirmed that the pre-*Shelby* version of the photo ID bill, without the later subtractions, had achieved the goal of upholding ballot integrity and voter confidence. This commonsense measure, Speaker Tillis said of the pre-*Shelby* bill, "will protect the integrity of the ballot box and restore confidence in our election system." Yet this affirmation did not deter Republicans in the legislature from imposing much stiffer restrictions in their post-*Shelby* bill.[45]

Studies show that strict photo voter ID laws fail to increase voter confidence in the integrity of elections. A national study by political scientists Shaun Bowler and Todd Donovan finds that "none of our model specifications yielded evidence that strict photo identification laws had any broad, unconditioned effects on voter confidence. The likelihood that a person perceived voter fraud as common was unrelated to how strict her state's voter identification laws were."[46]

Finally, Governor Pat McCrory invoked the need for "registration integrity" to justify the elimination of registration during the early voting period. However, the state Board of Elections report on voter fraud found only one case of registration fraud related to residency after adoption of early voting registration in 2007, compared to two cases before its adoption.[47]

From the post-Reconstruction era through "Operation Eagle Eye," calls for "election integrity" or "ballot security" have been used in efforts to discourage voting by minorities. More recently, in response to lawsuits in 1982 and again in 1987, the national Republican Party agreed to consent decrees in federal court that prohibited the party from engaging in antifraud activities that targeted minority voters. In a 2009 ruling, New Jersey federal district court judge Dickinson Debevoise denied a Republican National Committee (RNC) motion to end the consent decree. The U.S. Court of Appeals for the Third Circuit upheld his ruling. "Minority voters continue to overwhelmingly support Democratic candidates," Judge Debevoise wrote in his decision. "As long as that is the case, the RNC and other Republican groups may be tempted to keep qualified minority voters from casting their ballots, especially in light of the razor-thin margin of victory by which many elections have been decided in recent years." After reviewing all evidence of alleged voter fraud presented by the RNC, he held, "In fact, even a cursory investigation of the prevalence of voter intimidation demonstrates that ballot security initiatives have the potential to unfairly skew election results by disenfranchising qualified voters in far greater numbers than the instances of in-person fraud that may occur during any given race." After district court judge John Michael Vazquez let the consent decree expire in January 2018, the Democratic National Committee appealed his ruling to the Third Circuit.[48]

The special treatment of mail-in absentee ballots under VIVA further undermined the claim of upholding election integrity. Mail-in absentee ballots, which are disproportionately filed by white people, were exempted from the photo ID requirement. Yet absentee voting is far more susceptible to voter fraud than in-person voting because the perpetrators are nameless and faceless. It is far riskier and less efficient to walk into a polling place under false pretenses than it is to anonymously mail in a fraudulent ballot. Although absentee voting fraud is also rare, it is more common than voter impersonation. The North Carolina State Board of Elections compilation on voter fraud found forty-seven referrable cases of absentee voter fraud. Nationwide data reported in 2011 by News21 found that absentee voting fraud was the most common type of fraud, outnumbering voter impersonation by a ratio of forty-nine to one. A Government Accountability Office report released in October 2014 said that "no apparent cases of in-person voter impersonation [were] charged by DOJ's [Department of Justice's] Criminal Division or by U.S. Attorney's offices anywhere in the United States from 2004 through July 3, 2014."[49]

North Carolina Republicans noted that the photo ID component of VIVA had a two-year phase-in period during which registered voters could apply for free photo IDs from the DMV. Representative Ruth Samuelson, a primary bill sponsor, said, "I wanted to point out that, once again, the comparison to another state, South Carolina did not have a phase-in period. . . . The VIVA is going to be an outreach. It's going to be an outreach to churches. It will be an outreach to 12 community boards of elections. It will be an outreach to schools and other groups, and the kinds of people who are shut in." However, no other VIVA provision had a phase-in period, and the North Carolina General Assembly eliminated in VIVA many of the public education and outreach provisions of the pre-*Shelby* version. As of late January 2015, nearly a year and a half after VIVA's adoption, the state had issued only 771 free ID cards. This stands in stark contrast to the case in Pennsylvania. Before the courts invalidated Pennsylvania's never-implemented voter photo identification law, the state, which conducted an extensive campaign of public education and outreach, had issued 16,700 free voter ID cards in the first year and a quarter after the law's adoption.[50]

On the eve of a preliminary injunction hearing on VIVA in June 2015, the North Carolina legislature, fearful of an adverse verdict, modified the photo ID provision of the 2013 law to allow individuals without authorized photo IDs to vote provisional ballots if they signed a declaration indicating a reasonable impediment to obtaining such identification. This put off consideration of that provision until trial on the merits in January 2016. After a trial that lasted several weeks and created a record of 23,000 pages, federal district court judge Thomas D. Schroeder upheld VIVA in its entirety. Judge Schroeder wrote a detailed, 485-page opinion, but on July 29, 2016, a unanimous three-judge panel of the Fourth Circuit Court of Appeals overturned his findings and struck down every challenged provision of the law. Following Supreme Court guidelines for establishing intentional discrimination, the circuit court further ruled that in adopting VIVA, North Carolina had acted with the intent to discriminate against minority voters to achieve political advantages for Republicans.[51]

The appeals court found that "in holding that the legislature did not enact the challenged provisions with discriminatory intent, the [district] court seems to have missed the forest in carefully surveying the many trees. This failure of perspective led the court to ignore critical facts bearing on legislative intent, including the inextricable link between race and politics in North Carolina." As in the earlier *Garza* case, the court firmly rejected the claim that burdens placed on minority voters can be justified under the Constitution by political motivation. It noted that "the totality of circumstances ... cumulatively and unmistakably reveal that the General Assembly used [VIVA] 2013-381 to entrench itself. It did so by targeting voters who, based on race, were unlikely to vote for the majority party. Even if done for partisan ends, that constituted racial discrimination."[52]

The appeals court stated that provisions of the post-*Shelby* version of photo ID were deliberately designed to "*target African Americans with almost surgical precision,* they constitute inapt remedies for the problems assertedly justifying them and, in fact, impose cures for problems that did not exist. Thus, the asserted justifications cannot and do not conceal the State's true motivation." The court further found that "before enacting that law, the legislature requested data on the use, by race, of a number of voting practices. Upon receipt of the race data, the General Assembly enacted legislation that restricted voting and registration in five different ways, all of which disproportionately affected African Americans."[53]

A finding of intentional racial discrimination under the equal protection clause of the Fourteenth Amendment is rare and requires plaintiffs to surmount a high barrier of proof, which they did in this litigation. Despite the Supreme Court's invalidation of section 4 of the Voting Rights Act in the *Shelby* decision, this finding of intentional discrimination authorized the appeals court under section 3(c) of the act to "bail in" North Carolina to preclearance coverage. However, the court chose not to exercise this option.[54]

Even with this victory for black voting rights, the North Carolina case highlights the consequences of losing the preclearance provision of the Voting Rights Act. Black plaintiffs succeeded in overturning VIVA only after protracted, expensive, and complex litigation, with the full power and resources of the U.S. Justice Department behind them and a liberal appeals court in the Fourth Circuit, not a set of circumstances likely to be replicated for other instances of discriminatory state and local practices. Litigation under section 2 of the Voting Rights Act and the equal protection clause of the Fourteenth Amendment requires considerable resources, legal expertise, and the testimony of expert witnesses.

After the adverse VIVA ruling, for example, Republicans in North Carolina, unshackled by preclearance requirements, acted again to burden African Americans voting in the 2016 elections by reducing early voting locations in seventeen counties during the first week of early voting. These counties included the four counties with the largest African American populations. In some nine counties, local Republican election officials opened only one polling location for early voting's first week. Turnout during this period declined substantially in these seventeen counties as compared to the remainder of the state. The state also engaged in a flawed purge of registered voters that disproportionately impacted African Americans. Shortly before the election, U.S. District Court judge Loretta Copeland Biggs ordered the state to restore the purged voters. "Voter enfranchisement cannot be sacrificed when citizens through no fault of their own have been removed from the voter rolls," she ruled. Six months after the 2016 election, on May 15, 2017, the U.S. Supreme Court declined to take up an appeal by North Carolina on the VIVA case, leaving in place the appeals court's ruling.[55]

North Carolina was not alone in implementing after *Shelby* such seemingly small but consequential discriminatory measures. A 2016 study of a limited sample of 381 counties in formerly covered states found that since *Shelby,* 43 percent had closed polling places, piling up a total of 868 closures. The study found that 67 percent of counties in Alabama reduced the number of polling places, 61 percent in Louisiana, and 53 percent in Texas. In Arizona, nearly every county had closed polling places, erasing 212 polling locations. Although there may be "justifiable reasons" for closing polling places, the study concluded, "the loss of Section 5 means that there is no process to ensure that reductions are disclosed to the public, are conducted with the input of impacted communities, and do not discriminate against voters of color."[56]

In Arizona, for the 2016 presidential preference primary, Maricopa County reduced the number of polling places from more than two hundred in 2012 to sixty in 2016. Maricopa is the largest county in Arizona and the fourth largest in the United States, with a population of 4.2 million, including a 31-percent-Hispanic and 44-percent-minority component. The county's chief election official, Republican Helen Purcell, authorized this reduction despite having been warned ahead of time by county supervisor Steve Gallardo that sixty polling places was inadequate for the county. A study of polling place locations by the *Arizona Republic* found that "while both rich and poor areas were hurt by a lack of polling sites this year, a wide swath of predominantly minority and lower-income areas in west Phoenix and east Glendale, along with south Phoenix, were particularly lacking in polling sites compared with 2012." Most Arizona counties had about 2,500 eligible voters per polling place, compared to 21,000 per polling place in Maricopa County.[57]

In 2011, Alabama enacted a photo identification requirement for voting in person or absentee. It did submit the law for preclearance but delayed its implementation after the *Shelby* decision. Although driver's licenses are one of the limited forms of identification authorized under the law, in 2015 Alabama proposed to close thirty-one driver's license offices, mostly in rural areas of the state's black belt. After protests from civil rights groups, Alabama agreed to keep the offices open one day a week, still severely restricting access for residents of these substantially black counties.[58]

For eight years from 2011 to 2018, Texas defended patently discriminatory redistricting plans for congressional seats, also facilitated by the end of preclearance. The plan led to multiple lawsuits. From the 2000 to the 2010 U.S. Census, the population of Texas soared by 21 percent, which netted the state four new congressional seats, raising its apportionment to thirty-six seats. No other state gained more than two new districts. African Americans and Latinos accounted for 79 percent of this population growth, and all minorities combined accounted for 89 percent. Texas had become a majority-minority state, in both total and voting-age population. African Americans and Latinos comprised 39.5 percent of the state's citizen voting-age population, which translated into 14.2 congressional districts. All minorities combined comprised 43 percent of the citizen voting-age population, which translated into 15.5 districts, compared to 20.5 districts for whites.[59]

It was not easy, but by fragmenting and in some cases packing enough minority communities, the Republican legislature adopted a 2011 plan that created only ten districts in which minority voters had an effective opportunity to elect candidates of their choice. That left twenty-six districts in effect controlled by whites, over-representing whites by five and a half districts. The cracking and packing of minorities is illustrated by the districts that the Republican legislature drew in the heavily populated Dallas and Tarrant Counties of north Texas. From 2000 to 2010, in the region known as DFW, because it includes the cities of Dallas and Fort Worth, the Latino population grew by 84 percent (more than 440,000 people), the African American population grew by 34 percent (more than 179,000), and the population of other minorities by 12 percent (more than 63,000). The white population *declined* by 30 percent (more than 156,000). By 2010, minorities comprised 57 percent of the population in DFW, 53 percent of the voting-age population, and 40 percent of the citizen voting-age population. In defiance of these trends, the 2011 plan did not create a single additional minority opportunity congressional district in DFW, with the result that only one of eight districts (12.5 percent) that fell primarily within DFW provided minorities such an opportunity.

Republicans in the state legislature crammed additional African Americans into the already-packed congressional district 30, which had overwhelmingly elected a black candidate in every prior election. The plan upped the minority population of district 30 to 86 percent. The legislature then cracked or fragmented many minority communities in the region and created several bizarrely shaped districts controlled by whites. The legislature separated the Latino neighborhoods in Fort Worth from nearby African American neighborhoods by drawing a notorious "lightning bolt" district that shot into Tarrant County from white-controlled Denton County. The plan left many hundreds of thousands of minority voters stranded in white-dominated districts in which they had no ability to elect candidates of their choice to Congress or even influence election results.

The plan dismantled a minority opportunity district in Travis County, one of the state's most liberal counties, encompassing the city of Austin. The legislature cracked Travis County into five separate districts, all controlled by white Republicans. In Harris County, which encompasses the city of Houston, nearly all the substantial population growth was minority. Yet the legislature failed to create an additional minority opportunity district there even though minority advocacy groups presented alternative plans for the county that incorporated one.

In congressional district 23 in southwest Texas, the legislature used a different maneuver to dilute Hispanic votes. In 2006, the U.S. Supreme Court had found a voting rights violation in the prior version of this district and ordered a bolstering of the Hispanic population. To mask another voting rights violation, the legislature knowingly and intentionally reduced the effectiveness of the Hispanic vote without reducing the Hispanic voting-age percentage in the district. The map designers craftily switched out high-voting Democratic Hispanic areas with Hispanic areas that have lower turnout and moved in high-turnout white Republican areas. To achieve this end, the plan moved more than 600,000 people in and out of district 23 and split thirty-nine voting precincts. Texas's own redistricting expert, Professor John Alford of Rice University, conceded that district 23 "is probably less likely to perform than it was, and so I certainly wouldn't count and don't [and] haven't counted the 23rd as an effective minority district in the newly adopted plan."[60]

In defense of the plan, Texas attorney general Greg Abbott (who later became governor) admitted that it disparately burdened minority voters but raised the familiar, though often rejected, claim that the goal of advancing Republican interests immunized the plan from a constitutional violation of intentional discrimination, despite "incidental effects on minority voters." He observed, "DOJ's accusations of racial discrimination are baseless.... In 2011, both houses of the Texas Legislature were controlled by large Republican majorities, and their redistricting decisions were designed to increase the Republican Party's electoral prospects at the expense of the

Democrats. It is perfectly constitutional for a Republican-controlled legislature to make partisan districting decisions, even if there are incidental effects on minority voters who support Democratic candidates."[61]

The plan's defenders also dusted off the states'-rights plea by claiming that Texas should be free to formulate its redistricting plan without challenge from the Department of Justice. In an op-ed article in the *Washington Times* entitled "Obama's Scheme to Take Over Texas," Abbott wrote, "The Constitution makes elections the states' business, not the federal government's," and argued that the Department of Justice should not be challenging decisions made by the Texas legislature. Republican U.S. representative Blake Farenthold tweeted that the Department of Justice's "Attorney General Holder is trying to wage a war on Texas & states' rights," and "DOJ's push to overturn #TX voting laws: the govt's latest attempt at trying to tell states what they can & can't do."[62]

Abbott and Farenthold should have known that elections are not just the business of the states; both the Constitution and the Voting Rights Act have long protected minorities from discrimination by the states. In effect, Abbott and other Republican leaders in Texas have constructed an internally self-justifying rationale for intentionally discriminating against minorities. In their view, it is legitimate for Texas's Republican majority to discriminate against minorities because that is in the partisan interests of the Republican Party and consistent with states' rights. But it is apparently not legitimate for the U.S. Department of Justice to defend minority voting rights because that is in the partisan interests of the Democratic Party and interferes with state business. Yet the intent of the federal government is to enforce the Voting Rights Act and the Fourteenth Amendment to assure that minorities have the opportunity to participate fully in the political process and elect candidates of their choice. Change the names of the parties and the claims made by Texas Republicans in the twenty-first century replicated the arguments

made by Texas Democrats in the nineteenth century against enforcing the Fourteenth and Fifteenth Amendments.

Texas officials knew that the 2011 congressional redistricting plan
would not gain Justice Department preclearance. Instead, they
sought a judgment in favor of the plan from a three-judge panel of
the District Court for the District of Columbia. In a 2012 decision, the
district court unanimously ruled against the state. It held that the
plan had both the effect and intent of discriminating against minorities. The court found that "the parties have provided more evidence of
discriminatory intent than we have space, or need, to address here."[63]

As part of the tangled knot of litigation created by Texas's redistricting decisions, civil rights groups and Democratic interests sued
the state in 2011, charging violation of section 2 of the Voting Rights
Act and the Constitution. The Department of Justice later joined on
the lawsuit as a plaintiff. Before issuing a final ruling, a three-judge
court in San Antonio adopted an interim plan for the 2012 elections,
closely based on the 2011 plan and agreed to as part of a compromise
between the state and some, but not all, of the plaintiffs. The San Antonio court did not have the benefit of the District of Columbia
court's ruling at the time that it implemented the plan, and its order
made clear that the plan was interim only; it did not include any
final ruling on any pending voting rights or constitutional claims.
The interim plan fixed some but not all deficiencies of the 2011 plan.

In March 2017, the San Antonio court issued a final ruling on the
2011 congressional plan, agreeing with the DC court, whose ruling
had no legal standing after the *Shelby* decision, that the plan had
both the effect and intent of discriminating against minority voters.
The court rejected the state's claim "that they did not engage in
intentional vote dilution of minority voting strength, but only of
Democrat voting strength." For example, in DFW, it found that
"while there is certainly an overlap between cracking and packing
Democrats and cracking and packing minorities, the Court finds
that Plaintiffs have satisfied their burden of showing that inten-

tional minority vote dilution was a motivating factor in the drawing of district lines in DFW and that mapdrawers *intentionally diluted minority voting strength in order to gain partisan advantage.*" Across the state, the court held that "the record indicates not just a hostility toward Democratic districts, but a hostility to minority districts, and a willingness to use race for partisan advantage."[64]

Meanwhile, in a special session of the state legislature in 2013, Texas adopted the interim congressional plan as the official, permanent state plan. Although the legislative leadership ruled cosmetically that the legislature could make changes in the interim redistricting plans, it followed closely the initial call of Governor Rick Perry for the special session to adopt the interim plan with no changes. The Republican majority in the Texas legislature pushed the interim plan through along party lines with no changes, despite objections from minority advocacy groups and minority members of the legislature.[65]

In a subsequent August 2017 decision on the state's enactment in 2013 of the interim congressional plan, the San Antonio court again found that the state had engaged in intentional discrimination in certain parts of the state. It did not find intentional discrimination in DFW, not because it absolved the state of such intent but because it ruled that any further remedy of the plan's intentional discrimination would fail. It found that an additional single-race majority district could not be drawn in DFW and that a combined majority-minority district of African Americans and Hispanics failed to meet legal requirements because blacks and Hispanics diverged in their choice of candidates in Democratic primary elections. This decision is currently on appeal to the U.S. Supreme Court.[66]

Civil rights advocates achieved other victories in the courts. In 2013, federal district court judge Nelva Gonzales Ramos found that Texas's strict voter identification law violated section 2 of the Voting Rights Act and intentionally discriminated against minorities. Like North Carolina's VIVA law, the Texas statute included IDs more accessible to whites than minorities, notably licenses for the concealed carry of firearms, but excluded IDs more accessible to minorities, such as student, public assistance, and government employee IDs. A three-to-zero decision by a panel of the Fifth Circuit Court of Appeals and a nine-to-six *en banc* decision by the Fifth Circuit upheld Judge Ramos's finding that the Texas ID law violated the Voting Rights Act. It neither upheld nor overturned the finding of intentional discrimination in the enactment of the law but remanded the issue back to Judge Ramos for further consideration.[67]

The U.S. Supreme Court declined on January 23, 2017, to hear an appeal on the Fifth Circuit's ruling against the voter ID law brought by the state of Texas. Chief Justice John G. Roberts noted that the "issues will be better suited for certiorari review" after Judge Ramos issued a final order.[68] Upon remand from the Fifth Circuit, Ramos entertained briefings on the question of intentional discrimination. She again found discriminatory intent, ruling that actions of the state legislature "revealed a pattern of conduct unexplainable on nonracial grounds, to suppress minority voting."[69]

She subsequently rejected as inadequate a state revision of the ID law that changed none of its discriminatory requirements. The revision only enabled voters lacking an authorized ID to present an alternative photo or non-photo identification and sign an affidavit attesting to a "reasonable impediment" to obtaining an acceptable one. The new law subjected individuals who allegedly lied on the affidavit to felony prosecution with potential penalties of six months to two years in jail. Ramos found that "not one of the discriminatory features of [the old law] is fully ameliorated by the terms" of the new law. The revised law, she ruled, "trades one obstacle to voting with another—replacing the lack of qualified photo ID with an overreaching affidavit threatening severe penalties for perjury."[70]

Combined with the decision of the District of Columbia District Court and two decisions from the San Antonio court on redistricting, federal courts have ruled four times since 2012 that the state of Texas had intentionally discriminated against minority voters. So too did the appeals court in North Carolina. A district court in Louisiana also found in August 2017 that the state of Louisiana had intentionally discriminated against African American voters by maintaining an at-large system for electing judges in the state's Thirty-Second Judicial District.[71] These intent findings in three jurisdictions, which pre-*Shelby* had been covered under the preclearance provision of the Voting Rights Act, provide further evidence that contrary to the reasoning in the *Shelby* decision, racial discrimination has not faded away in previously covered jurisdictions.

More than fifteen years after the *Page v. Bartels* litigation, the Supreme Court recognized the discriminatory effects of packing minorities into districts, common practice for Republican-controlled legislatures. By confining minority voters to a relatively few districts, packing impedes their ability to elect candidates of their choice—typically Democrats—in additional districts. The threshold percentage of minorities for a packed district is a factually intensive inquiry and is usually much higher for Hispanics than for African Americans. Even in districts with less than a voting-age majority, black voters can still elect candidates of their choice in partisan elections. They have done so in many instances, by winning in Democratic primaries, with white voters primarily participating in Republican contests, and then drawing enough crossover votes from whites to elect their chosen candidates in general elections.

During its 2017 term, the Supreme Court upheld anti-packing decisions in Virginia and North Carolina. In Virginia, a three-judge federal court found that Republicans in the legislature had unduly packed minorities into congressional district 3, represented by African American Democrat Bobby Scott. In 2016, with unanimous approval from the Supreme Court, the lower court implemented a new plan that unpacked district 3 and enabled African Americans to elect candidates of their choice in neighboring district 4. In North Carolina, three-judge courts found that the state's plans for both

Congress and state legislatures had impermissibly used race to pack African Americans into certain districts. The decisions covered two congressional districts, nineteen state house districts, and nine state senate districts. The Supreme Court upheld both the congressional and state legislative findings of discrimination.[72]

In reaching these findings on excessively packed minority districts, the courts drew on Supreme Court precedent from the 1990s that prohibited jurisdictions from drawing districts predominantly based on race, absent a showing that the districts were narrowly drawn to meet a compelling state interest, such as complying with the Voting Rights Act. The packing of districts to create wasted minority votes would clearly not qualify as a legitimate state interest of any kind. Writing for a court majority in the North Carolina congressional case, Supreme Court justice Elena Kagan rejected the state's defense that it drew district lines based on politics, not race. "The sorting of voters on the grounds of their race remains suspect even if race is meant to function as a proxy for other (including political) characteristics," she wrote.[73]

One of the ironies of voting rights jurisprudence is the unexpected consequences of the racial gerrymandering prohibitions of the 1990s that advocates initially believed would thwart the ability to create minority opportunity districts. Instead, as the recent rulings indicate, these 1990s restraints have checked the packing of minorities by Republican legislatures intent on confining minorities to racially packed districts and expanding the political power of Republicans elsewhere across redistricting maps.

In January 2018, a three-judge court in North Carolina also turned against the state of North Carolina its claims of political gerrymandering as a defense against racial gerrymandering. In what the media dubbed a "bombshell ruling," the court struck down as an unconstitutional political gerrymander the congressional redistricting plan that North Carolina had adopted to remedy its nullified racial gerrymander. Never before in American history had a federal court strode boldly into the "political thicket" to invalidate a congressional redistricting plan as an unconstitutional partisan gerrymander. The court found that the plan violated the equal protection clause because the North Carolina General Assembly enacted it "with intent of discriminating against voters who favored non-Republican candidates." The plan violated the First Amendment "by unjustifiably discriminating against voters based on their previous political expression and affiliation," and "Article I, section 2's grant of authority to 'the People' to elect their Representatives." The court denounced that partisan gerrymandering for "undermining the right to vote—the principle [sic] vehicle through which the public secures other rights and prevents government overreach." It said that the state had no legitimate interest in "the drawing of legislative district lines to subordinate adherents of one political party and entrench a rival party in power." The Supreme Court stayed implementation of a new redistricting plan and may ultimately review this ruling as part of its unprecedented roster of partisan gerrymandering cases.[74]

Even before the North Carolina case, the Supreme Court was reconsidering the legality of partisan gerrymandering, with potentially far-reaching effects on the balance of party power in Congress and state and local legislatures. Although political gerrymandering recognizes no party boundaries, Republican victories in gubernatorial and state legislative elections in 2010 gave the party control of far more state governments than Democrats, including such large swing states as Pennsylvania, Michigan, Florida, Ohio, and Wisconsin. Republicans used their control of state governments to enact political gerrymanders during the redistricting that followed the 2010 U.S. Census. Republican control of the redistricting process followed from a carefully planned effort to gain control of government in key states during the 2010 elections. According to a report by the Republican State Legislative Committee (RSLC), "As the 2010 Census approached, the RSLC began planning for the subsequent election cycle, formulating a strategy to keep or win Republican control of state legislatures with the largest impact on Congressional redistricting as a result of reapportionment." The Republican "REDistricting MAjority Project (REDMAP), focused critical resources on legislative chambers in states projected to gain or lose Congressional seats in 2011 based on Census data."[75]

In the swing state of Pennsylvania, REDMAP put "critical resources" into elections to assure a GOP majority in the state's general assembly in the 2010 elections and corresponding control over the 2011 redistricting process. This effort paid off with one of the nation's most consequential political gerrymanders. Barack Obama won Pennsylvania with 52.7 percent of the two-party vote in 2012, and Democrats won 51 percent of the statewide, two-party congressional vote. Yet under a plan drawn by a Republican-controlled legislature, Republicans in Pennsylvania won thirteen U.S. House seats (72%) and Democrats only five (28%). Republicans held this two-thirds majority of seats through 2016. In its report on the REDMAP initiative, the Republican State Legislative Committee bragged about the importance of party gerrymandering in securing a nationwide congressional majority:

> Voters pulled the lever for Republicans only 49 percent of the time in Congressional races, suggesting that 2012 could have been a repeat of 2008, when voters gave control of the White House and both chambers of Congress to Democrats.... Instead, Republicans enjoy a 33-seat margin in the U.S. House seated yesterday in the 113th Congress, having endured Democratic successes atop the ticket and over one million more votes cast for Democratic House candidates than Republicans.... All components of a successful Congressional race, including recruitment, message development and resource allocation, rest on the Congressional district lines, and this was an area where Republicans had an unquestioned advantage.[76]

The Pennsylvania State Supreme Court, voting along party lines in February 2018, struck down the state's congressional redistricting plan as a violation of the state constitution. After the Republican-controlled state legislature and the Democratic governor dead-locked, the court drew its own plan. The Pennsylvania ruling shows the value of litigating state constitutions, which, unlike the U.S. Constitution, usually mandate affirmative voting rights. See also *Martin v. Kohls*, 2104 Ark. 427, striking down Arkansas's voter ID law. On March 19, 2018, a panel of three federal judges and the U.S. Supreme Court rejected petitions by Republican legislators to halt implementation of the court's plan.[77]

Earlier, in a challenge to the redistricting plan for the Wisconsin State Assembly, a federal court for the first time struck down as unconstitutional a statewide redistricting plan. Unlike the North Carolina case, where the court found that plaintiffs had presented sufficient social science evidence using multiple methodologies to prove its case, the three-judge court in Wisconsin proposed to fill the gap left by the Supreme Court's *Vieth* ruling, which failed to establish a standard for identifying an unconstitutional partisan gerrymander.

The Wisconsin court relied on the so-called efficiency gap, a measure of the relative number of wasted votes for each party that resulted from a redistricting plan. An excessive number of wasted votes for the disadvantaged party equal to 7 percent or more of total turnout in elections would establish a prima facie case for a partisan gerrymander of legislative redistricting plans. The Wisconsin case is pending before the U.S. Supreme Court. The Court also agreed to hear a case in the state of Maryland, where Republicans have alleged that Democrats shifted a single congressional district from Republican to Democratic in violation of Republican voters' rights of free expression under the First Amendment. The Court took up the case although the lower court had not yet conducted a trial.[78]

As part of its new wave of voting rights litigation, the Supreme Court has revisited the issue of purging voters from registration rolls. In Ohio, the Sixth Circuit Court of Appeals found that the state's "Supplemental Process" for purging individuals from the registration rolls violated the provision of the National Voter Registration

Act that prohibits a state from using procedures that "result in the removal of the name of any person from the official list of voters registered to vote in an election for Federal office by reason of the person's failure to vote." Under its supplemental process, Ohio purged registrants who had not voted in two years, failed to respond to a state-issued mailing, and did not vote for another four years.

The circuit court noted that registrants are automatically removed under this supplemental process in Ohio "even if he or she did not move and otherwise remains eligible to vote." In the North Carolina VIVA litigation, scrutiny of the state's online voter files for 2012, for example, disclosed that 37,489 North Carolina citizens registered as of 2002 first voted in 2012 after a ten-year gap. The court ruled in the Ohio case that "it is clear that the Supplemental Process does include a trigger [two years of nonvoting], and that that trigger constitutes perhaps the plainest possible example of a process that 'result[s] in removal of a voter from the rolls by reason of his or her failure to vote.'" The case is now before the Supreme Court on appeal by the state.[79]

The question of whether not voting for a period of time should be a basis for denying the right to vote at a future time is fundamental to the franchise for potentially millions of voters nationwide. Seventeen states, all controlled by Republicans, filed an amicus brief in the Supreme Court to support the Ohio law. Twelve states, mostly controlled by Democrats, filed an amicus brief in opposition to the law.[80]

With the Supreme Court deciding in January 2018 to also review the lower court's finding of intentional discrimination in the formulation of Texas's congressional redistricting plan, it has taken more important voting cases than at any time in recent history. The fate of American voting rights for the foreseeable future may well depend on decisions reached by a closely divided court ideologically. Justice Anthony Kennedy will likely provide the critical swing vote as he has done in prior voting rights cases that split the other eight justices four to four, across a conservative / liberal divide.

In the presidential election of 2016, an unprecedented threat to the vote in America emerged from a hostile foreign power. On October 7,

2016, the Department of Homeland Security and Office of the Director of National Intelligence issued a joint statement concluding that "the U.S. Intelligence Community (USIC) is confident that the Russian Government directed the recent compromises of e-mails from US persons and institutions, including from US political organizations. . . . These thefts and disclosures are intended to interfere with the US election process." On January 6, 2017, the U.S. intelligence agencies released a second report that pinned this interference on Russian president Vladimir Putin and said that its purpose was to aid in the election of Donald Trump, not just to disrupt America's democracy. This interference had three interlocking components: the hacking of Democratic emails; propaganda from state-controlled media, Twitter, and Facebook ads; and the use of internet trolls and bots to poison political debate.[81]

Later, in 2018, intelligence officials indicated that Russian hackers had tried to penetrate registration rolls—though not the voting machines—in some twenty-one states, and likely succeeded in several. Officials have not reported that the hackers altered the registration rolls to block citizens' ability to vote in the election. This hacking again exploited the fragmented American election system where localities are responsible for the conduct of elections and a lack of national standards or funding for technological improvements continues to exist. The hacking has the potential to corrupt the vote in America by adding or deleting names from registration rolls, requesting and submitting phony absentee ballots, and even altering or deleting the votes cast in voting machines. Michael Bahar, a former Democratic staffer for the House Intelligence Committee, warned that "the integrity of the entire system is in question. So you need the system to push back and find out what happened and why, so it never happens again."[82]

Russian manipulation of the 2016 elections extended beyond the presidential contest to aiding Republican congressional candidates in selected districts. They did so by releasing detrimental information to Republican operatives on Democratic candidates that

Russian hackers had stolen from the Democratic Congressional Campaign Committee. The Russians did not assist any Democratic candidates in 2016 or release any information from Republican sources that their hackers had breached prior to election day.[83]

Former acting CIA director Michael Morell and former Republican representative and chair of the House Intelligence Committee Mike Rogers have warned that Russian manipulation of American elections did not end in 2016. "The United States has failed to establish deterrence in the aftermath of Russia's interference in the 2016 election," they wrote. "We know we failed because Russia continues to aggressively employ the most significant aspect of its 2016 tool kit: the use of social media as a platform to disseminate propaganda designed to weaken our nation." In February 2018, President Trump's intelligence officials confirmed that Russia will continue to target American elections in the 2018 midterms and beyond.[84] Hacking into the voting machinery to alter or scramble results may be next on the Russian agenda. At a cybersecurity conference held in Las Vegas during July 2017, attendees easily hacked into thirty voting machines of various types. According to Fox News, "With every machine successfully breached in less than a day, the conference proved the devices are not up to par with modern technologies."[85]

Donald Trump and his administration have shown no inclination to protect the vote from manipulation by the Russians or another malevolent foreign power. Instead, he has harped on the bogus issue of voter fraud, claiming that, contrary to all evidence and plain commonsense, he would have won the popular vote had it not been for 3 to 5 million illegal voters. These phantom millions presumably all voted for Hillary Clinton—Trump said, "none of 'em come to me"—and then somehow disappeared without detection, including by the Republicans who administered elections in most states. It would have been the most extraordinary conspiracy in the history of the United States. Yet Trump's outlandish charge gained some traction. According to a Morning Consult/Politico poll released on July 26,

2017, 47 percent of Republicans said they believed that Trump won the 2016 election's popular vote. Even 25 percent of independents and 12 percent of Democrats professed this belief.[86]

In fact, Trump lagged Hillary Clinton by 2.9 million popular votes, equal to 2.1 percent of the votes cast in the election. No Electoral College winner has ever lost the popular vote by a larger numerical margin, and only in the disputed election of 1876 did the Electoral College winner lose the popular vote by a larger percentage margin.

Rather than deal with the foreign threat to our democracy, President Trump launched a new voter fraud commission with the potential to suppress voting in the United States. Kansas's Republican secretary of state Kris W. Kobach, co-chair with Vice President Mike Pence of the Presidential Advisory Commission on Election Integrity, has asked for the registration records of every American, including personal information such as addresses, dates of birth, political affiliation, military service, voting history, criminal convictions, and the last four digits of social security numbers. Kobach's data-mining request met considerable resistance from state officials including Mississippi's Republican secretary of state Delbert Hosemann, who said, "They can go jump in the Gulf of Mexico and Mississippi is a great state to launch from."[87]

Kobach has used false claims of widespread voter fraud to justify making voting more difficult, especially for the minorities and young people that primarily vote Democratic. In 2011, Kobach drafted and the Republican-controlled Kansas state legislature adopted the Secure and Fair Elections Act. It requires that voters at the polls present photo identification, absentee voters provide their driver's license numbers and have their signatures verified, and all new registrants present documentary proof of American citizenship.

Kobach bragged at the time in a *Wall Street Journal* op-ed that "although a few states, including Georgia, Indiana and Arizona, have enacted one or two of these reforms, Kansas is the only state to enact all three." A federal court temporarily enjoined the proof of citizenship requirement for voters using the federal form, and a trial on the merits of the full law commenced in March 2018. At trial, Kobach's expert witness, Jesse Richman, a political science professor at Old Dominion University, said he was unaware of any research that supported Trump's claim that millions of illegal votes cast ballots in the 2016 presidential election.[88]

In June 2017, a federal magistrate sanctioned Kobach, fining him one thousand dollars for his "deceptive conduct and lack of candor" in response to requests for the discovery of information in his possession. The court found that he had made "patently misleading representations to the court about the documents" requested. In upholding the sanction, federal district court judge Julie A. Robinson noted that Kobach had exhibited a "pattern" in federal litigation of "statements made or positions taken by Secretary Kobach that have called his credibility into question."[89] Kobach's claims of rampant voter fraud to justify the omnibus 2011 law were equally misleading. The Republican National Lawyers Association's study found one prosecution for voter fraud in Kansas from 1997 through 2011. When Kobach claimed lax enforcement of voter fraud, the legislature in 2015 made him the only secretary of state in the nation authorized to investigate and prosecute cases of voter fraud.

Kobach has tacitly endorsed President Trump's claim of millions of illegal votes cast nationwide, saying, "We will probably never know the answer to that question" of who won the popular vote. In support of his fraud claims, in September 2017, on Breitbart, Kobach claimed that "now there's proof" that illegal voters turned the 2016 New Hampshire election to the Democrats, because some 5,313 voters lacked either a New Hampshire driver's license or a registered vehicle in the state. New Hampshire's Democratic secretary of state Bill Gardner, a commission member, debunked Kobach, because New Hampshire law authorizes temporary residents, such as college students, with out-of-state driver's licenses and no vehicles registered in the state to vote legally.[90]

In Kansas, as of late August 2017, the zealous fraud hunter Kobach has charged just twelve people for fraud in all prior elections out of millions of ballots cast. Ten cases involved people who double-voted. Only two involved noncitizen voting, despite Kobach's claim that in his state, "the total number [of noncitizens] could be in excess of 18,000 on our voter rolls."[91] Despite the absence of significant voter fraud, the strict voter photo ID law in Kansas resulted in a 1.9 to 2.2 percent decline in voter turnout in Kansas according to a study by the nonpartisan U.S. Government Accountability Office. Black turnout dropped by 3.7 percentage points more than white turnout, and turnout by eighteen-year-olds declined by 7.1 percent more than among people aged forty-four to fifty-three.[92]

This finding for Kansas is consistent with the results of nation-wide studies of how voter photo ID laws have impacted turnout. A study published in the April 2017 *Journal of Politics* using validated voter data demonstrates that photo ID laws functioned as intended: "The analysis shows that strict identification laws have a differentially negative impact on the turnout of racial and ethnic minorities in primaries and general elections. We also find that voter ID laws skew democracy toward those on the political right." The authors conclude that voter ID laws are only one of the ways in which states are restricting the opportunity to vote:

> What makes voter ID laws more disturbing is that they are just one of the many different ways in which the electoral system is being altered today. Shortened early voting periods, repeal of same-day voter reg-istration, reduced polling hours, a decrease in poll locations, and increased restrictions on voting by felons are all being regularly im-plemented at the state or local level, and all have been cited as having the potential to skew the electorate and American democracy.[93]

Kobach has advocated the crosscheck of voter registration rolls with other lists, for example, of felons, double-registered, and deceased people. Such crosschecks lead to voter suppression because they generate far more false than true positives. A study by professors at Harvard, the University of Pennsylvania, and Stanford found that purging registration rolls using the crosscheck system "would eliminate about 300 registrations used to cast legitimate votes for every one registration used to cast a double vote." As applied by advocates like Kobach, matching has relied on flawed lists biased against minority voters as in Florida's 2000 election. In 2004, a public outcry stopped Florida officials from using a similarly flawed purge list.[94]

Kobach has stacked the commission with like-minded members, one of whom, Hans Von Spakovsky, argued against appointing any Democrats or "mainstream Republicans" to the commission, because such membership "would guarantee its failure." Had it continued, the commission might well have recommended crosscheck purges, strict voter photo ID laws, proof of citizenship requirements, and other restrictive measures. One invited witness at a commission hearing went so far as to propose making every voter pass the background check used for gun purchases, which would disenfranchise millions of otherwise eligible voters. The commission has been plagued with more than fifteen lawsuits against its data requests and allegedly secret practices, including a successful case filed by one of the commissioners, Matthew Dunlap, Maine's Democratic secretary of state, charging that he had been denied access to internal documents and commission activities.[95]

On January 3, 2018, President Trump abruptly dissolved the fraud commission by executive order. A White House statement said that the president had terminated the commission because "many states have refused to provide [it] with basic information relevant to its inquiry" and because the president sought to avoid "endless legal battles at taxpayer expense." However, the statement reiterated the claim that there is "substantial evidence of voter fraud," even though the fraud hunters on the commission had uncovered no such evidence in its eight months of work. The statement indicated that the failed fraud-hunting of the commission could reemerge under the auspices of the Department of Homeland Security, with no input from Democrats or any independent review. An indictment by Special Counsel Robert Mueller of thirteen Russian nationals and three companies charged that Russian trolls in 2016 echoed Trump's false claims of rampant voter fraud by Democrats. Republican senatorial candidate Roy Moore, who lost a December 2017 special election for U.S. Senate in heavily Republican Alabama, struck a similar theme, blaming fraudulent voting for his defeat by more than 21,000 votes. However, a state judge dismissed Moore's effort to block certification of the election, and Alabama's Republican secretary of state, John Merrill, who supported Moore, found not a single instance of any type of election fraud.[96]

The advent of the Trump administration has threatened Justice Department backing for voting rights litigation. Attorney General Jeff Sessions reversed his department's position on the Texas voter identification law, now taking the stand that the law did not intentionally target minority voters. He similarly reversed the department's opposition to Ohio's voter purging law, now asserting that the state's practice is consistent with federal law, and he dropped the department's support for the ruling of a three-judge court that Texas's congressional redistricting plan intentionally discriminated against minorities. In 1986, a Republican Senate had rejected Sessions's nomination by President Ronald Reagan for a federal judgeship, because of credible allegation of the nominee's racism. He was only the second nominee in fifty years to be denied a federal judgeship by the Senate.[97]

With America standing nearly alone among nations in lacking a constitutional right to vote, our democracy finds itself at a crossroads, with crucial decisions pending in courtrooms and legislatures. The U.S. Supreme Court has an opportunity in pending cases cited above in Wisconsin, Maryland, and North Carolina for the first time to strike down redistricting plans as illicit partisan gerrymanders. The Court is reviewing a congressional redistricting plan that a lower court found had intentionally discriminated against minorities and a voter purge law in Ohio in which nonvoting triggers a process for removing people from the registration rolls.

Pending in the legislatures of most states are bills to either expand or restrict opportunities to register and vote. Expansive measures include legislation to automatically register citizens who apply for driver's licenses, to expand early voting, to adopt independent redistricting commissions, and to authorize registration on election day. Restrictive measures include voter photo ID laws, documentary proof of citizenship for registration, onerous residency requirements, and cutbacks in early voting. At least a dozen states are poised to adopt stringent voter purge legislation if the Supreme Court sanctions the Ohio law. With positions on voting rights mostly falling along party lines, the nation may increasingly become bound to a dual system of political rights, one for blue states and another for red states. Americans' right to vote is in danger of becoming dependent on their place of residence, just as it once depended on their property-holding, their race, or their sex.

An international assessment reflects the fragile state of democracy in the United States. The toxic mix of low turnout, partisan gerrymandering, and rising cynicism in government has cost the United States its leadership place as the world's beacon of democracy. The 2017 report of the Economic Intelligence Unit in Great Britain, which tracks the status of democracy among 167 nations across the world, classified only nineteen nations, with 4.5 percent of the world's population, as "full democracies" and fifty-seven nations, with 44.8 percent of the population, as "flawed democracies." It classified the remaining nations with slightly more than half the world's population as "authoritarian" or "hybrid" regimes (with a mix of democratic and authoritarian features). Among democracies, the

United States had for the first time in 2016 fallen from a full to a flawed democracy, a classification that remained unchanged in 2017, with a ranking of just twenty-first, tied with Italy.[98]

The United States has declined in its rank among democracies because of partisan gerrymandering and public cynicism about government, fueled in part by repeated, unsubstantiated claims of voter fraud. According to a September 2016 AP-NORC poll, "35 percent of respondents said there is a great deal of election fraud in the United States, 39 percent say there is some election fraud. This poll found that only 24 percent say there is hardly any voter fraud, which is consistent with the outcome of multiple studies and court findings."[99]

Freedom House, another international monitor, found that the election of Donald Trump accelerated the decline of democracy in the United States. It reported that the Trump administration's lack of transparency, disregard for ethical standards, and failure to safeguard U.S. elections from foreign manipulation posed unprecedented threats to American democracy. It found that 2017 "brought further, faster erosion of America's own democratic standards than at any other time in memory." America's decline as a beacon of freedom and democracy, the study found, contributed to the erosion of democracy worldwide and the emboldening of authoritarian rulers. "Democracy is facing its most serious crisis in decades," warned Freedom House's president, Michael J. Abramowitz. "Democracy's basic tenets—including guarantees of free and fair elections, the rights of minorities, freedom of the press, and the rule of law—are under siege around the world."[100]

White House spokesperson Sarah Huckabee Sanders indicated on March 20, 2018, that the Trump administration had abandoned America's historic role as a champion of democratic elections worldwide. When asked if Vladimir Putin's sham reelection as Russian president was "free and fair," Sanders responded, "We're focused on our elections. We don't get to dictate how other countries operate.

What we do know is that Putin has been elected in their country, and that's not something that we can dictate to them—how they operate."[101]

America can reclaim its place in the front ranks of the world's democracies. The United States, which once inspired emerging democracies across the world, now has much to learn from the experiences of other nations and its own history. Simple, practical reforms are within reach to enhance access to the vote in America, end discriminatory practices, and help assure that people's votes will count effectively in the election of public officials. But reform will come only if the American people are willing to see past the smokescreen of voter fraud, and demand real change to expand opportunities to register and vote. Despite the lack of a constitutional guarantee, the right to vote remains the bedrock of all other rights in a democratic nation.

8

REFORMING AMERICAN VOTING

Did I end up finding a little blue pill to cure America's
electoral dysfunction? Unfortunately, it's not that simple.

—MO ROCCA, COMEDIAN, 2012

In May 1949, just four years after the collapse of Adolf Hitler's Third
Reich, the American and European occupiers in the western part
of a divided Germany supervised the drafting of a new German constitution. It guaranteed that every adult national "shall be entitled
to vote." Three months later, the German people exercised their
voting rights in the first free election in their homeland since Hitler
had seized power in 1933. "Deep in everyone's heart is the question
whether someday today's voters may be punished for this," said one
voter. But vote they did. Emblematic of broad voter participation was
the balloting in the small town of Stauffenberg, where an aged
countess lined up with small farmers, shopkeepers, and laborers at the
polls. Across West Germany, more than 70 percent of adult citizens
cast ballots in a quiet election with no incidents at any polling place.[1]

Seven decades later, the people of America still lack the explicit
constitutional right to vote that most democratic nations have enshrined in their constitutions. The Constitution of the United States

establishes the civil liberties necessary for a functioning democracy but not the right to vote. The original Constitution deferred voting qualifications to the states, and subsequent amendments specified only what states could not do with respect to denying suffrage based on race, sex, and age. Today's Congress has shown no interest in acting on proposals for an affirmative right-to-vote amendment to the Constitution. Yet not only the postwar German constitution but other constitutions drawn under American supervision in nations such as Japan and Iraq guarantee the right to vote. The International Covenant on Civil and Political Rights that the United States ratified in 1992 (with the reservation that it did not supersede domestic law) likewise guarantees the right "to vote and to be elected at genuine periodic elections which shall be by universal and equal suffrage."[2]

Despite the lack of a constitutional guarantee, the U.S. Supreme Court has at times interpreted the vote as a "fundamental right," which would subject any abridgement to the highest level of judicial review known as "strict scrutiny." The standard requires that a challenged law must meet a compelling state interest and be narrowly tailored to meet that end. It would establish a high bar for the state to surmount in enacting any law or regulation that burdens the right to vote.

However, the courts have typically not treated the right to vote as fundamental and subject to strict scrutiny. This places the vote on a lower plane than enumerated rights in the Constitution such as freedom of speech, which government cannot abridge. According to legal scholar Pamela S. Karlan,

The Supreme Court long ago expressed itself "unanimously of the opinion that the Constitution of the United States does not confer the right of suffrage on any one." And it reinforced this view in the notorious *Bush* v. *Gore* decision, with its almost offhanded declaration that "[t]he individual citizen has no federal constitutional right to vote for electors for the President of the United States unless and until the state legislature chooses a statewide election as the means to implement its power to appoint members of the Electoral College."

In the *Crawford* decision as in other high court cases, Justice John Paul Stevens applied a "balancing test" to validate Indiana's voter photo identification law. The test weighs the impact on the asserted right against the importance of the government's interest. This more permissive standard provides states greater latitude than strict scrutiny to adopt measures that restrict opportunities for registration and voting.[3]

An affirmative right-to-vote amendment, like the version of the Fifteenth Amendment that Congress rejected in 1869, would bring America into line with most other democratic nations and with international conventions. It would not invalidate every restriction on the vote, any more than the right of free speech invalidates libel and slander laws. But it would rebalance the scales of justice in favor of the voter, not the state. The Fourteenth Amendment spanned 435 words, but an affirmative right-to-vote amendment could be crafted with just 50 words, as illustrated by the text that Democratic representative Mark Pocan of Wisconsin proposed in 2013:

> SECTION 1. Every citizen of the United States, who is of legal voting age, shall have the fundamental right to vote in any public election held in the jurisdiction in which the citizen resides.
>
> SECTION 2. Congress shall have the power to enforce and implement this article by appropriate legislation.[4]

A right-to-vote amendment would likely doom felon disenfranchisement laws. The United States remains one of the few democracies that still withholds the ballot from felons who have completed their sentences, including probation and parole, and paid their legal debt to society. A comparative study of forty-five democracies found that only three other nations had similarly stringent disenfranchisement laws: Armenia, Belgium, and Chile. Twenty-one nations imposed no restrictions on felon voting even while in prison, fourteen imposed selective bans on prisoners, and only ten banned prison voting.[5]

In America as of 2017, forty-eight states and the District of Columbia prohibit voting by imprisoned felons; only the small states of Maine and Vermont impose no suffrage penalties on felons. As of 2016, thirty-four states prohibit voting by paroled felons and twenty-one states ban voting by felons on probation. Twelve states ban voting by ex-felons or some category of ex-felons who have completed their sentences. Restoration of voting rights is possible in most states, but the process is typically slow, cumbersome, and uncertain.[6]

An estimated 6.1 million felons in 2016 had temporarily or permanently lost their voting rights, up from 1.7 million in 1976, 3.34 million in 1996, and 5.85 million in 2010. The disenfranchised include 7.4 percent of adult African Americans, compared to 1.8 percent of adult whites. About 3.1 million people are disenfranchised after completing their sentences. In the swing state of Florida, which disenfranchises ex-felons, 21 percent of adult African Americans have lost their voting rights, more than enough to decide the outcome of a close local or statewide election. In February 2018, a federal district court judge struck down Florida's subjective, laborious, and ineffective process for restoring voting rights to ex-felons one by one. Floridians will vote in November 2018 on a referendum for a constitutional amendment to restore the franchise to former felons.[7]

Nationwide, the confusing patchwork of laws on felon disenfranchisement has led some former felons to vote illegally in restrictive states because they mistakenly thought that their voting rights had been restored. Unintentional voting by former felons adds to the tally of alleged fraud, fueling demands for further restrictions on the vote. A restoration of voting rights for ex-felons alone and those on parole or probation would enfranchise 77 percent of the 6.1 million currently denied the ballot.[8]

In the 1974 case of *Richardson v. Ramirez,* the U.S. Supreme Court held that a law disenfranchising former felons did not violate the equal protection clause of the Fourteenth Amendment. The court found that section 2 of the Fourteenth Amendment justified the law. This section reduces a state's representation in Congress if the state has denied the right to vote for any reason "except for participation in rebellion, or other crime." The Court seized on this exception as a justification for felon disenfranchisement.[9]

A constitutional right to vote with no exceptions for criminal conviction would likely supersede this part of section 2. In Canada, its supreme court struck down felon disenfranchisement for violating the right to vote inscribed in the Canadian Charter of Rights and Freedoms. That court held that "the argument that only those who respect the law should participate in the political process cannot be accepted. Denial of the right to vote on the basis of attributed moral unworthiness is inconsistent with the respect for the dignity of every person that lies at the heart of Canadian democracy [and] runs counter to the plain words of s. 3 of the *Charter*." Section 3 guarantees that "every citizen of Canada has the right to vote in an election of members of the House of Commons or of a legislative assembly."[10]

A constitutional right to vote would help but not cure the dismal participation of voters in the United States. Turnout has been lower in recent elections than at any time since the 1920s, despite rebounding in the South after enactment of the Voting Rights Act. Although the turnout gap between the South and North narrowed considerably in the 1960s, falling northern turnout sent national turnout into a downward spiral. Both presidential and congressional turnout of voting-age citizens in the North declined by about 10 percentage points from 1928 to 1964 on average as compared to the average in later years. Nationally for these two periods, presidential turnout slid from 60 to 56 percent and midterm congressional turnout from 42 to 39 percent. A constitutional guarantee of voting rights would both strike down some current restrictions and guard against future burdens on the vote.[11]

In America's hard-fought and closely contested presidential election of 2016, only 59 percent of voting-age citizens cast a ballot, equaling about 86 million lost votes. Donald Trump won the presidential election of 2016 with 63 million votes, just 28 percent of America's voting-age citizens. In the 2014 midterm elections, only 38 percent of American citizens participated, equaling about 140 million lost votes. In closely contested U.S. Senate races across the nation in 2014, candidates typically won seats with votes equal to about one-fifth of the state's citizens of voting age. Turnout is yet lower in local elections. A 2014 study by two University of Wisconsin researchers found that turnout in 144 mayoral elections across the nation averaged only 25.6 percent of the citizen voting-age population. Thus, candidates could win mayoral elections with support from just over 10 percent of their citizen voting-age constituents.[12]

Turnout is similarly bleak in primary elections that set the choices for voters in the general elections. In 2016, when both parties had spirited contests for their presidential nominations, about 28 percent of voting-age citizens participated in the Republican and Democratic presidential primaries combined. In states holding caucuses, turnout averaged merely 7 percent. Only about 8 percent of American citizens chose Hillary Clinton as the Democratic nominee and only about 6 percent chose Donald Trump as the Republican nominee. In midterm elections, primary turnout is yet lower. In 2014, just 28.4 million voters participated in the primary elections in forty-five states that had at least one contested statewide primary for both parties, equaling about 15 percent of the citizen voting-age population in those states.[13]

In 1900, the United States led the democratic world in the voting participation of its citizens. Now roles have reversed and America trails most comparable democracies in voter turnout. According to a 2017 Pew Research Center study of thirty-five nations in the Organization for Economic Cooperation and Development, the United States ranked twenty-eighth in voter turnout.[14]

Political gerrymandering and public cynicism about government help explain declining northern and national voter turnout, even as

the Voting Rights Act of 1965 removed barriers to minority participation. The gerrymandering of legislative districts to favor one party
over another at every level of government kills political competition
and the incentive to vote. It lets candidates choose their voters, rather
than voters choose their candidates. In the general elections of
2016, 42 percent of state representative seats went uncontested. In
congressional elections, 12 percent of seats were uncontested.
However, only about 10 percent of the remaining seats were competitive, with a winning margin of less than 10 percentage points.
Not surprisingly, relatively few voters turned out in uncontested or
lopsided elections.[15]

Since the early 1960s, Americans have lost faith in their government. According to data from the Pew Research Center, in 1964,
77 percent of Americans "trusted the federal government to do what
is right just about always / most of the time." By 1980, Americans'
trust in government had fallen steadily and steeply to just 28 percent.
Only once and briefly in the aftermath of the September 11, 2001,
attacks did trust in government rise above 50 percent. It then
steadily declined again to an average of just 19 percent from 2013 to
2017. The paradox here is that a lack of faith in government deters
voting, but government will better serve ordinary Americans if
they vote in larger numbers.[16]

A consequence of nonvoting, partisan gerrymandering, and
public cynicism is an American government that is especially
responsive to the wealthiest citizens, a throwback to the early republic when tax and property qualifications prevailed across the
nation. A study by Ellen Shearer of the Medill School of Journalism
at Northwestern University found that 61 percent of 2012 voters
earned $50,000 or more per year, compared to 41 percent of non-
voters. Only 12 percent of nonvoters earned more than $75,000,
compared to 31 percent of voters.[17]

Low turnout, an economically stratified electorate, and noncom-
petitive elections create a political vacuum filled by special-interest

groups. The upper-income bias of American turnout produces election results favorable to the wealthy and business. Organizations with money, power, and inside connections can tilt the outcomes of low-turnout contests by targeting only a relatively few voters and backing favored candidates and parties. These interests can operate in the dark as advocacy groups with no financial reporting requirements and the receipt of unlimited funds from wealthy corporations under a recent Supreme Court decision.[18]

Uncontested and lightly contested elections open legislators to the influence of lobbyists that proliferate in Congress, state legislatures, and local governing bodies. In 2016, more than eleven thousand registered lobbyists plied their trade in Washington, most of them representing business interests. Nineteen of the top twenty spenders on lobbying in 2017 were business associations or major corporations like AT&T and Boeing. Heading the list with a combined spending of $164 million were the U.S. Chamber of Commerce, the National Association of Realtors, and the Business Roundtable. Adding to the total of registered lobbyists were at least an equal number of unregistered "shadow lobbyists." Although comparable data is hard to compile, much larger numbers of lobbyists are likely active in state and local governments. John Delaney, a successful businessman who won a Maryland seat in Congress, warned that "representative democracy is in crisis in the United States. . . . Our electoral process has created perverse incentives that have warped our democracy and empowered special interests and a vocal minority."[19]

A shattering study by political science professors Martin Gilens of Princeton University and Benjamin Page of Northwestern University validated Delaney's warning. They found that wealthy interests seeking profit, power, and control significantly shape policy outcomes in the United States. The analysts found that when controlling for the power of economic elites and organized interest groups, the influence of ordinary Americans registers at a "nonsignificant, near-zero level." They found that the policy preferences of business and the rich often sharply diverge from those of ordinary citizens, and when they do, the economic elites and business interests almost always win. An expanded suffrage might not break the golden rule of politics—those who have the gold rule—but it would serve as an important corrective.[20]

Without electoral reform, voter turnout will continue to stagnate in the United States, and a small minority of the nation's citizens will nominate and elect the public officials who govern the nation. Changes in electoral laws and regulations are not a magic wand for raising turnout, but they do matter, as shown by the experiences of high-turnout nations. According to data compiled for 2016 by the U.S. Census Bureau's Current Population Survey, 15 percent of respondents reported that they could not vote because they were unregistered, and another 15 percent were not asked, responded "did not know," or refused to answer the question.

Registration reform holds the greatest promise for an expanded American turnout. Unlike the United States, most high-turnout nations employ a form of government-initiated registration known as "automatic registration." In Sweden, for example, the National Tax Administration maintains a civil registry (including a twelve-digit personal identification number) that the Swedish Election Authority uses to compile an electoral roll of eligible voters thirty days before an election. The information is maintained electronically, with day-to-day updates by local tax offices, to ensure that the lists given to voting stations are accurate. By law, residents are required to update information with changes at their local tax office. From the list of eligible voters, the government automatically issues a voter registration card to be presented at a polling place (alternately, voters can provide some other proof of identity). Nearly every adult Swede is registered to vote, and turnout typically reaches or exceeds 80 percent of the nation's voting-age population.[21]

The American people, with their tradition of federalism and distrust of centralized authority, would not likely embrace the Swedish model of top-down registration. The states, not the federal government, maintain civil registries, which are less comprehensive than in Sweden. Each state has an Office of Vital Records or Statistics that keeps records of birth and death certificates (and sometimes more), and individual county clerks keep marriage certificates, housing deeds, and other information. The United States lacks the sort of list that Sweden has which would enable individual states to compile a register of every single eligible voter in their state. Our country also lacks the European precedent of an independent national bureaucracy.

A more plausible means for expanding the voter rolls is government-assisted registration, which has precedent in the Motor Voter Law of 1993. Beginning with Oregon in 2015, some states have expanded the motor voter mandate. The so-called Oregon Motor Voter Act requires state officials to register automatically every non-registered citizen who appears at a motor vehicle bureau to apply for, renew, or replace an Oregon driver's license, nonoperator ID card, or driver's permit. The automatic registration applies only to people eighteen years or older who are coded as citizens by the Department of Motor Vehicles. In Oregon, individuals must provide proof of citizenship or legal status to obtain a driver's license or ID card. The state sends eligible people a mailing explaining that they will be automatically registered to vote unless they return an opt-out card, included in the mailing with prepaid postage.[22]

The Oregon Motor Voter Act has worked as intended to expand both registration and turnout. A study by the Center for American Progress found that in the act's first year and a half since its implementation in January 2016, the new system registered more than 270,000 additional voters, including 98,000 who participated in the general election of 2016. In this case, expanded registration led to expanded voter turnout. The study estimated that the law registered an additional 116,000 people "who were unlikely to have registered otherwise, and more than 40,000 of these previously disengaged people voted in the November election." That expanded turnout equals about 2.5 percent of Oregon's eligible voter population, which projected nationally would add some 3.5 million new presidential voters in 2016. In Oregon, voter turnout increased by 4.1 percent between 2012 and 2016, more than double the national increase of 1.6 percentage points.[23]

By early 2018, eight other states and the District of Columbia had adopted some form of expanded motor voter legislation, including the Republican-controlled states of Alaska, Georgia, and West Virginia. This record indicates some support across party lines, despite vetoes of such legislation by Republican governors in Nevada and New Jersey. Legislators have introduced versions of the Oregon bill in most other states.[24]

Some states have had in place for decades an even closer analogue to automatic registration: election day registration, which allows individuals to register when they show up to vote at the polls. Maine, Minnesota, and Wisconsin first adopted election day registration in the mid-1970s, with New Hampshire, Idaho, and Wyoming following suit in the 1990s. The turnout rates in these six states have consistently topped the national average by wide margins, with just four allegations of registration fraud from 2000 to 2011, according to a News21 survey. Most academic studies have found that election day registration boosts voter turnout, with the estimated size of the increment ranging from the low single digits to nearly 10 percentage points.[25] As of late 2017, fourteen states and the District of Columbia have adopted election day registration, most of them since 2010. Two other states authorize registration during their early voting period. Given the range of statistical estimates, the adoption of election day registration nationwide would likely increase turnout by anywhere from 3 to 15 million votes in presidential elections.[26]

There are models now available for eliminating the most egregious effects of partisan gerrymandering. Other democracies avoid the gerrymandering of legislative districts through proportional representation. Voters do not opt for individual candidates in single-member districts but vote for an entire list of candidates submitted by competing parties. Each party gains seats in proportion to the vote for its lists. However, proportional representation is too radical a change in the relationship between voters and representatives for adoption in the United States. American legislators have a powerful incentive to maintain rather than drastically shift the election systems under which they have gained political power. To date, no American state has seriously considered the adoption of proportional representation.

Within the American tradition, the state of Florida, despite its history of minority vote suppression, offers an anti-gerrymandering model for the nation. In 2010, 63 percent of Florida voters backed state constitutional amendments to restrict partisan gerrymandering for Congress and the state legislature. The new rules required that "no apportionment plan or individual district shall be drawn with the intent to favor or disfavor a political party or an incumbent; and districts shall not be drawn with the intent or result of denying or abridging the equal opportunity of racial or language minorities to participate in the political process or to diminish their ability to elect representatives of their choice." Districts "shall be compact; and districts shall, where feasible, utilize existing political and geographical boundaries."[27] After years of resistance from Republicans in the state legislature, the courts compelled the redrawing of district lines in conformity with the amendment. Although reform could not entirely wipe out prior Republican gerrymandering, the results were striking. In 2016, the first congressional election under new lines, Florida elected ten new members of Congress, compared to forty-five in all other states. Five party seats changed hands in Florida, compared to just seven in all other states.[28]

A nationwide Florida-style anti-gerrymandering provision, enacted by Congress for federal elections, could be effectively combined with redistricting conducted by an independent commission rather than elected officials. In 2015, the U.S. Supreme Court upheld the authority of states through initiatives adopted by the voters to take redistricting out of the hands of state legislatures and delegate this task to independent commissions. Writing for a five-justice majority, Ruth Bader Ginsburg cited "the animating principle of our Constitution that the people themselves are the originating source of all the powers of government." She added, "Banning lawmaking by initiative to direct a State's method of apportioning Congressional districts would do more than stymie attempts to curb partisan gerrymandering, by which the majority in the legislature draws district lines to their party's advantage. It would also cast doubt on numerous other election laws adopted by the initiative method of legislating."[29]

Some fourteen states have bipartisan or nonpartisan commissions for congressional or legislative districts, or both. The results are mixed but on balance positive. Political scientist Bruce E. Cain finds that "independent citizen commissions are the culmination of a reform effort focused heavily on limiting the conflict of interest implicit in legislative control over redistricting." His research determines that they "have succeeded to a great degree in that goal," but adds the qualifier that "they have not eliminated the inevitable partisan suspicions associated with political line-drawing and the associated risk of commission deadlock."[30]

Cain concludes that the most effective redistricting commissions have members who are relatively insulated from partisan commitments and super-majority decision-making so that the final product results from bargaining and compromise among members. The combination of such commissions, which Congress could mandate for U.S. House elections, with Florida-style anti-gerrymandering requirements would considerably reduce the baleful effects of redistricting plans that unfairly advantage one party over another.

Congress also has the power to restore the preclearance provision of the Voting Rights Act, which the Supreme Court invalidated in

2013. It could do so by adopting a new, updated formula for determining which state and localities would be covered by preclearance. The reinstatement of preclearance would block discriminatory voting and registration laws before they took effect and avoid the difficult, expensive, and tedious process of challenges under section 2 of the Voting Rights Act. Various proposals for an updated formula have been pending in Congress for several years. However, there is little chance for the necessary bipartisan support given present Republican opposition to any revival of the preclearance provision.

America's antiquated systems for state and local control over the conduct of elections needs updating with national requirements binding on all federal elections. A paper trail on all voting machines would help secure the integrity of the vote, which is now threatened by foreign interference. This reform tallies votes concretely on paper as a check against possible technological errors or the hacking of electronic results. A revised Help America Vote Act should set minimum standards for ballot design and election technology. It should include renewed federal funding for technological upgrades and the training of election officials and poll workers. The nation needs a blue-ribbon national commission, not on phony voter fraud but on safeguarding our voting technology from hacking and other malicious interference.

The United States has continued its eighteenth-century procedure for the indirect election of presidents through the Electoral College. In 2016, for the second time in sixteen years, the Electoral College produced a president who lost the popular vote. Prior to 2000, the popular and electoral votes had not diverged since 1888. Campaigns now focus on about ten to fifteen so-called swing states, ignoring, among others, four of the nation's five most populous states: California, Texas, New York, and Illinois. Despite public support, there is little chance for a constitutional amendment for the popular election of presidents. The small states, which are now guaranteed at least three electoral votes each, hold a veto over any prospects for a two-thirds vote in the Senate for an amendment and a three-quarters vote of the states for ratification.

Republicans are unlikely to join an effort to abolish the Electoral College. In both 2000 and 2016, Republican presidential candidates lost the popular vote but won the electoral vote tally. The reason is that in recent elections, Democrats have gained a rising majority of millions of popular votes in just two states, New York and California. Democratic presidential candidates led Republicans in these states by 4 million popular votes in 2000 and 6 million in 2016. For the Electoral College, these are wasted votes, because even a victory by Democratic presidential candidates in these states by just a few votes would still secure their electoral votes. There are no comparable Republican-leaning states that yield the Republicans even roughly comparable popular vote margins. The closest analogue is Texas, which Donald Trump won by 807,000 votes in 2016.

Two states, Maine and Nebraska, allocate electoral votes according to a mixed system that harkens back to the early republic. These states allocate one electoral vote to the winner of each congressional district and two votes to the statewide victor. If adopted nationwide, this system would infect presidential elections with the political gerrymandering of congressional districts, widening the gap between the popular and Electoral College votes. In 2012, for example, Republican candidate Mitt Romney would have won most of Pennsylvania's electoral votes even though he lost the popular vote to Barack Obama by 5.4 percent. Nationwide, Romney would have garnered an Electoral College majority and won the presidency, despite trailing Obama by 5 million votes and 4 percentage points in the popular tally.[31]

The United States also differs from most other democracies in holding national elections during the week on a regular work day. The great majority of nations across the world hold elections on either a weekend or a declared national holiday. There is a lack of compelling evidence that making election day a holiday in the

United States would appreciably increase turnout, but it would make voting fun again and not just a civic exercise. Why not serve refreshments (nonalcoholic), bring on bands and songs, and have a celebration of voting at the polling place? Such incentives are certainly worth a try.

The combination of several practical reforms—eliminating felon disenfranchisement (even just for former felons), expanded motor voter registration, election day registration, and a combined antigerrymandering rule and independent redistricting commissions—would transform voting and politics in the United States. The first three reforms would likely increase presidential turnout by at least 10 percent, adding about 14 million or more new voters in presidential elections.

Gerrymandering reform would make elections more fair and competitive and likely boost turnout as well. An election day holiday might not appreciably increase turnout but would help restore the joy and communal spirit to elections. A new formula for preclearance would help assure that state and local governments did not discriminate against minorities in their voting laws and practices. An upgrading of ballot safeguards and effective technology would facilitate voting and guard against the hacking of electoral systems.

So far, electoral reform has plodded along in America, state by state, through a scattershot process that widens the divide in access to the vote between red and blue states. Yet the national government has authority to legislatively enact these reforms for federal elections under the Constitution's elections clause, which authorizes Congress to "make or alter" the "times, places, or manner" of federal elections. The federal government has significantly exercised this authority since 1842 when it required the states to elect members of the House of Representatives from districts, each of which could elect only a single member of Congress. The Congress has since repealed, readopted, and repealed again this requirement. In 1845, Congress again overrode the autonomy of states and mandated a national election day for presidential electors on the first Tuesday after the second Monday in November. It expanded this requirement to Senate elections in 1866 and House elections in 1872. In 1967, Congress mandated that states must hold elections for the U.S. House of Representatives in single-member districts.[32]

The National Voter Registration Act in 1993 launched the most ambitious federal effort to regulate registration and voting. Several circuit courts rejected constitutional challenges to the law, and in 1996 the Supreme Court declined to take up the matter. A year later, in unrelated litigation on conflicts between federal election law and Louisiana's "open primary," the U.S. Supreme Court held as "settled doctrine" that the "Election Clause grants Congress 'the power to override state regulations' by establishing uniform rules for federal elections, binding on the States."[33]

Yet another reform at the state level could substantially increase voter turnout in local elections, over which only the states, not the federal government, have jurisdiction. This state-by-state reform would shift all local elections to the national election day in midterm and presidential years. Local primary elections would also have to fall in line with congressional and presidential primaries. The study by Zoltan L. Hajnal and Paul G. Lewis found that the turnout effects of holding city elections on election day in presidential and midterm years rather than off-cycle are substantial: "Presidential elections are associated with turnouts of registered voters in city elections that are 36% higher than off-cycle elections; midterm Congressional elections and presidential primaries are associated with municipal turnouts of 26% and 25% more registered voters, respectively."[34]

An obstacle to reform is gaining support from Republicans, many of whom believe that low turnout, especially among minorities, benefits their party. In 1980, during the campaign to elect Ronald Reagan, prominent Republican strategist Paul Weyrich, a founder of the contemporary conservative movement, criticized what he called the "goo-goo syndrome—good government. They want everybody to vote." He said, "I don't want everybody to vote. Elections are not won by a majority of people. . . . As a matter of fact our leverage in the elections quite candidly goes up as the voting populace goes down."[35]

More recently Republicans have said restrictions on voting such as photo identification laws help their party win elections by diminishing the opposition vote. In 2012, the Republican Pennsylvania state house majority leader, Mike Turzai, said, "Voter ID, which is going to allow Governor Romney to win the state of Pennsylvania, done." In 2013, while commenting on Virginia's voter ID law and long lines at the polls, Scott Tranter of the Republican consulting firm Optimus (which specializes in election analysis) commented, "A lot of us are campaign professionals and we want to do everything we can to help our sides. Sometimes we think that's voter ID, sometimes we think that's longer lines, whatever it may be." Also in 2013, Don Yelton, a Republican precinct chair in North Carolina, said that voter ID laws were acceptable to him if it kept "lazy blacks" from voting. "The law is going to kick the Democrats in the butt," he added. His comments were so blatantly racist that Yelton had to resign his position. Ken Emanuelson, a Republican Tea Party leader in Texas, was holding a 2013 meeting of Battlefield Dallas County, a group dedicated to turning out Republican voters, when a black pastor asked him, "What are the Republicans doing to get black people to vote?" Emanuelson responded, "Well, I'm going to be real honest with you. The Republican Party doesn't want black people to vote if they're going to vote nine to one for Democrats."[36]

In 2016, Republican representative Glenn Grothman of Wisconsin, a backer of the state's photo ID law, said, "I think Hillary Clinton is about the weakest candidate the Democrats have ever put up. And now we have photo ID, and I think photo ID is going to make a little bit of a difference as well." Also in Wisconsin, then-Republican state senate staffer Rodd Allbaugh testified under oath in court that at a closed door meeting, several Republican members of the state legislature were "giddy" and "politically frothing at the mouth" in anticipation of a voter ID law that would make it more difficult for likely Democratic supporters to vote. Although Allbaugh was a lifelong Republican, he said that the experience led him to leave the party.[37]

Not every Republican leader shares these sentiments. Some believe that as the electorate becomes less white, Republicans should focus on winning over minority voters rather than on tamping down turnout. According to national exit polls, from 1980 to 2016, the non-Hispanic white share of the presidential electorate fell from 88 to 71 percent and will surely continue to tumble in future elections. Republican senator Rand Paul of Kentucky, one of the party's most prominent conservative leaders, warned Texas Republicans that its hostility to minorities is counterproductive and that they will eventually lose their grip on Texas, with its growing minority population, unless they change their approach. Senator Paul, who grew up in Texas and whose father, Ron Paul, was a long-serving member of the Texas congressional delegation and a candidate for the Republican presidential nomination, said in February 2014, "What I do believe is Texas is going to be a Democrat state within 10 years if we don't change. That means we evolve, it doesn't mean we give up on what we believe in, but it means we have to be a welcoming party."[38]

Long-serving Wisconsin Republican senator Dale Schultz chided his party "for pouring all of its energy into election mechanics. We should be pitching as political parties our ideas for improving things in the future rather than mucking around in the mechanics and making it more confrontational at the voting sites and trying to suppress the vote." Veteran Republican representative James Sensenbrenner of Wisconsin sponsored legislation to restore the preclearance provision of the Voting Rights Act under a revised formula. He said in a 2016 *New York Times* op-ed, "Ensuring that every eligible voter can cast a ballot without fear, deterrence and prejudice is a basic American right. I would rather lose my job than suppress votes to keep it."[39]

Electoral reforms to make registration and voting easier and to protect voting machines from malicious hacking and errors has widespread public support. The 2016 Survey of the Performance of American Elections, a robust survey of 10,200 registered voters nationwide, found that 63 percent of respondents strongly or somewhat supported automatically registering all citizens over age eighteen to vote, 57 percent supported election day registration, 65 percent supported making election day a national holiday, and 85 percent supported a paper trail for electronic voting machines. Another poll by the independent media and research group Government Technology conducted in December 2016 found that "eight in 10 voters and nearly 90 percent of poll workers believe upgrades to the nation's voting technology will strengthen and build trust in elections."[40]

Low turnout and distrust of government in the United States is no less a cultural than a legal and constitutional issue. Yet changes in law can change hearts and minds. It was only after enactment of the Civil Rights Act of 1964 that, for the first time, white southerners came to reject segregation of the races. Prior to the 1967 Supreme Court decision striking down laws against interracial marriage, nearly 60 percent of Americans supported such regulations. Three years after the decision, poll responses had reversed. Recent polls now show 90 percent opposition to prohibiting interracial marriage by law.

Reform of American suffrage may be simpler than comedian Mo Rocca has suggested in the quotation that begins this chapter.[41] The only cure for an ailing democracy is more participation in voting and representation by ordinary Americans. Even if amendments to guarantee the right to vote and popularly elect the president remain beyond practical reach, well-tested, commonsense reforms, most of them within the authority of Congress, would recharge the dimmed beacon of American democracy, bringing governance closer to the will of the people. But reform will take place only if the American people demand change forcefully enough and do not just opt out of political engagement. "Let us never forget that government is ourselves," said Franklin Roosevelt, "and not an alien power over us. The ultimate rulers of our democracy are not a President and Senators and Congressmen and Government officials, but the voters of this country."[42]

CONCLUSION

The Embattled Vote

And here, in this very first paragraph of the declaration, is the assertion of the natural right of all to the ballot; for, how can "the consent of the governed" be given, if the right to vote be denied.

—SUSAN B. ANTHONY, 1872

For more than two hundred years, women and other excluded Americans have struggled against stout resistance from elite white men for their right to vote. Women gained the vote in 1920 after a campaign that began in the 1840s and only ended after suffragists picketed in front of the White House gates, braved arrest, organized hunger strikes in prison, and suffered forced-feedings. At the height of the suffrage movement, most states were making voting more difficult through registration and residency requirements. In the South, where most African Americans lived, only white women realistically secured the right to vote in 1920. African Americans lost the vote in the antebellum years, regained the vote during the post–Civil War Reconstruction, and soon lost their rights to white supremacists who "redeemed" southern governments. They secured the right to vote again only during the "Second

Reconstruction" of the 1960s, after voting rights protesters suffered beatings, arrests, and even death.

The struggle for the vote has historically come from the bottom up, not the top down, with victories tempered by setbacks and defeats. Frederick Douglass, Susan B. Anthony, Carrie Chapman Catt, and Martin Luther King, Jr., among other noted figures, led grassroots campaigns for the vote. In recent years, however, groups with the resources to sustain and finance voting rights litigation have achieved victories against voter photo ID laws, racial and partisan gerrymandering, and legislation intended to restrict the registration and voting opportunities for minority groups. The U.S. Supreme Court has authorized the use of independent commissions to draw redistricting plans. Still, the centuries-long battle for full suffrage rights for all Americans remains unfinished. In our own time, restrictions on voting still pose barriers to the franchise for tens of millions of Americans, with burdens falling most heavily on African Americans and other minorities. The outcome of efforts to stymie partisan gerrymandering remains uncertain, and wealthy special interests have an outsized influence on the outcomes of elections and public policy in America's national, state, and local governments.

The vote has been embattled for centuries in the United States in large part because Americans lack an explicit constitutional right to vote. American patriots fought the Revolutionary War not just to gain independence from Britain's harsh rule but to establish a radical new principle for their time: sovereignty of the people. The American people, not the birthright of kings and nobles, would determine the destiny of the new republic. Still, the people would rule indirectly through elected representatives in what became a democratic republic. To balance popular sovereignty with the threat to order and liberty posed by voters who supposedly lacked the will and ability to resist dangerous demagogues, the founding fathers opposed universal voting. In their view, the vote should be granted only to men who possessed the economic status that ensured an investment in the land and a wise and independent vote. Beyond the fearful rhetoric of mob rule in America, hard, practical politics also motivated this restrictive view of the franchise. America's slave-holding and commercial elite believed that voting by men of property and standing would best protect their economic interests and preserve their control over the government.

With the Constitution silent on the matter, the individual states decided who could vote and who could not. States initially granted the franchise primarily to men who held property or paid taxes. Yet in some ways voting in the early republic was less restrictive than today. Almost no one had to register prior to voting or present forms of written identification. Voters at the polls only had to swear to their identity. Some states allowed voting by noncitizens who owned property or paid taxes. Most states only laxly enforced voting requirements. Some technically ineligible voters cast ballots by simply showing up at the polls.

The vote has been a controversial issue through to the present day, with no simple, linear progression of expanded voting rights. As the states eased economic requirements for voting and expanded the range of elected offices in the antebellum period, they implemented the idea of a white man's republic by shutting off votes for African Americans and continuing to exclude women and Native Americans from the franchise. The Fifteenth Amendment nominally secured votes for African Americans but left the door open for disenfranchisement through literacy tests, poll taxes, and white primaries.

Even the Voting Rights Act of 1965 did not preclude the restriction of minority voting through felon disenfranchisement, voter purges, photo ID laws, and racially and politically gerrymandered legislative districts. The elimination of Justice Department preclearance by the U.S. Supreme Court has enabled states and localities to discriminate against minority voters through the reduction of polling places and other small but consequential and unchecked maneuvers. Advocates of voting rights do not have the ability to file court challenges against every discriminatory change in voting practice.

The stakes in the ongoing battle over the vote could not be higher, especially with Americans voting for half a million elected offices, one for about every five hundred adult citizens in the United States. Nonvoters can influence politics in various ways, through lobbying, demonstrations, fundraising, and participation in political debates. Most of these activities, however, are weighted toward the wealthy.

Americans become decision-makers only if they vote in elections and can make their vote count. The issue of voter turnout has clouded the history of voting in the United States, with authorities disputing the role of voter apathy versus structural impediments. Even though Americans have fought and died for the vote, the United States ranks near the bottom among other democratic nations in voter turnout of its citizens. Low turnout creates a political vacuum that enables wealthy special interest groups to gain undue influence over American elections and policy, to the detriment of the common good. Partisan and racial gerrymandering has also robbed voters of the opportunity to participate in truly competitive elections.

Despite dismal turnout, many states have enacted a new wave of restrictive voting laws in the twenty-first century. In a contentious national debate that has spilled into courtrooms, defenders argue that such measures reasonably ensure the integrity and smooth administration of elections, while critics claim that they resurrect discriminatory burdens on voting by racial minorities, the poor, and young people. The debate is bitterly partisan, fueled by intense polarization between Republicans and Democrats and racially linked patterns of voting for the parties. The alleged targets of restrictive new laws on registration and voting, adopted almost exclusively by Republican-controlled state governments, are their Democratic opponents. Multiple studies and court findings have proved that claims of voter fraud have no validity and are nothing more than smokescreens for measures to limit the votes of political opponents.

As the second decade of the twenty-first century nears its end, American democracy is in crisis. Cynicism about government has soared to record levels, and voter turnout lags most other developed nations. As many states moved to facilitate voting, a counter-revolution fueled by extreme partisanship and polarization made voting more difficult, especially for minorities. The Russians, who compromised the presidential election of 2016, will strive to do so again, and neither the president nor Congress has shown an inclination to retaliate or adopt strong preventive measures. The nation remains mired in a fragmented, eighteenth-century system of election administration by more than ten thousand localities, and the Trump administration has not yet provided national assistance for safeguarding registration rolls and voting machines. Instead, the administration has abetted the push for voter restrictions by making false claims about illegal voting in American elections.

In some ways, modern American democracy resembles the economic stakeholder model of more than two centuries ago. Restrictions on registration and voting, and alienation from politics have combined to produce a "party of nonvoters" that is disproportionately minority, young, and economically disadvantaged. A Pew Research Center survey of the 2014 midterm electorate found that 43 percent of nonvoters were nonwhite, compared to 22 percent of voters; 34 percent of nonvoters were under the age of thirty, compared to 10 percent of voters; and 46 percent of nonvoters had family incomes under thirty thousand dollars per year, compared to 19 percent of voters.[1]

Experience in the United States and abroad demonstrates that there are pathways to reforming the vote in America. A constitutional right to vote, expanded motor voter registration, same-day registration, anti-gerrymandering requirements, independent redistricting commissions, the revival of voting rights preclearance, mandates for paper ballot trails, and secure voting technology would advance the democratic goal of assuring that America is governed truly by the consent of the governed. Still, reform of the vote will not come easily from the politicians. It may not be necessary any longer to risk dying for the vote, but change will come only through the kind of concerted, grassroots action that prompted Congress to enact the Voting Rights Act. "When too many Americans don't vote or participate, some see apathy and despair," said the late Minnesota senator Paul Wellstone. "I see disappointment and even outrage. And I believe that out of this frustration can come hope and action."[2]

NOTES

Introduction

1. Sam Roberts, "Bonard Fowler, Alabama Officer in Shooting That Led to Selma March, Dies at 81," *New York Times,* 9 July 2015, https://www .nytimes.com/2015/07/10/us/bonard-fowler-alabama-officer-in-shooting -that-led-to-selma-march-dies-at-81.html?_r=0.

2. George Wythe Munford, *The Two Parsons; Cupid's Sports; the Dream; and the Jewels of Virginia* (Richmond, VA: J. D. K. Sleight, 1884), p. 208.

3. United States Election Project, "Voter Turnout," http://www .electproject.org/home/voter-turnout/voter-turnout-data.

4. William E. Gladstone, "Kin beyond Sea," *North American Review,* Sept.–Oct. 1878, p. 185.

1. The Founding Fathers' Mistake

1. George Washington to Theodorick Bland, 18 Nov. 1786; Washington to Edmund Randolph, 28 Mar. 1787, W. W. Abbot et al., eds., *The Papers of George Washington, Confederation Series* (Charlottesville: University Press of Virginia, 1992–1997), 4:377–379, 5:112–114.

2. George Washington to Bushrod Washington, 15 Nov. 1786; George Washington to Marquis de Lafayette, 15 Aug. 1787, ibid., 4:368–370, 5:294–297.

3. George Mason to George Mason, Jr., 1 June 1787, Kate Mason Rowland, *The Life of George Mason, 1725–1792* (New York: Russell and Russell, 1964), 2:129–130.

4. Leonard L. Richards, *Shays's Rebellion: The American Revolution's Final Battle* (Philadelphia: University of Pennsylvania Press, 2002).

5. George Washington to Henry Lee, Jr., 31 Oct. 1786; George Washington to Henry Knox, 26 Dec. 1786, Abbot et al., eds., *Papers of George Washington, Confederation Series,* 4:318–320, 481–483.

6. *The Debates in the Several State Conventions on Adoption of the Federal Constitution* (Philadelphia: J. B. Lippincott, 1881), 1:486; Glenn A. Phelps, *George Washington and American Constitutionalism* (Lawrence: University Press of Kansas, 1993), pp. 91–120.

7. John Adams to Thomas Brand Hollis, 5 Apr. 1788, *Papers of John Adams,* Digital Edition, http://rotunda.upress.virginia.edu/founders/ADMS.

8. Benjamin Rush to Elias Boudinot, 9 July 1788, L. H. Butterfield, ed., *The Letters of Benjamin Rush* (Philadelphia: American Philosophical Society, 1951), 1:475.

9. Thomas Jefferson to Edward Rutledge, 18 July 1788, Julian P. Boyd, ed., *The Papers of Thomas Jefferson* (Princeton, NJ: Princeton University Press, 1950–2016), 13:377–379.

10. James Wilson, "Remarks to Pennsylvania Ratifying Convention," 26 Nov. 1787, David Mark Hall and Kermit L. Hall, eds., *Collected Works of James Wilson* (Indianapolis: Liberty Fund, 2007), 1:182.

11. Alexander Hamilton, James Madison, and John Jay, *The Federalist Papers* (New York: SoHo Books, 2012), no. 39, p. 108.

12. "On Some of the Principles of American Republicanism," Baltimore *Federal Gazette,* 8 May 1797, p. 3.

13. A Voter, "For the Centinel," Georgetown, District of Columbia, *Centennial of Liberty,* 19 Aug. 1800, p. 3.

14. An American Citizen, "Commentary Number IV," *Pennsylvania Gazette,* 24 Oct. 1787, p. 3.

15. John Adams to James Sullivan, 26 May 1776, *Papers of John Adams.*

16. Alexander Hamilton, *The Farmer Refuted &c,* 23 Feb. 1775, Founders Online, https://founders.archives.gov/documents/Hamilton/01-01-02-0057.

17. Max Farrand, *Records of the Federal Convention of 1787* (New Haven, CT: Yale University Press, 1911), 2:202, 203–204.

18. Ibid., 2:203, 204.

19. Ibid., 2:201.

20. "Northwest Ordinance," Primary Documents of American History, Library of Congress, https://www.loc.gov/rr/program/bib/ourdocs /northwest.html; Peter S. Onuf, *Statehood and Union: History of the Northwest Ordinance* (Bloomington: Indiana University Press, 1987).

21. Jerrold G. Rusk, *A Statistical History of the American Electorate* (Washington, DC: CQ Press, 2001), pp. 23–24.

22. Ibid., pp. 31–33; Donald Ratcliffe, "The Right to Vote and the Rise of Democracy, 1787–1828," *Journal of the Early Republic* 33 (2013): 230–243. An excellent online database of voter turnout in the early republic is now available: Phillip Lampi, "A New Nation Votes," http://elections.lib.tufts .edu/.

23. Rusk, *A Statistical History*, pp. 23–24, 31–33.

24. Ibid., pp. 25–32, 50–54.

25. James Madison, "Speech to Virginia Ratifying Convention," 20 June 1788, V. Gaillard Hunt, ed., *The Writings of James Madison* (New York: G. P. Putnam's Sons, 1900–1910), 5:223; Colleen A. Sheehan and Gary L. McDowell, eds., *Friends of the Constitution: Writings of the "Other" Federalists, 1787–1788* (Indianapolis: Liberty Fund, 1998), p. 194.

26. A Friend of Society and Liberty, "To the INHABITANTS of the Western Counties of Pennsylvania," *Pennsylvania Gazette,* 23 July 1788, p. 2.

27. Samuel Adams, "To the Legislature of Massachusetts," 16 Jan. 1795, Samuel Adams Heritage Society, http://www.samuel-adams-heritage.com /documents/address-to-massachusetts-legislature.html.

28. *The Federalist,* no. 10, pp. 26–27.

29. John Adams to William Stephens Smith, 21 Dec. 1786, *Papers of John Adams.*

30. *The Federalist,* no. 63, p. 184.

31. "From Correspondents," *Philadelphia Gazette,* 17 Feb. 1790, p. 3.

32. Thomas Jefferson to James Madison, 20 Dec. 1787, *Papers of Thomas Jefferson,* 12:438–447.

33. Christian G. Fritz, *American Sovereigns: The People and America's Constitutional Tradition before the Civil War* (New York: Cambridge University Press, 2008), p. 179; Jacob Katz Cogan, "Imagining Democracy: Popular

Sovereignty from the Constitution to the Civil War" (Ph.D. dissertation, Princeton University, 2002), p. 29.

34. *The Federalist,* no. 65, p. 188.

35. "The Convention of Massachusetts," *Connecticut Courant,* 3 Mar. 1788, p. 1.

36. "Mr. Martin's Information to the House of Assembly," *Pennsylvania Packet,* 1 Feb. 1788, p. 2.

37. Amicus, "Hints," Charleston *Columbian Herald,* 28 Aug. 1788, p. 2.

38. Harvey Flaumenhaft, *The Effective Republic: Administration and Constitution in the Thought of Alexander Hamilton* (Durham, NC: Duke University Press, 1992), p. 151.

39. *Annals of Congress,* House of Representatives, 1st Congress, 1st session, 15 Aug. 1789, pp. 761–762, https://memory.loc.gov/cgi-bin/ampage?collId=llac&fileName=001/llac001.db&recNum=51.

40. Seth Cotlar, "Languages of Democracy in America from the Revolution to the Election of 1800," in *Re-Imagining Democracy in the Age of Revolutions,* ed. Joanna Innes and Mark Philip (New York: Oxford University Press, 2013), p. 21.

41. *Annals of Congress,* 15 Aug. 1789, pp. 761–762, 766.

42. Ibid., pp. 767, 770.

43. Christopher Terranova, "The Constitutional Life of Legislative Instructions in America," *New York University Law Review* 84 (Nov. 2009): 1346.

44. Matthew Schoenbachler, "Republicanism in the Age of Democratic Revolution: The Democratic-Republican Societies of the 1790s," *Journal of the Early Republic* 18 (Summer 1998): 248–250.

45. James P. Martin, "When Repression Is Democratic and Constitutional: The Federalist Theory of Democratic Representation and the Sedition Act of 1798," *University of Chicago Law Review* 66 (1999): 132; George Washington to Burgess Ball, 25 Sept. 1794, Dorothy Twohig et al., eds., *Papers of George Washington, Presidential Series* (Charlottesville: University Press of Virginia, 1987–2016), 16:722–723.

46. Jeffrey L. Pasley, "The Cheese and the Words: Popular Political Culture and Participatory Democracy in the Early American Republic," in *Beyond the Founders: New Approaches to the Political History of the Early Republic,* ed. Jeffrey L. Pasley, Andrew W. Robertson, and David Waldstreicher (Chapel Hill: University of North Carolina Press, 2004), pp. 31–56; Simon P. Newman, *Parades and the Politics of the Street: Festive Culture in*

the Early American Republic (Philadelphia: University of Pennsylvania Press, 1997); Robert W. T. Martin, *Government by Dissent: Protest, Resistance, and Radical Democratic Thought in the Early American Republic* (New York: NYU Press, 2013).

47. *The Federalist*, no. 60, p. 175; *Powell v. McCormack*, 395 U.S. 486 (1969); *U.S. Term Limits, Inc. v. Thornton*, 514 U.S. 779 (1995); *Cook v. Gralike*, 531 U.S. 510 (2001).

48. "Constitution of Maryland—1776"; "Constitution New Jersey—1776"; "Constitution of South Carolina—1790," Francis Newton Thorpe, ed., *The Federal and State Constitutions* (Washington, DC: U.S. Government Printing Office, 1909), 3:1691, 5:2594–2595, 6:3258–3260.

49. Farrand, *Records*, 2:240, 242.

50. Robert G. Natelson, "The Original Scope of the Constitution to Regulate Elections," *Journal of Constitutional Law* 13, no. 1 (2010): 39–40; Govtrack, "House Vote #11 in 1789," https://www.govtrack.us/congress/votes/1-1/h11.

51. "Philadelphia," Philadelphia *Federal Gazette*, 7 Feb. 1791, p. 3.

52. Juniatta Mann, "A Mistaken Principle in Government," Philadelphia *Independent Gazetteer*, 10 Apr. 1790, p. 2.

53. On the apportionment of legislative districts in the early republic, see Rosemarie Zagarri, *The Politics of Size: Representation in the United States, 1776–1850* (Ithaca, NY: Cornell University Press, 2010); state systems for electing members of Congress is at p. 108.

54. Robert G. Dixon, Jr., *Democratic Representation: Reapportionment in Law and Politics* (New York: Oxford University Press, 1968), pp. 72–75; "Constitution of Delaware—1782"; "Constitution of Georgia—1789," Thorpe, ed., *The Federal and State Constitutions*, 1:571, 2:785. Population data is from the 1800 U.S. Census.

55. Dixon, *Democratic Representation*.

56. Robert J. Dinkin, *Voting in Revolutionary America* (Westport, CT: Greenwood Press, 1982), pp. 90–107.

57. Chilton Williamson, *American Suffrage: From Property to Democracy, 1760 to 1860* (Princeton, NJ: Princeton University Press, 1960), p. 123.

58. See, for example, "Universal Suffrage," Hartford *American Mercury*, 26 May 1803, p. 3; "New York," New York *Citizen*, 5 Dec. 1801, p. 2; "To the Public," *New York Evening Post*, 15 Jan. 1802, p. 2; "Respecting the Selectmen of Charleston," Boston *Independent Chronicle*, 8 Apr. 1804, p. 2; "Speech of Dr. Lieb," *Carlisle Gazette*, 12 June 1807, p. 1; "Thursday November 11, 1811,"

Richmond Enquirer, 26 Nov. 1811, p. 2; John T. Dempsey, "Control by Congress over the Seating and Disciplining of Members" (Ph.D. dissertation, University of Michigan, 1956), pp. 330–331.

59. William Shakespeare, *Othello,* ed. E. A. J. Honigmann (London: Thomson Learning, 1997), p. 156.

2. A White Man's Republic

Epigraph: Lincoln–Douglas debates, Fifth Joint Debate, 7 Oct. 1858. Senator Stephen Douglas was the leading Democratic politician of the 1850s. He clashed with Abraham Lincoln in the famous Lincoln–Douglas debates during the Illinois Senate campaign of 1858. After defeating Lincoln in the state legislature's vote for senator, Douglas lost to Lincoln in the presidential election of 1860.

1. "Universal Suffrage," *Connecticut Courant,* 11 May 1803, p. 2; Boston *New England Palladium,* 17 May 1803, p. 1; *New York Evening Post,* 27 May 1803, p. 2; *New York Herald,* 1 June 1803, p. 2.

2. Connecticut General Assembly, *The Public Statute Laws of the State of Connecticut, Book 1* (Hartford: Hudson and Goodwin, 1808), p. 300; "The Charter of Connecticut 1662," Connecticut State Library, http://cslib .cdmhost.com/cdm/ref/collection/p128501coll2/id/188289; Jerrold G. Rusk, *A Statistical History of the American Electorate* (Washington, DC: CQ Press, 2001), pp. 24, 33; "Connecticut," New Hampshire *Farmer's Cabinet,* 4 Nov. 1847, p. 3.

3. Christopher Malone, *Between Freedom and Bondage: Race, Party, and Voting Rights in the Antebellum North* (New York: Routledge, 2007), p. 4.

4. Washington Farewell Address, 19 Sept. 1796, John C. Fitzpatrick, ed., *The Writings of George Washington* (Washington, DC: U.S. Government Printing Office, 1931–1944), 35:214–238.

5. Elisabeth S. Clemens, *The People's Lobby: Organizational Innovation and the Rise of Interest Group Politics in the United States, 1890–1925* (Chicago: University of Chicago Press, 1997), pp. 20–22.

6. Allan J. Lichtman, "Elections and Electoral Eras," in *The Concise Princeton Encyclopedia of American Political History,* ed. Michael Kazin (Princeton, NJ: Princeton University Press, 2011), p. 198.

7. On the acts, see Terri Diane Halperin, *The Alien and Sedition Acts of 1798: Testing the Constitution* (Baltimore: Johns Hopkins University Press, 2016).

8. *Annals of Congress,* U.S. House of Representatives, 5th Congress, 1st session, July 1797, p. 430.

9. William Cranch to Abigail Smith Adams, 7 Jan. 1800, *Papers of John Adams,* Digital Edition, http://rotunda.upress.virginia.edu/founders/ADMS.

10. George Washington to Alexander Spotswood, Jr., 22 Nov. 1798, Dorothy Twohig et al., eds., *Papers of George Washington, Retirement Series* (Charlottesville: University Press of Virginia, 1998–1999), 3:216–217.

11. Alex Ayres, ed., *The Wit and Wisdom of Abraham Lincoln* (New York: Meridian, 1992), p. 1858.

12. *Annals of Congress,* U.S. House of Representatives, 8th Congress, 1st session, 28 Oct. 1803, pp. 516–517.

13. Ibid., 26 Oct. 1803, p. 493.

14. Thomas Jefferson, *Notes on the State of Virginia* (Paris: s.n., 1784), p. 157.

15. Lucius Crassus, "Examination No. VII," 7 Jan. 1802, Harold C. Syrett, ed., *The Papers of Alexander Hamilton* (New York: Columbia University Press, 1961–1987), 25:491–495.

16. John Adams to John Adams Smith, 12 May 1821, *Adams Papers.*

17. John Thomas Scharf, *History of Maryland from the Earliest Days to the Present Day* (Hatboro, PA: J. B. Piet, 1879), 2:611.

18. J. R. Pole, "Constitutional Reform and Election Statistics in Maryland, 1790–1812," *Maryland Historical Magazine* 55 (1960): 279.

19. "Wilmin. Mirroa," Maryland *Hornet,* 7 Dec. 1802, p. 4.

20. David S. Bogen, "The Annapolis Poll Books of 1800 and 1804: African American Voting in the Early Republic," *Maryland Historical Magazine* 86 (1991): 57–65.

21. William Griffith, *Eumenes* (Trenton: G. Craft, 1799), pp. 33, 36; Jan Ellen Lewis, "Rethinking Women's Suffrage in New Jersey, 1776–1807," *Rutgers Law Review* 63 (2011): 1031–1035; "House Committee on Elections Report," *New Jersey Journal,* 17 Dec. 1802, p. 2.

22. Lewis, "Rethinking Women's Suffrage in New Jersey," p. 1032.

23. David N. Gellman and David Quigley, eds., *Jim Crow New York: A Documentary History of Race and Citizenship, 1777–1877* (New York: NYU Press, 2003), pp. 164–165, 103.

24. Ibid., pp. 107–108, 125.

25. Ibid., pp. 128, 141–142.

26. Ibid., pp. 120, 180. There is an extensive literature on the social construction of "whiteness" in American history. See, for example, "Toward a

Bibliography of Critical Whiteness Studies," Center on Democracy in a Multiracial Society, University of Illinois at Urbana-Champaign, Nov. 2006, pp. 20–26, http://nathanrtodd.netfirms.com/documents/Spanierman_Todd_Neville(2006)Whiteness_Bib.pdf.

27. Gellman and Quigley, eds., *Jim Crow New York*, p. 185.

28. George E. Walker, *The Afro-American in New York City, 1827–1860* (New York: Garland, 1993), p. 116.

29. Gellman and Quigley, eds., *Jim Crow New York*, pp. 124–126, 132.

30. *Corfield v. Coryell*, 6 Fed. Cas. 546, no. 3, 230 C.C.E.D.Pa. (1823). Through much of American history Supreme Court justices also sat at times on appeals court panels.

31. Andrew Jackson, First Annual Message, 8 Dec. 1829, American Presidency Project, http://www.presidency.ucsb.edu/ws/?pid=29471.

32. Peter Argersinger, *Structure, Process, and Party: Essays in American Political History* (Armonk, NY: M. E. Sharpe, 1992), p. 37.

33. S. Croswell and R. Sutton, *Debates and Proceedings in the New York State Convention for the Revision of the Constitution* (Albany: Albany Argus, 1846), 30 Sept. 1846, p. 777; 2 Oct. 1846, p. 796; 1 Oct. 1846, pp. 783–785.

34. Ibid., 6 Oct. 1846, pp. 822–823.

35. Hanes Walton, Jr., Sherman C. Puckett, and Donald R. Deskins, Jr., *The African American Electorate: A Statistical History* (Thousand Oaks, CA: Sage, 2012), p. 151.

36. "Constitution of New York, 1846," Francis Newton Thorpe, ed., *The Federal and State Constitutions* (Washington, DC: U.S. Government Printing Office, 1909), 5:2656.

37. "Constitution of the Commonwealth of Pennsylvania, 1790," ibid., 5:3096.

38. *Reports of Cases Argued and Determined in the Supreme Court of Pennsylvania,* vol. 6, *May–September 1837* (Philadelphia: Kay and Brothers, 1880), *Hobbs v. Fogg* (Sunbury, July 1837), pp. 553–560.

39. *Proceedings and Debates of the Constitutional Convention of the Commonwealth of Pennsylvania, Held on the Second Day of May 1837* (Harrisburg, PA: Packer, Barrett, and Parks, 1837), 19 June 1837, 2:476; 23 June 1837, 3:84.

40. *Opinion of the Honorable John Fox against the Exercise of Negro Suffrage in Pennsylvania* (Harrisburg, PA: Packer, Barrett, and Park, 1838).

41. Eric Ledell Smith, "The End of Black Voting Rights in Pennsylvania: African Americans and the Pennsylvania Constitutional Convention of 1837–1838," *Pennsylvania History* 65 (1998): 279–299.

42. Ibid.; "The Appeal of Forty Thousand Citizens Threatened with Disenfranchisement to the People of Pennsylvania," 14 Mar. 1918, Digital History, http://digitalhistory.hsp.org/pafrm/doc/appeal.

43. Van Gosse, "We Are Americans: The Ideology of Black Republicanism before the Civil War," Harriet Tubman Institute for Research on Africa and Its Diasporas, 2004, http://avery.cofc.edu/wp-content/uploads/2012/08/gosse.pdf.

44. "Right of Suffrage in Ohio," *The North Star*, 13 June 1850, p. 4.

45. *Proceedings and Debates of the Virginia State Convention of 1829–1830* (Richmond: Ritchie and Cooke, 1830), 26 Oct. 1829, p. 47; 11 Nov. 1829, p. 257.

46. Ibid., 3 Nov. 1829, pp. 158–159; 20 Nov. 1829, pp. 398–399, 409; 23 Nov. 1829, pp. 437, 438.

47. Ibid., 21 Nov. 1829, p. 412; 13 Oct. 1829, p. 27; 26 Oct. 1829, p. 50.

48. John Marshall to James M. Garnett, 20 May 1829, Charles F. Hobson, ed., *The Papers of John Marshall, Correspondence, Papers, and Selected Judicial Opinions, April 1827–December 1830* (Chapel Hill: University of North Carolina Press, 1974–2006), 11:246–250.

49. *Proceedings and Debates of the Virginia State Convention,* 14 Nov. 1829, pp. 315–316.

50. Ibid., 13 Oct. 1829, p. 28; 26 Oct. 1829, p. 51.

51. "Constitution of Virginia, 1830," Thorpe, ed., *Federal and State Constitutions,* 7:3821–3827.

52. *Proceedings and Debates of the Virginia State Convention,* 23 Nov. 1829, p. 439.

53. "Constitution of Virginia, 1851," Thorpe, ed., *Federal and State Constitutions,* 7:3832–3837.

54. The details of Dorr's Rebellion in the following paragraphs come from Erik J. Chaput, *The People's Martyr: Thomas Wilson Dorr and His 1842 Rhode Island Rebellion* (Lawrence: University Press of Kansas, 2013).

55. Ibid., p. 9.

56. Ibid., pp. 165–166.

57. *Luther v. Borden,* 48 U.S. 1 (1849). For a recent application of the "political thicket" doctrine by several U.S. Supreme Court justices, see *Vieth v. Jubelirer,* 541 U.S. 267 (2004).

58. *Journal of the Convention, Ohio, 1802* (Columbus: F. Orge Nashbee, 1827); Constitution of Ohio, 1802, Thorpe, ed., *Federal and State Constitutions,* 7:2901–2913.

59. Ohio Constitution of 1851, http://textbook2.infohio.org/images /section8images/1851_Ohio_Constitution_Transcript.pdf.

60. Walton, Puckett, and Deskins, *The African American Electorate*, p. 147; John Rozett, "Racism and Republican Emergence in Illinois, 1848–1860: A Reevaluation of Republican Negrophobia," *Civil War History* 22 (1976): 102.

61. Alexander Keyssar, *The Right to Vote: The Contested History of Democracy in the United States,* rev. ed. (New York: Basic Books, 2009), p. 48.

62. Joseph P. Ferrie, "The End of American Exceptionalism? Mobility in the U.S. since 1850," NBER Working Paper, May 2005, p. 23, http://www.nber .org/papers/w11324.pdf.

63. Ronald Hayduk, *Democracy for All: Restoring Immigrant Voting Rights in the United States* (New York: Routledge, 2006), pp. 19–20.

64. Other authorities indicate that fewer than 10 percent of adult white males were disenfranchised, but these estimates do not account for the significant effect of residency requirements and the smaller effects of disenfranchising paupers, felons, illiterates, and people of unsound mind.

65. Max Farrand, *Records of the Federal Convention of 1787* (New Haven, CT: Yale University Press, 1911), 2:241.

66. Ralph Ketcham, *James Madison: A Biography* (New York: Macmillan, 1971), p. 275; "Madison's Election to the First Federal Congress, October 1788–February 1789," Founders Online, https://founders.archives .gov/documents/Madison/01-11-02-0219.

67. Peter Argersinger, *Representation and Inequality in Later Nineteenth Century America* (New York: Cambridge University Press, 2012), p. 8.

68. Elmer C. Griffith, *The Rise and Development of the Gerrymander* (Chicago: Scott, Foresman, 1907), pp. 123–124; Andrew Hacker, *Congressional Districting: The Issue of Equal Representation* (Washington, DC: Brookings Institution, 1964), pp. 40–41.

69. Alec C. Ewald, *The Way We Vote: The Local Dimension of American Suffrage* (Nashville, TN: Vanderbilt University Press, 2009), pp. 40–46, 46 (quotation).

70. For an alternative view, see Keyssar, *The Right to Vote*, pp. 55–56.

71. Farrand, *Records,* 2:202–204.

72. *Votes and Proceeding of the Senate of the State of Maryland,* Nov. 1800 session (Annapolis, MD: Frederick Green, 1801), p. 48; Maryland State Archives, Session Laws, p. 1600, http://msa.maryland.gov/megafile/msa /speccol/sc4800/sc4872/003181/html/m3181-1600.html.

73. Gellman and Quigley, eds., *Jim Crow New York*, pp. 150–151; Chilton Williamson, *American Suffrage: From Property to Democracy, 1760 to 1860* (Princeton, NJ: Princeton University Press, 1960), p. 204.

74. James M. McPherson, *Abraham Lincoln and the Second Revolution* (New York: Oxford University Press, 1991), p. 50.

3. Constructing and Deconstructing the Vote

Epigraph: "Reconstruction," *Atlantic Monthly,* Dec. 1866. The escaped slave Frederick Douglass became a nationally renowned orator, abolitionist, and leader of the movements for African American and women's suffrage.

1. Allan J. Lichtman, "Elections and Electoral Eras," in *The Concise Princeton Encyclopedia of American Political History,* ed. Michael Kazin (Princeton, NJ: Princeton University Press, 2011), 1:200.

2. Henry Louis Gates, Jr., *Lincoln on Race and Slavery* (Princeton, NJ: Princeton University Press, 2009), pp. 82–83.

3. Joshua A. Lynn, "Preserving the White Man's Republic: The Democratic Party and the Transformation of American Conservatism, 1847–1860" (Ph.D. dissertation, University of North Carolina at Chapel Hill, 2015), p. 61.

4. Lichtman, "Elections and Electoral Eras," 1:201.

5. Jerrold G. Rusk, *A Statistical History of the American Electorate* (Washington, DC: CQ Press, 2001), p. 33.

6. Abraham Lincoln, "Second Inaugural Address," 4 Mar. 1865, The Avalon Project, http://avalon.law.yale.edu/19th_century/lincoln2.asp.

7. Andrew Johnson, "Speech on the Gag Resolution," 31 Jan. 1844, LeRoy P. Graff and Ralph W. Haskins, eds., *The Papers of Andrew Johnson* (Knoxville: University of Tennessee Press, 1967–2000), 1:140.

8. "The Speech at St. Louis," *New Orleans Tribune,* 16 Sept. 1866, p. 4; H. Lowell Brown, *High Crimes and Misdemeanors in Presidential Impeachment* (New York: Palgrave Macmillan, 2010), p. 149; Elizabeth R. Varon, "Andrew Johnson and the Legacy of the Civil War," Oxford Research Encyclopedia, Mar. 2016, http://americanhistory.oxfordre.com/view/10.1093/acrefore/9780199329175.001.0001/acrefore-9780199329175-e-11.

9. David Warren Bowen, *Andrew Johnson and the Negro* (Knoxville: University of Tennessee Press, 1989), pp. 1–7.

10. John H. and Lawanda Cox, *Politics, Principle, and Prejudice, 1865–1866: Dilemma of Reconstruction America* (New York: Atheneum, 1969), p. 163.

11. Hanes Walton, Jr., Sherman C. Puckett, and Donald R. Deskins, Jr., *The African American Electorate: A Statistical History* (Thousand Oaks, CA: Sage, 2012), pp. 148–158.

12. Gloria J. Browne-Marshall, *The Voting Rights War: The NAACP and the Ongoing Struggle for Justice* (Lanham, MD: Rowman and Littlefield, 2016), p. 34.

13. Walton et al., *The African American Electorate,* pp. 233–234.

14. Benjamin B. Kendrick, "The Journal of the Joint Committee of Fifteen on Reconstruction" (Ph.D. dissertation, Columbia University, 1914), pp. 50–60.

15. Herman V. Ames, The *Proposed Amendments to the Constitution of the United States during the First Century of Its History* (Washington, DC: U.S. Government Printing Office, 1896), pp. 227–228.

16. *Congressional Globe,* 39th Congress, 1st session, 20 May 1866, p. 2765, https://memory.loc.gov/ammem/amlaw/lwcglink.html#anchor40.

17. See, for example, *North Carolina State Conference of the NAACP v. Mc-Crory,* 182 F. Supp. 3d 320 (M.D.N.C. 2016).

18. *Congressional Globe,* 39th Congress, 1st session, 8 May 1866, p. 2462.

19. Ibid., p. 2459.

20. See, for example, *Saunders v. Wilkins,* 152 F.2d 235 (4th Cir. 1945), cert. denied, 328 U.S. 870 (1946). See also Arthur Earl Bonfield, "Right to Vote and Judicial Enforcement of Section 2 of the Fourteenth Amendment," *Cornell Law Quarterly* 46 (1960): 108–137.

21. Walton et al., *The African American Electorate,* pp. 151–160.

22. *Congressional Globe,* 40th Congress, 3rd session, 29 Jan. 1869, p. 727, https://memory.loc.gov/cgi-bin/ampage?collId=llcg&fileName=085 /llcg85.db&recNum=204.

23. Ibid., 28 Jan. 1869, p. 668; 29 Jan. 1869, p. 707.

24. "Republican Party Platform of 1868," American Presidency Project, http://www.presidency.ucsb.edu/ws/?pid=29622.

25. *Congressional Globe,* 40th Congress, 3rd session, 4 Feb. 1869, pp. 858, 991.

26. Ibid., 28 Jan. 1869, p. 672.

27. Ibid., 29 Jan. 1969, p. 706; 4 Feb. 1869, p. 859.

28. Ibid., 8 Feb. 1869, pp. 990–991; 5 Feb. 1869, p. 902.

29. Ibid., 8 Feb. 1869, p. 1010.

30. Ibid., pp. 995–996.

31. Ibid., p. 1011.

32. Ibid., 28 Jan. 1869, p. 690.

33. Ibid., 4 Feb. 1869, pp. 694, 861.

34. Ibid., 9 Feb. 1869, p. 1014; 5 Feb. 1869, p. 900.

35. Ibid., 8 Feb. 1969, p. 1013; 9 Feb. 1989, pp. 1039, 1029, 1040; 15 Feb. 1869, p. 1226; 20 Feb. 1869, pp. 1425–1428; 25 Feb. 1869, p. 1563; 26 Feb. 1869, p. 1641.

36. Ibid., 9 Feb. 1869, p. 1037.

37. "The Fifteenth Amendment," *New York Times,* 12 Apr. 1869, p. 4.

38. On ratification, see William Gillette, *The Right to Vote: Politics and the Passage of the Fifteenth Amendment* (Baltimore: Johns Hopkins University Press, 1965), pp. 133–152; and "Tennessee Ratifies Fifteenth Amendment," *Deseret News,* 4 Apr. 1997, https://www.deseretnews.com/article/552624 /Tennessee-ratifies-15th-Amendment.html.

39. "The First Amendment, and the Last Their Bearings," Philadelphia *Christian Recorder,* 19 Feb. 1870, p. 2.

40. Hugh Davis, *"We Will Be Satisfied with Nothing Less": The African American Struggle for Equal Rights in the North during Reconstruction* (Ithaca, NY: Cornell University Press, 2011), p. 71.

41. *Report of the Select Committee on Affairs in Alabama,* 43rd Congress, 2nd session, House Report no. 262 (Washington, DC: United States Government Printing Office, 1875), pp. 1–1325; Mary Ellen Curtin, *Black Prisoners and Their World, Alabama, 1865–1900* (Charlottesville: University Press of Virginia, 2000), pp. 55–56.

42. Robert L. Kaczorowski, *The Politics of Judicial Interpretation: The Federal Courts, Department of Justice, and Civil Rights, 1866–1876* (New York: Fordham University Press, 2005), pp. 80–92.

43. *Congressional Record,* 43rd Congress, 2nd session, 27 Feb. 1875, pp. 1893, 1918, http://memory.loc.gov/ammem/amlaw/lwcrlink.html; "Negro Politics," *Atlanta Constitution,* 20 Nov. 1874, p. 2.

44. *Congressional Record,* 27 Feb. 1875, p. 1918.

45. *Slaughter-House Cases,* 83 U.S. 36 (1873); "The Question of Races," *Chicago Tribune,* 2 Jan. 1875, p. 4.

46. *Congressional Record,* 27 Feb. 1875, p. 1922.

47. Ibid., pp. 1903, 1907.

48. Ibid., 26 Feb. 1875, p. 1852.

49. *U.S. v. Cruikshank,* 92 U.S. 542 (1875).

50. Lichtman, "Elections and Electoral Eras," 1:201.

51. "The 'Negro Riots' Season," *New York Times,* 1 Apr. 1880, p. 4.

52. J. Morgan Kousser, *The Shaping of Southern Politics: Suffrage Restrictions and the Establishment of the One-Party South, 1880–1910* (New Haven,

CT: Yale University Press, 1974), pp. 11–82; Michael Perman, *Struggle for Mastery: Disfranchisement in the South, 1888–1908* (Chapel Hill: University of North Carolina Press, 2001); Angela Behrens, Christopher Uggen, and Jeff Manza, "Ballot Manipulation and the 'Menace of Negro Domination': Racial Threat and Felon Disenfranchisement in the United States, 1850–2002," *American Journal of Sociology* 109 (2003): 559–605.

53. *McKay v. Campbell,* 2 Abb. U.S. 120 (1870).

54. *United States v. Reese,* 92 U.S. 214 (1875).

55. *Washington v. State,* 75 Ala. 582 (1884).

56. Henry Cabot Lodge and T. V. Powderly, "The Federal Election Bill," *North American Review,* Sept. 1890, p. 259; Perman, *Struggle for Mastery,* pp. 39–42.

57. Kousser, *The Shaping of Southern Politics,* pp. 238–264; Kent Redding and David R. James, "Estimating Levels and Modeling Determinants of Black and White Voter Turnout in the South, 1880 to 1912," *Historical Methods* 34 (2001): 141–158; Rusk, *A Statistical History,* pp. 51–52. These low percentages reflect the disenfranchisement of women in most states.

58. Emma Lou Thornbrough, "The National Afro-American League, 1887–1908," *Journal of Southern History* 27 (1961): 506. See also Shawn Lee Alexander, *An Army of Lions: The Civil Rights Struggle before the NAACP* (Philadelphia: University of Pennsylvania Press, 2012), and Benjamin R. Justesen, *Broken Brotherhood: The Rise and Fall of the National Afro-American Council* (Carbondale: Southern Illinois University Press, 2008).

59. W. E. B. Du Bois, *The Souls of Black Folk* (New York: Oxford University Press, 2007), pp. 41–42; Russell Brooker, *The American Civil Rights Movement, 1865–1950: Black Agency and People of Good Will* (Lanham, MD: Lexington Books, 2017), p. 180.

4. Votes for Women

Epigraph: Speech, 16 Nov. 1895. Susan B. Anthony was one of the most important and prominent leaders of the nineteenth-century women's movement. She cofounded several women's rights organizations and, with Elizabeth Cady Stanton and others, coauthored the influential six-volume *History of Woman Suffrage.*

1. "Remarks of Susan B. Anthony at Her Trial for Illegal Voting," 19 June 1873, The Elizabeth Cady Stanton and Susan B. Anthony Papers Project, Rutgers University, http://ecssba.rutgers.edu/docs/sbatrial.html.

2. "Severe Storm," *Washington Federalist,* 2 Dec. 1800, p. 2.

3. On New Jersey and women's suffrage in the early republic, see Jan Ellen Lewis, "Rethinking Women's Suffrage in New Jersey, 1776–1807," *Rutgers Law Review* 63 (2011): 1017–1035; and Judith Apter Klinghoffer and Lois Elkis, "The Petticoat Electors: Women's Suffrage in New Jersey, 1776–1807," *Journal of the Early Republic* 12 (1992): 159–193.

4. "Address to the People Called Quakers," *Trenton Federalist,* 19 Sept. 1808, p. 2; Lewis, "Rethinking Women's Suffrage," p. 1032.

5. Elizabeth Cady Stanton, Susan B. Anthony, and Matilda Joslyn Gage, eds., *History of Woman Suffrage,* vol. 1 (New York: Fowler and Wells, 1881), pp. 53–62.

6. Jacob Katz Cogan and Lori D. Ginzberg, "The 1846 Petition for Woman's Suffrage, New York State Constitutional Convention," *Signs* 22 (1997): 431.

7. Sherman Croswell and R. Sutton, *Debates and Proceedings in the New York State Convention* (Albany: Albany Argus, 1846), 1 Oct. 1846, p. 783.

8. Sally G. McMillen, *Seneca Falls and the Origins of the Women's Rights Movement* (New York: Oxford University Press, 2008), pp. 237–239.

9. Ibid., pp. 93–94.

10. Faye Dudden, *Fighting Chance: The Struggle over Woman Suffrage and Black Suffrage in Reconstruction America* (New York: Oxford University Press, 2011), p. 19.

11. J. V. Smith, *Official Report of Debates and Proceedings in the Convention to Form a New Constitution for the State of Ohio* (Columbus, OH: Bascom and Scott, 1851), 2:1182.

12. Eve LaPlante, *Marmee and Louisa: The Untold Story of Louisa May Alcott and Her Mother* (New York: Simon and Schuster, 2012), p. 168; Abby Hills Price, "Statement," Massachusetts Convention of 1853, http://www.hope1842.com/priceconstconv.html.

13. Price, "Statement"; "Concord Women Cast First Votes," 29 Mar. 1880, Mass Moments, http://www.massmoments.org/moment.cfm?mid=97.

14. "Moneka Women's Rights Association," Kansas Historical Society, https://www.kshs.org/kansapedia/moneka-woman-s-rights-association/15158; Marilyn Schultz Blackwell, "The Politics of Motherhood: Clarina Howard Nichols and School Suffrage," *New England Quarterly* 78 (2005): 570–598.

15. Dudden, *Fighting Chance,* p. 62.

16. Ibid., pp. 70–71.

17. Ibid., p. 71.

18. Richard M. Re and Christopher M. Re, "Voting and Vice: Criminal Disenfranchisement and the Reconstruction Amendments," *Yale Law Journal* 121 (2012): 1615.

19. Dudden, *Fighting Chance*, pp. 68–70, 94.

20. *Congressional Globe,* 39th Congress, 1st session, 23 Jan. 1866, p. 380, https://memory.loc.gov/cgi-bin/ampage?collId=llcg&fileName=070 /llcg070.db&recNum=106.

21. Elizabeth Cady Stanton, Susan B. Anthony, and Matilda Joslyn Gage, *The History of Woman Suffrage, 1861–1876,* vol. 2 (Rochester, NY: Charles Vann, 1887), p. 173.

22. Ibid., p. 269; "Mr. Greeley on Female Suffrage," *New York Times,* 3 Oct. 1867, p. 4.

23. *Congressional Globe,* 40th Congress, 3rd session, 4 Feb. 1869, p. 862, https://memory.loc.gov/cgi-bin/ampage?collId=llcg&fileName=086 /llcg86.db&recNum=4.

24. Carolyn Summers Vacca, *A Reform against Nature: Woman Suffrage and the Rethinking of American Citizenship, 1840–1920* (New York: Peter Lang, 2004), p. 134. See also Tracy A. Thomas, *Elizabeth Cady Stanton and the Feminist Foundations of Family Law* (New York: NYU Press, 2016), p. 12.

25. Ellen Carol DuBois, "Outgrowing the Compact of the Fathers: Equal Rights, Woman Suffrage, and the United States Constitution, 1820–1878," *Journal of American History* 74 (1987): 849.

26. Eleanor Flexnor and Ellen Fitzpatrick, *Century of Struggle: The Woman's Right Movement in the United States* (Cambridge, MA: Belknap Press of Harvard University Press, 1996), pp. 136–148.

27. "The Fifteenth Amendment in Peril," *New York Times,* 4 June 1869, p. 4.

28. Flexnor and Fitzpatrick, *Century of Struggle,* pp. 152–156; T. A. Larson, "The Woman Suffrage Movement in Washington," *Pacific Northwest Quarterly* 67 (1976): 49–62.

29. *Minor v. Happersett,* 88 U.S. 162 (1875).

30. Flexnor and Fitzpatrick, *Century of Struggle,* pp. 155–156; Larson, "The Woman Suffrage Movement," pp. 54–55.

31. *Congressional Record,* 49th Congress, 2nd session, 25 Jan. 1887, p. 984, https://congressional-proquest-com.proxyau.wrlc.org/congressional/result /pqpresultpage.gispdfhitspanel.pdflink/$2fapp-bin$2fgis-congrecord $2f3$2f1$2fc$2ff$2fcr-1887-0125_from_1_to_60.pdf/entitlementkeys=1234%7 Capp-gis%7Ccongrecord%7Ccr-1887-0125.

32. "Woman's Suffrage in the Senate," *Baltimore Sun,* 29 Jan. 1887, p. 5; *Congressional Record,* 25 Jan. 1887, pp. 983–986.

33. "Woman's Suffrage in the Senate," *New York Times,* 26 Jan. 1887, p. 4.

34. "Women Who Ask to Vote," *Washington Post,* 26 Jan. 1887, p. 2.

35. Elizabeth Cady Stanton, "To the Editor of the World," 26 Apr. 1894, Ann D. Gordon, ed., *The Selected Papers of Elizabeth Cady Stanton and Susan B. Anthony* (New Brunswick, NJ: Rutgers University Press, 1997–2013), 5:596–598.

36. "The Woman Suffrage Waterloo in New York," *Baltimore Sun,* 21 July 1894, p. 4.

37. "Woman Suffrage Defeated: The Constitutional Convention Decides against It," *New York Times,* 16 Aug. 1894, p. 1.

38. "Will Carry on the Fight," *New York Times,* 17 Aug. 1894, p. 5.

39. Sarah Smith, "Make It a Woman's World: The 1911 California Woman Suffrage Campaign," *Chapman University Historical Review* 7 (2015): 94.

40. Ibid., pp. 101–102.

41. "Assembly Concurrent Resolution 42: Relative to Chinese Americans in California," 17 July 2009, California Legislative Information, http://leginfo.legislature.ca.gov/faces/billNavClient.xhtml?bill_id=200920100ACR42.

42. William B. Fisch, "Constitutional Referendum in the United States of America," *American Journal of Comparative Law* 54 (2006): 495.

43. H. S. Gilbertson, "Popular Control under the Recall," *Annals of the American Academy of Political and Social Science* 38 (1911): 833.

44. Charles Edward Merriam and Louise Overacker, *Primary Elections* (Chicago: University of Chicago Press, 1928), pp. 60–107; Louise Overacker, "The Presidential Primary since 1924," *American Political Science Review* 22 (1928): 108–109.

45. Shigeo Hirano and James M. Snyder, Jr., "The Direct Primary and Candidate-Centered Voting in U.S. Elections," Working Paper, 2012, http://www.columbia.edu/~sh145/papers/primaries_personal_vote.pdf.

46. U.S. House of Representatives, 62nd Congress, 1st session, Report of the Committee on Election of President, Vice President, and Representatives in Congress, "Election of Senators by the People," 12 Apr. 1911, *United States Congressional Series Set* (Washington, DC: U.S. Government Printing Office, 1911), p. 4.

47. Smith, "Make It a Woman's World," pp. 96–98; Equal Suffrage League, "Declares Women Suffragists Have Made Great Record in Progressive Legislation in Colorado," *Baltimore Sun,* 18 Jan. 1911, p. 6.

48. An Iowa Woman, "Woman Suffrage Is Not Coming If the Men Take It Seriously," *The Woman Patriot,* 19 Apr. 1919, p. 8.

49. Mary Jane Smith, "Laura Clay (1849–1941): States' Rights and Southern Suffrage Reform," in *Kentucky Women,* ed. Melissa A. McEuen and Thomas H. Appleton (Athens: University of Georgia Press, 2015), p. 129.

50. Elna C. Green, *Southern Strategies: Southern Women and the Woman Suffrage Question* (Chapel Hill: University of North Carolina Press, 1997), p. 95.

51. "Final Vote Today on Women's League," *New York Times,* 26 Mar. 1919, p. 10; Paul E. Fuller, *Laura Clay and the Woman's Rights Movement* (Lexington: University Press of Kentucky, 1975), pp. 145–161; "Louisiana's Honest Suffragists," *The Woman Patriot,* 24 Apr. 1920, p. 4.

52. Aileen S. Kraditor, *The Ideas of the Woman Suffrage Movement, 1890–1920* (New York: Columbia University Press, 1965), p. 139. On race, ethnicity, and suffrage, see Glenda Gilmore, *Gender and Jim Crow: Women and the Politics of White Supremacy in North Carolina, 1896–1920* (Chapel Hill: University of North Carolina Press, 1996); Marjorie Spruill Wheeler, *New Women of the New South: The Leaders of the Woman Suffrage Movement in the Southern States* (New York: Oxford University Press, 1993); Rosalyn Terborg-Penn, *African-American Women in the Struggle for the Vote, 1850–1920* (Bloomington: Indiana University Press, 1998); and Vacca, *A Reform against Nature.*

53. Allan J. Lichtman, *White Protestant Nation: The Rise of the American Conservative Movement* (New York: Grove / Atlantic, 2008), p. 22.

54. Mary Isabel Brush, "State of Wisconsin to Be Pivotal Point of Woman's Suffrage in November," *Chicago Daily Tribune,* 4 Feb. 1912, p. I1.

55. Robert Booth Fowler and Spencer Jones, "Carrie Chapman Catt and the Last Years of the Struggle for Woman Suffrage: 'The Winning Plan,'" in *Votes for Women: The Struggle for Suffrage Revisited,* ed. Jean H. Baker (New York: Oxford University Press, 2002), pp. 130–142.

56. Full statistical analysis available from the author. On the New York campaign, see Susan Goodier and Karen Pastorello, *Women Will Vote: Winning Suffrage in New York State* (Ithaca, NY: Three Hills, 2017). New York suffrage returns for counties and assembly districts are available in the *New York Times,* 4 Nov. 1915, p. 2, and 8 Nov. 1917, pp. 1, 3. The structure of the assembly districts changed between 1915 and 1917, thus demographic data is drawn from the censuses of both 1910 and 1920.

57. Kraditor, *The Ideas of the Woman Suffrage Movement,* pp. 231–248; Linda Ford, "Alice Paul and the Politics of Nonviolent Protest," in Baker, ed.,

Votes for Women, pp. 174–188. See also generally Mary Walton, *A Woman's Crusade: Alice Paul and the Battle for the Ballot* (New York: Palgrave Macmillan, 2010).

58. "Makes Suffrage Plea," *Washington Post,* 8 Jan. 1918, p. 5.

59. Walton, *A Woman's Crusade,* pp. 193–207, 203 (quotation).

60. "No Vote Changed by Wilson's Plea to Let Women Vote," *Atlanta Constitution,* 1 Oct. 1918, p. 1.

61. "Suffrage Wins in Senate: Now Goes to States," *New York Times,* 5 June 1919, p. 1.

62. "Suffrage Now Up to States," *Baltimore Sun,* 5 June 1919, p. 1; Arthur Sears Henning, "U.S. Senate Votes for Woman Suffrage," *Chicago Tribune,* 5 June 1919, p. 1.

63. Carol Lynn Yellin, "Countdown in Tennessee, 1920," *American Heritage* 30 (1978): 27–35.

64. "Planning to Win 37th State," *Atlanta Constitution,* 19 Aug. 1920, p. 1.

65. "Better Citizens Now Women's Aim, Says Mrs. Catt," *Atlanta Constitution,* 19 Aug. 1920, p. 3.

66. Barbara Stuhler, *For the Public Record: A Documentary History of the League of Women Voters* (Westport, CT: Greenwood Press, 2000), p. 41.

67. Ibid., pp. 52, 110; National League of Women Voters, "Statements of Policy, Jan. 1923–Nov. 1925," League of Women Voters Papers, microfilm reel 5, Harry S. Truman Presidential Library, Independence, Missouri (hereafter League Papers).

68. National League of Women Voters, "Minutes, National Convention," 29 Apr. 1924, League Papers, part 2, reel 4.

69. Stuhler, *For the Public Record,* pp. 41–42; "Jubilee Convention of the National American Woman Suffrage Association," 24–29 Mar. 1919, League Papers, part 2, reel 1.

70. National League of Women Voters, "Meeting of the Executive Committee," 9–11 July 1924, League Papers, part 1, reel 2; National Convention, 14–20 Apr. 1926, League Papers, part 2, reel 3.

71. Liette Gidlow, *The Big Vote: Gender, Consumer Culture, and the Politics of Exclusion, 1890s–1920s* (Baltimore: Johns Hopkins University Press, 2004).

72. "Women in Politics," *Youth's Home Companion,* 27 Nov. 1924, p. 786.

73. "Electoral Quotas for Women: An International Overview," 14 Nov. 2013, Parliament of Australia, http://www.aph.gov.au/About_Parliament/Parliamentary_Departments/Parliamentary_Library/pubs/rp/rp1314/ElectoralQuotas.

74. Abagail Geiger and Lauren Kent, "Number of Women Leaders around the World Has Grown, but Still a Small Group," Pew Research Center, 8 Mar. 2017, http://www.pewresearch.org/fact-tank/2017/03/08/women -leaders-around-the-world/.

5. The Absent Voter

1. "The Campaign of 1888 in Indiana," *Indiana Magazine of History* 10 (1914): 47–50. Even with party ballots it was still possible to split tickets by striking out the names of candidates and substituting an alternative.

2. Gary W. Cox and J. Morgan Kousser, "Turnout and Rural Corruption: New York as a Test Case," *American Journal of Political Science* 25 (1981): 655.

3. "Campaign Corruption Funds," *New York Times,* 27 Feb. 1905, p. 6.

4. Jill Lepore, "Rock, Paper, Scissors: How We Used to Vote," *New Yorker,* 13 Oct. 2008, http://www.newyorker.com/magazine/2008/10/13/rock-paper -scissors; Wallace S. Hutcheon, Jr., "The Louisville Riots of August, 1855," *Register of the Kentucky Historical Society* 69 (1971): 150–172.

5. Melvin G. Holli, "Urban Reform," in *The Progressive Era,* ed. Lewis L. Gould (Syracuse, NY: Syracuse University Press, 1974), p. 137.

6. "A Really Secret Ballot," *New York Times,* 18 Dec. 1888, p. 4.

7. Arthur Ludington, "The Present Status of Ballot Laws in the United States," *American Political Science Review* 3 (1909): 252.

8. Ibid., pp. 256–261; Peter H. Argersinger, "A Place on the Ballot: Fusion Politics and Anti-Fusion Laws," *American Historical Review* 85 (1980): 287–306; "Limitations on Access to the General Election Ballot," *Columbia Law Review* 37 (1937): 86; "Straight-Ticket Voting States," National Conference of State Legislatures, 31 May 2017, http://www.ncsl.org/research/elections-and -campaigns/straight-ticket-voting.aspx.

9. Phillip Loring Allen, "The Multifarious Australian Ballot," *North American Review* 191 (1910): 602–611; Alan Ware, "Anti-Parties and Party Control of Political Reform in the United States: The Case of the Australian Ballot," *British Journal of Political Science* 30 (2000): 1–29.

10. "Ex-Gov. Stone's Warning," *New York Times,* 28 Sept. 1900, p. 3.

11. Ware, "Anti-Parties and Party Control"; Erik J. Engstrom, "The Rise and Decline of Turnout in Congressional Elections: Electoral Institutions, Competition, and Strategic Mobilization," *American Journal of Political Science*

56 (2012): 373–386; Jac. C. Heckelman, "The Effect of the Secret Ballot on Voter Turnout Rates," *Public Choice* 81 (1995): 107–124.

12. Joseph P. Harris, *Election Administration in the United States* (Washington, DC: Brookings Institution, 1934), p. 247.

13. H. W. Dodds, "City Manager Government in American Municipalities," *British Journal of Comparative Legislation and International Law* 6 (1924): 183–192; Zoltan L. Hajnal and Paul G. Lewis, "Municipal Institutions and Voter Turnout in Local Elections," *Urban Affairs Review* 38 (2003): 660.

14. Chandler Davidson and George Korbel, "At-Large Elections and Minority Group Representation: A Re-Examination of Historical and Contemporary Evidence," *Journal of Politics* 43 (1981): 982–1005.

15. Sarah F. Anzia, "Partisan Power Play: The Origins of Local Election Timing as an American Political Institution," *Studies in American Political Development* 26 (2012): 24–49; statistic on p. 24.

16. Hajnal and Lewis, "Municipal Institutions," pp. 645–646, 655.

17. Sarah F. Anzia, "Election Timing and the Electoral Influence of Interest Groups," *Journal of Politics* 73 (2011): 412–427; Clinton Rogers Woodruff, ed., *Proceedings of the Pittsburgh Conference for Good City Government and the Fourteenth Annual Meeting of the National Municipal League* (Pittsburgh: National Municipal League, 1908), p. 89.

18. Charles R. Adrian, *Governing Urban America: Structure, Politics, and Administration* (New York: McGraw-Hill, 1955), p. 72; Zoltan L. Hajnal and Jessica Trounstine, "Where Turnout Matters: The Consequences of Uneven Turnout in City Politics," *Journal of Politics* 67 (2005): 515–535.

19. See *State Ex Rel. Klein v. Hillenbrand,* Ohio St. 130 N.E. 29 (1920).

20. *Ahern v. Elder,* 195 N.Y. 493 N.E. 1059 (1909).

21. Permanent registration means renewal is required only when changing addresses. Joseph P. Harris, *The Registration of Voters in the United States* (Washington, DC: Brookings Institution, 1929), p. 106.

22. *Report of the President's Commission on Registration and Voting Participation, November 1963* (Washington, DC: U.S. Government Printing Office, 1963); Curtis B. Gans, *Creating the Opportunity: How Voting Laws Affect Voter Turnout* (Washington, DC: Committee for the Study of the American Electorate, 1987).

23. Michael Perman, *Struggle for Mastery: Disfranchisement in the South, 1888–1908* (Chapel Hill: University of North Carolina Press, 2001), pp. 15, 109.

24. *Mills v. Green,* 25 U.S. App. 383, 69 Fed. 852 (1895); 159 U.S. 651 (1895).

25. *Williams v. Mississippi,* 170 U.S. 213 (1898); *Giles v. Harris,* 189 U.S. 475 (1903).

26. "South Is within the Law in Suffrage Legislation," *Atlanta Constitution,* 8 May 1904, p. 4; Arthur W. Machen, Jr., "Is the Fifteenth Amendment Void?" *Harvard Law Review* 23 (1910): 169.

27. Arthur W. Bromage, "Literacy and the Electorate," *American Political Science Review* 24 (1930): 951.

28. Ibid., p. 962.

29. David McCormack, "Harvard Students Take the 1964 Louisiana Literacy Test That Black Voters Had to Pass before Being Allowed to Go to the Polls—And Every Single Person FAILED," London *Daily Mail,* 12 Nov. 2014, http://www.dailymail.co.uk/news/article-2831095/Harvard-students-sit -1964-Louisiana-Literacy-Test-black-voters-pass-allowed-polls-single -person-FAILED.html.

30. Ron Hayduk, *Democracy for All: Restoring Immigrant Voting Rights in the United States* (New York: Routledge, 2006), pp. 19–25; Gerald L. Neuman, "We Are the People: Alien Suffrage in German and American Perspective," *Michigan Journal of International Law* 13 (1992): 297–298.

31. Hayduk, *Democracy for All,* p. 25; J. W. Gardner and Alpheus Henry Snow, "Participation of the Alien in the Political Life of the Community," *Proceedings of the American Society of International Law at Its Annual Meeting* 5 (1911): 172–192.

32. Leon E. Aylsworth, "The Passing of Alien Suffrage," *American Political Science Review* 25 (1931): 134; Hayduk, *Democracy for All,* pp. 25–31.

33. *U. S. v. Thind,* 261 U.S. 204 (1923); *Gong Lum v. Rice,* 275 U.S. 78 (1927). On race and citizenship, see Desmond King, *Making Americans: Immigration, Race, and the Origins of the Diverse Democracy* (Cambridge, MA: Harvard University Press, 2000); Natalia Molina, *How Race Is Made in America: Immigration, Citizenship, and the Historical Power of Racial Scripts* (Berkeley: University of California Press, 2014); Haney Lopez, *White by Law Tenth Anniversary Edition: The Legal Construction of Race* (New York: NYU Press, 2006); and Evelyn Nakano Glenn, *Unequal Freedom: How Race and Gender Shaped American Citizenship and Labor* (Cambridge, MA: Harvard University Press, 2004).

34. Helen L. Peterson, "American Indian Political Participation," *Annals of the American Academy of Political and Social Science* 311 (1957): 121–122.

35. *Porter v. Hall,* 34 Ariz. 308 (1928).

36. *Harrison v. Laveen,* 67 Ariz. 337 (1948).

37. *Trujillo v. Garley,* no. 1350 (D.N.M. 1948).

38. Bethany R. Berger, "Red: Racism and the American Indian," *UCLA Law Review* 56 (2009): 645–646.

39. Jeanette Wolfley, "Jim Crow, Indian Style: The Disenfranchisement of Native Americans," *American Indian Law Review* 16 (1991): 192–202; Laughlin McDonald, "Expanding Coverage of Section 5 in Indian Country," in *The Future of the Voting Rights Act,* ed. David L. Epstein et al. (New York: Russell Sage, 2006), pp. 163–200.

40. Frank Kent, "The Great Game of Politics," *Baltimore Sun,* 5 Feb. 1923, p. 7; 8 Feb. 1923, p. 7.

41. Jerrold G. Rusk, *A Statistical History of the American Electorate* (Washington, DC: CQ Press, 2001), pp. 52, 54.

42. Ibid.

43. Mark Lawrence Kornbluh, *Why America Stopped Voting: The Decline of Participatory Democracy and the Emergence of Modern American Politics* (New York: NYU Press, 2000), pp. 99–111. See, generally, Elisabeth S. Clemens, *The People's Lobby: Organization Innovation and the Rise of Interest Group Politics* (Chicago: University of Chicago Press, 1997). All North Dakota presidential and congressional turnout statistics are from Rusk, *A Statistical History,* pp. 72–101.

44. Samuel P. Huntington, *The Third Wave: Democratization in the Late Twentieth Century* (Norman: University of Oklahoma Press, 1991), p. 26.

6. The Voting Rights Act of 1965

1. James Samuel Stemmons, "Negro Suffrage and the South," *Southwest Review* 16 (1931): 181–182.

2. "What the Ballot Means to Us," *Chicago Defender,* 19 Oct. 1918, p. 16.

3. National Colored Republican Conference, "Memorandum of Conference," Mar. 1924, Papers of Calvin Coolidge, microfilm reel 93, Library of Congress, Washington, DC.

4. Republican Party Platform of 1928, 12 June 1928, American Presidency Project, http://www.presidency.ucsb.edu/ws/index.php?pid=29637.

5. Allan J. Lichtman, *White Protestant Nation: The Rise of the American Conservative Movement* (New York: Grove / Atlantic, 2008), p. 49; Neval Thomas, "The Republican Party Is Dead," Baltimore *Afro-American,* 22 Sept. 1928, p. 1.

6. Lichtman, *White Protestant Nation,* p. 92.

7. Ibid., p. 65; Allan J. Lichtman, "Elections and Electoral Eras," in *The Concise Princeton Encyclopedia of American Political History*, ed. Michael Kazin (Princeton, NJ: Princeton University Press, 2011), p. 203.

8. Will Alexander to Rexford Tugwell, "Negroes in the Next Election," 12 July 1935, OFC-300, Colored Folder, Franklin D. Roosevelt Presidential Library, Hyde Park, New York.

9. C. P. Trussell, "Roosevelt Scores Levying Poll Tax," *New York Times*, 14 Feb. 1942, p. 1; C. P. Trussell, "Poll Tax Repeal Virtually Dead," *New York Times*, 10 Nov. 1942, p. 1; "Poll Tax Upheld as Senate Defeats Cloture," *New York Times*, 21 Nov. 1942, p. 1; "The Poll Tax Barbarians," *Chicago Defender*, 5 Dec. 1942, p. 14; Kimberly Johnson, *Reforming Jim Crow: Southern Politics and the State in the Age before Brown* (New York: Oxford University Press, 2010), pp. 97–98.

10. *Guinn v. United States*, 238 U.S. 347 (1915).

11. *Lane v. Wilson*, 307 U.S. 268 (1939).

12. *Nixon v. Herndon*, 273 U.S. 536 (1927).

13. *Nixon v. Condon*, 286 U.S. 73 (1932); *Grovey v. Townsend*, 295 U.S. 45 (1935); *Smith v. Allwright*, 321 U.S. 649 (1944).

14. *Schnell v. Davis*, 336 U.S. 933 (1949); *Lassiter v. Northampton County*, 360 U.S. 45 (1959).

15. *Breedlove v. Suttles*, 302 U.S. 277 (1937).

16. Clark M. Clifford, "Memorandum for the President," 19 Nov. 1947, Clark Clifford Political File, box 20, Truman Papers, Harry S. Truman Presidential Library, Independence, MO; Kari Frederickson, *The Dixiecrat Revolt and the End of the Solid South, 1932–1968* (Chapel Hill: University of North Carolina Press, 2001), pp. 118–149.

17. Lichtman, *White Protestant Nation*, p. 165; Frederickson, *The Dixiecrat Revolt*, pp. 150–186.

18. Lichtman, *White Protestant Nation*, pp. 165–166.

19. Earl Brown, "Civil Rights Scuttled," *New York Amsterdam News*, 20 Oct. 1949, p. 12.

20. *Brown v. Board of Education*, 347 U.S. 483 (1954); *Plessy v. Ferguson*, 163 U.S. 537 (1896).

21. David A. Nichols, *A Matter of Justice: Eisenhower and the Beginning of the Civil Rights Revolution* (New York: Simon and Schuster, 2007).

22. Allan J. Lichtman, "The Federal Assault against Voting Discrimination in the Deep South: 1957–1967," *Journal of Negro History* 54 (1969): 346–367; "The 1963 Report of the United States Commission on Civil Rights," *Congressional*

Record, 89th Congress, 1st session, 19 May 1965, p. 11020. All Congressional Record references for 1965 are at https://www.govinfo.gov/app/collection /crecb/_crecb/Volume%20111%20(1965).

23. "Statement by Attorney General Nicholas deB. Katzenbach before the House Judiciary Committee on the Proposed Voting Rights Act of 1965," U.S. Department of Justice, 18 Mar. 1965, pp. 5–9, https://www.justice.gov /sites/default/files/ag/legacy/2011/08/23/03-18-1965.pdf.

24. Ibid.; Lichtman, "The Federal Assault," pp. 366–367.

25. Diane McWhorter, *Carry Me Home: Birmingham, Alabama, the Climactic Battle of the Civil Rights Revolution* (New York: Simon and Schuster, 2001).

26. John F. Kennedy, "Radio and Television Report to the American People on Civil Rights," 11 June 1963, John F. Kennedy Library and Museum, https://www.jfklibrary.org/Research/Research-Aids/JFK-Speeches/Civil -Rights-Radio-and-Television-Report_19630611.aspx.

27. "Presidential Job Approval: John F. Kennedy," American Presidential Project, http://www.presidency.ucsb.edu/data/popularity.php?pres=35.

28. Lichtman, *White Protestant Nation,* pp. 232, 247, 255.

29. "Democrats Charge G.O.P. Poll Watch Today Will Harass Negroes and the Poor," *New York Times,* 3 Nov. 1964, p. 22.

30. Lichtman, *White Protestant Nation,* p. 257.

31. *Baker v. Carr,* 369 U.S. 186 (1962).

32. *Wesberry v. Sanders,* 376 U.S. 1 (1964); *Reynolds v. Sims,* 377 U.S. 533 (1964).

33. Stephen Ansolabehere and James M. Snyder, *The End of Inequality: One Person, One Vote and the Transformation of American Politics* (New York: Norton, 2008); Gary W. Cox and Jonathan N. Katz, *Elbridge Gerry's Salamander: The Electoral Consequences of the Reapportionment Revolution* (New York: Cambridge University Press, 2002); Charles S. Bullock III, *Redistricting: The Most Political Activity in America* (Lanham, MD: Rowman and Littlefield, 2010); Thomas E. Mann, "Redistricting Reform," *The National Voter,* June 2005, https://www.brookings.edu/wp-content/uploads/2016/06/po4-07.pdf.

34. Robert Mann, *When Freedom Would Triumph: The Civil Rights Struggle in Congress, 1954–1968* (Baton Rouge: Louisiana State University Press, 2007), pp. 221–222.

35. Allan J. Lichtman, "The Story behind Selma," The Hill, 29 Jan. 2015, http://thehill.com/blogs/pundits-blog/civil-rights/231061-the-story -behind-selma.

36. "Lyndon B. Johnson: Voting Rights Address," 15 Mar. 1965, Great American Documents, http://www.greatamericandocuments.com/speeches/lbj -voting-rights.html.

37. *Congressional Record,* 19 May 1965, pp. 11008, 11013–11014; 26 May 1965, pp. 11718, 11721; 10 May 1965, p. 10050; Mary McGrory, "An Implacable Man from Plaquemines," *Los Angeles Times,* 2 Apr. 1965, p. A6.

38. *Congressional Record,* 10 May 1965, p. 10032.

39. For the text of the 1965 version of the act, see "Public Law 89–110, Voting Rights Act of 1965," http://library.clerk.house.gov/reference-files /PPL_VotingRightsAct_1965.pdf.

40. *Harper v. Virginia State Board of Elections,* 383 U.S. 663 (1966).

41. *South Carolina v. Katzenbach,* 383 U.S. 301 (1966).

42. "History of Voting Rights Laws: The Voting Rights Act of 1965," U.S. Department of Justice, https://www.justice.gov/crt/history-federal-voting -rights-laws.

43. Ibid.; *City of Mobile v. Bolden,* 446 U.S. 55 (1980).

44. Lichtman, "The Federal Assault," p. 365. There are several fine books that deal with the enforcement of the Voting Rights Act. See, for example, Chandler Davidson and Bernard Grofman, eds., *Quiet Revolution in the South: The Impact of the Voting Rights Act, 1965–1990* (Princeton, NJ: Princeton University Press, 1994).

45. For section 5 objections, see "Section 5 Objection Letters," U.S. Department of Justice, https://www.justice.gov/crt/section-5-objection -letters.

46. *United States v. Dallas County Commission,* 548 F. Supp. 794 (S.D. Ala. 1982).

47. *U.S. v. Dallas County Commission,* 850 F.2d 1430 (1988).

48. *Garza v. County of Los Angeles,* 756 F.Supp. 1298 (C. D. Cal. 1990).

49. *Garza v. County of Los Angeles,* 918 F.2d 763 (9th Cir. 1990).

50. Robert G. Retana, "Case Note Addendum: *Garza v. County of Los Angeles,*" *La Raza Law Journal* 4 (1991): 128.

51. *Page v. Bartels,* 144 F. Supp. 2d 346 (D.N.J. 2001); Sam Hirsch, "Unpacking *Page v. Bartels:* A Fresh Redistricting Paradigm Emerges in New Jersey," *Election Law Journal* 1 (2002): 7–23.

52. "The Americans with Disabilities Act," U.S. Department of Justice, Civil Rights Division, Disability Rights Section, https://www.ada.gov/ada _voting/ada_voting_ta.htm; Sally B. Hurme and Paul S. Appelbaum, "Defining and Assessing Capacity to Vote: The Effect of Mental Impairment on the Rights of Voters," *McGeorge Law Review* 38 (2007): 931–1014; Kimberly

Leonard, "Keeping the 'Mentally Incompetent' from Voting," *The Atlantic,* 17 Oct. 2012, https://www.theatlantic.com/health/archive/2012/10/keeping -the-mentally-incompetent-from-voting/263748/; Dinesh Bhugra et al., "Mental Illness and the Right to Vote: A Review of Legislation across the World," *International Review of Psychiatry* 28 (2016): 395–399.

53. *Congressional Record,* 102nd Congress, 1st session, 18 July 1991, pp. S10318–S10319, http://webarchive.loc.gov/congressional-record/2016042514 0950/http://thomas.loc.gov/home/backcr/cr1021.html.

54. "Bush Rejects 'Motor Voter' Legislation," CQ Almanac 1992, https:// library.cqpress.com/cqalmanac/document.php?id=cqal92-1107023; Royce Crocker, "The National Voter Registration Act of 1993: History, Implemen- tation, and Effects," Congressional Research Service, 18 Sept. 2013, pp. 3–6, https://fas.org/sgp/crs/misc/R40609.pdf.

55. Joint Center for Political and Economic Studies, "50 Years of the Voting Rights Act," http://jointcenter.org/sites/default/files/VRA%20report%2C%203 .5.15%20%281130%20am%29%28updated%29.pdf; Louis DeSipio, "Latino Po- litical and Civic Participation," in *Hispanics and the Future of America,* ed. Marta Tienda and Faith Mitchell (Washington, DC: National Academies Press, 2006), pp. 447–480.

56. Lichtman, *White Protestant Nation,* pp. 412–416.

57. Ibid.

58. Americans for Democratic Action, "2016 Congressional Voting Record," https://adaction.org/wp-content/uploads/2018/02/2016.pdf.

59. On the legal issues raised in the Florida recount and the various court decisions, see Samuel Issacharoff, Pamela S. Karlan, and Richard H. Pildes, *When Elections Go Bad: The Law of Democracy and the Presidential Elec- tion of 2000* (St. Paul, MN: Foundation Press, 2001).

7. The New Wars over the Vote

1. U.S. Election Atlas, "2000 Election Timeline," 2017, https://uselectionatlas .org/INFORMATION/ARTICLES/pe2000timeline.php; Richard L. Hasen, *The Voting Wars: From Florida 2000 to the Next Election Meltdown* (New Haven, CT: Yale University Press, 2012).

2. U.S. Election Atlas, "2000 Election Timeline."

3. Ibid.

4. Allan J. Lichtman, *White Protestant Nation: The Rise of the American Conservative Movement* (New York: Grove / Atlantic, 2008), p. 1.

5. *Bush v. Gore,* 531 U.S. 98 (2000); Julia Campbell, "U.S. Supreme Court Overturns Florida Court," ABC News, 13 Dec. 2000, http://abcnews.go.com /Politics/story?id=1222392Page=1; Andrew Glass, "Gore Concedes to Bush," *Politico,* 13 Dec. 2012, http://www.politico.com/story/2012/12/this-day-in -politics-084997.

6. Walter R. Mebane, Jr., "The Wrong Man Is President! Overvotes in the 2000 Presidential Election in Florida," *Symposium: U.S. Elections* 2 (2004): 12–13.

7. Allan J. Lichtman, "Report on the Racial Impact of the Rejection of Ballots Cast in the 2000 Presidential Election in the State of Florida," U.S. Commission on Civil Rights, June 2001, http://www.usccr.gov/pubs /vote2000/report/appendix/app7.htm; Allan J. Lichtman, "What Really Happened in Florida's 2000 Presidential Election," *Journal of Legal Studies* 32 (2003): 221–243.

8. Paul M. Schwartz, "Voting Technology and Democracy," *New York University Law Review* 77 (2002): 633–634; David Kidwell and Joseph Tanfani, "Faulty Part May Have Voided Ballots," *Miami Herald,* 12 Nov. 2001, p. 1A.

9. "Ten Years Later Infamous 2000 Election Ballot Recount Still Defines Palm Beach County to Many," *Palm Beach Post,* 9 Nov. 2010, http://www.palmbeachpost.com/news/ten-years-later-infamous-2000 -election-ballot-recount-still-defines-palm-beach-county-many /uscC5niN1BtOOs7d33V8GL/.

10. U.S. Election Assistance Commission, "The Election Administration and Voting Survey, 2016 Comprehensive Report," 27 June 2017, p. 29, https://www.eac.gov/assets/1/6/2016_EAVS_Comprehensive_Report.pdf.

11. Wendy Underhill, "Election 2000: Before and After," National Conference of State Legislatures, Sept. 2012, http://www.ncsl.org/research /elections-and-campaigns/election-2000-before-and-after.aspx.

12. Martin Luther King, Jr., *Where Do We Go from Here: Chaos or Community?* (New York: Harper and Row, 1967), p. 11.

13. National Conference of State Legislatures, "Voter ID History," 31 May 2017, http://www.ncsl.org/research/elections-and-campaigns/voter-id -history.aspx.

14. *Crawford v. Marion County Election Board,* 553 U.S. 181 (2008).

15. National Conference of State Legislatures, "Voter ID History."

16. Republican National Lawyers Association, "Vote Fraud Survey," Nov. 2011, http://www.rnla.org/survey.asp; "Election Fraud in America," News21, 12 Aug. 2012, https://votingrights.news21.com/interactive/election

-fraud-database/. See also, generally, Lorraine C. Minnite, *The Myth of Voter Fraud* (Ithaca, NY: Cornell University Press, 2010).

17. *Applewhite v. Commonwealth of Pennsylvania,* 330 M.D. 2012 (2014); *One Wisconsin Institute Inc. v. Thompson,* 198 F.Supp. 3d 896 (W.D. Wis. 2016); Gary O. Bartlett, executive director, North Carolina State Board of Elections, to Committees of the North Carolina General Assembly, 11 Mar. 2013, attachment F, "Documented Cases of Voter Fraud in North Carolina," http://www.ncleg.net/documentsites/committees/JointAppropriationsGeneralGovernment/2013%20Session/03-07-13%20Meeting/sbe_GA_response_with_attachments.pdf.

18. Ray Christensen and Thomas J. Schultze, "Identifying Voter Fraud Using Orphan and Low Propensity Voters," *American Politics Research* 42 (2014): 311–337; John S. Ahlquist, Kenneth R. Mayer, and Simon Jackman, "Alien Abduction and Voter Impersonation in the 2012 U.S. General Election: Evidence from a Survey List Experiment," *Election Law Journal* 13 (2014): 460–475; M. V. Hood III and William Gillespie, "They Just Don't Vote Like They Used To: A Methodology to Empirically Assess Voter Fraud," *Social Science Quarterly* 93 (2012): 76–94.

19. Michael Schneider, "Federal, State Investigators Say No Widespread Fraud in Election," *Easton Star,* 24 Aug. 1995, p. 5.

20. Steve Schultze, "GOP Wants to Tighten Voter Laws," *Milwaukee Journal Sentinel,* 4 Nov. 2004, http://freerepublic.com/focus/f-news/1270231/posts.

21. Steven H. Huefner et al., *From Registration to Recounts: The Election Ecosystems of Five Midwestern States* (Columbus: Ohio State University Moritz College of Law, 2007), pp. 120–121, http://moritzlaw.osu.edu/electionlaw/projects/registration-to-recounts/book.pdf; Republican National Lawyers Association, "Voter Fraud Survey," Wisconsin section; "Election Fraud in America," News21, 12 Aug. 2012.

22. Allan J. Lichtman, "When the Dead Speak," Gazette.net, 16 Oct. 1998, http://www.gazette.net/stories/101698/poliadmiss_31866.shtml.

23. Robert Farley, "Trump's Bogus Voter Fraud Claims," FactCheck.org, 19 Oct. 2016, https://www.factcheck.org/2016/10/trumps-bogus-voter-fraud-claims/.

24. Robert Barnes, "Stevens Second Thoughts on 2008 Photo-ID Ruling," *Washington Post,* 16 July 2016, p. A15; John Schwartz, "Judge in Landmark Case Disavows Support for Voter ID," *New York Times,* 16 Oct. 2013, p. 16.

25. *Frank v. Walker,* 773 F.3d 783, 796–797 (7th Cir. 2014).

26. Brendon Mock, "Institute Index: Running the Numbers on NC's Discriminatory Voter Law," Facing South, 15 Aug. 2013, https://www.facingsouth.org/2013/08/institute-index-running-the-numbers-on-ncs-discrim.html.

27. "7 Things to Know about Polarization in America," 12 June 2014, Pew Research Center, http://www.pewresearch.org/fact-tank/2014/06/12/7-things-to-know-about-polarization-in-america/; Drew De Silver, "The Polarized Congress of Today Has Its Roots in the 1970s," 12 June 2014, Pew Research Center, http://www.pewresearch.org/fact-tank/2014/06/12/polarized-politics-in-congress-began-in-the-1970s-and-has-been-getting-worse-ever-since/.

28. "A Deep Dive into Party Affiliation," 17 Apr. 2015, Pew Research Center, http://www.people-press.org/2015/04/07/a-deep-dive-into-party-affiliation/.

29. Registration by race is from the online database of the North Carolina State Board of Elections. The board reports its data as white voters and African American voters, including Hispanics, that is, the board's data does not separately break out Hispanic voters. The separation of Hispanics into their own category would slightly widen the gap, because Hispanics self-identify more as white than black in North Carolina.

30. Ari Berman, "The 94-Year-Old Civil-Rights Pioneer Who Is Now Challenging North Carolina's Voter-ID Law," The Nation, 25 Jan. 2016, https://www.thenation.com/article/the-92-year-old-civil-rights-pioneer-who-is-now-challenging-north-carolinas-voter-id-law/; "President Obama's Letter to the Editor," New York Times, 12 Aug. 2015, https://www.nytimes.com/2015/08/16/magazine/president-obamas-letter-to-the-editor.html.

31. Berman, "The 94-Year-Old Civil-Rights Pioneer"; Allan Smith, "94-Year-Old Rosanell Eaton Is Center of Voting Rights Case," Business Insider, 25 Jan. 2016, http://www.businessinsider.com/rosanell-eaton-voter-id-rights-north-carolina-2016-1.

32. Hasen, The Voting Wars. See also Ari Berman, Give Us the Ballot: The Modern Struggle for Voting Rights in America (New York: Farrar, Straus and Giroux, 2015); Tova Wang, The Politics of Voter Suppression: Defending and Expanding Americans' Right to Vote (Ithaca, NY: Cornell University Press, 2012); Michael Waldman, The Fight to Vote (New York: Simon and Schuster, 2016), pp. 173–268; Abigail Thernstrom, Voting Rights—and Wrongs: The Elusive Quest for Racially Fair Elections (Washington, DC: AEI Press, 2009); Jesse H. Rhodes, Ballot Blocked: The Political Erosion of the Voting Rights Act (Stanford, CA: Stanford University Press, 2017); Charles S. Bullock III, Ronald

Keith Gaddie, and Justin J. Wert, *The Rise and Fall of the Voting Rights Act* (Norman: University of Oklahoma Press, 2016); and Alexander Keyssar, *The Right to Vote: The Contested History of Democracy in the United States,* rev. ed. (New York: Basic Books, 2009), pp. 258–294.

33. *Shelby County v. Holder,* 570 U.S. 2 (2013).

34. Jim Malewitz and Alexa Ura, "As Court Scoldings Pile Up, Will Texas Face a Voting Rights Reckoning?" *Texas Tribune,* 17 June 2017, https://www .texastribune.org/2017/06/16/voter-wars-kickoff/; J. Morgan Kousser, "Do the Facts of Voting Rights Support Chief Justice Roberts's Opinion in Shelby County?" *Transatlantica* 1 (2015): 1–50.

35. Unless otherwise indicated the data presented below is from my North Carolina trial testimony, available at http://moritzlaw.osu.edu/elec tionlaw/litigation/documents/TranscriptofTrialDay5heldon7172015.pdf; http://moritzlaw.osu.edu/electionlaw/litigation/documents/Transcriptof TrialDay7heldon7212015.pdf; and http://moritzlaw.osu.edu/electionlaw/liti gation/documents/TranscriptofTrialDay14heldon7302015.pdf.

36. "House Passes Bipartisan Voter ID Bill," nchouse117.com, 25 Apr. 2013, https://nchouse117.com/category/elections/page/2/; Brian Warner, "N.C. House Passes Voter ID Bill," *Jones Street Chronicles,* 25 Apr. 2013, http:// thevoterupdate.com/jones/?p=903#.VLc6uCvF9SI.

37. Rhonda Amoroso, "Voter ID Update: House Leaders Introduce Voter ID Bill," USA Dot Com, 4 Apr. 2013, http://usadotcom.blogspot.com/2013_03 _31_archive.html.

38. "North Carolina Voter ID Bill Moving Ahead with Supreme Court Ruling," WRAL.com, 25 June 2013, http://www.wral.com/nc-senator-voter-id -bill-moving-ahead-with-ruling/12591669/; David Zucchino, "Changes Loom for N.C. Electorate," *Los Angeles Times,* 30 June 2013, http://articles.latimes .com/2013/jun/30/nation/la-na-voting-rights-20130630; "Swift Impact of Voting Decision," *Durham Herald Sun,* 27 June 2013, p. A8.

39. North Carolina Division of Motor Vehicles, "Requirements and Documents for No-Fee Voter ID Cards," https://www.ncdot.gov/dmv /driver/id/.

40. General Assembly of North Carolina, "When Is the General Assembly in Session," http://www.ncga.state.nc.us/gascripts/Help/KnowledgeBase /viewItem.pl?nID=35.

41. General Assembly of North Carolina, session 2013–14, House Bill 589, http://www.ncga.state.nc.us/gascripts/BillLookUp/BillLookUp.pl?Session =2013&BillID=h%20+589&submitButton=Go.

42. John B. Holbein and D. Sunshine Hillygus, "Erratum to *Making Young Voters: The Impact of Preregistration on Youth Turnout*," *American Journal of Political Science* 61 (2017): 507.

43. "Current Issues in the State of North Carolina," Feb. 2011, High Point University Survey Research Center, www.highpoint.edu/src/; SurveyUSA Market Research Study no. 20443, 11–14 Apr. 2013, http://www.surveyusa .com/client/PollPrint.aspx?g=8c5c6269-5692-483a-a5f0-9662c4e5567e&d =0; "North Carolinians Oppose Voting Bill Signed Today," Public Policy Polling, 12 Aug. 2013, http://www.publicpolicypolling.com/pdf/2011/PPP _Release_NC_812.pdf; "Elon Poll," *High Country Press,* 17 Apr. 2013, http://www .hcpress.com/news/elon-poll-nc-citizens-oppose-several-state-legislative -proposals-view-results-spanning-various-issues.html.

44. Laura Leslie, "Tillis: Fraud 'Not the Primary Reason' for Voter ID Push," WRAL.com, 17 Mar. 2013, http://www.wral.com/tillis-actual-voter -fraud-not-the-primary-reason-for-voter-id-push-/12231514/.

45. Abby Cavenaugh, "State House Passes Voter ID Bill: Next Stop Is Senate Approval," *Anson Record,* 1 May 2013, p. A1.

46. Shaun Bowler and Todd Donovan, "A Partisan Model of Electoral Reform: Voter Identification Laws and Confidence in State Elections," *State Politics and Policy Quarterly* 16 (2016): 351; Stephen Ansolabehere and Nathan Persily, "Vote Fraud in the Eye of the Beholder: The Role of Public Opinion in the Challenge to Voter Identification Requirements," *Harvard Law Review* 121 (2008): 1759.

47. Bartlett to Committees of the North Carolina General Assembly, 11 Mar. 2013, attachment F.

48. *DNC v. RNC,* 671 F. Supp. 2d 575 (D.N.J. 2009); *DNC v. RNC,* 673 F.3d 192 (2012); "Statement: DNC to Appeal Ruling to Continue RNC Consent Decree," Democrats.org, 2 Feb. 2018, https://www.democrats.org/Post/statement -dnc-to-appeal-to-continue-rnc-consent-decree.

49. U.S. Election Assistance Commission, *Election Crimes: An Initial Review and Recommendations for Additional Study,* Dec. 2006, p. 9, https://www .eac.gov/assets/1/6/Initial_Review_and_Recommendations_for_Further _Study.pdf; Natasha Khan and Corbin Carson, "Comprehensive Database of U.S. Voter Fraud Uncovers No Evidence That Photo Id Is Needed," News21, 12 Aug. 2012, http://votingrights.news21.com/article/election-fraud/; Wayne Slater, "Few North Carolina Voter-Fraud Cases Would Have Been Prevented by Photo ID Law," Dallasnews.com, 8 Sept. 2013, http://www.dallasnews.com /news/politics/headlines/20130908-few-North Carolina-voter-fraud-cases -would-have-been-prevented-by-photo-id-law-review-shows.ece; U.S. Gov-

ernment Accountability Office, *Issues Related to State Voter Identification Laws,* Sept. 2014, https://www.gao.gov/assets/670/665966.pdf.

50. "Pennsylvania Voter ID Law Back in Court: Can It Be Enforced?" *Christian Science Monitor,* 15 July 2013, https://www.csmonitor.com/USA /Justice/2013/0715/Pennsylvania-voter-ID-law-back-in-court-Can-it-be -enforced.

51. *North Carolina State Conference of the NAACP v. McCrory,* 182 F. Supp. 3d 320 (M.D.N.C. 2016).

52. *North Carolina State Conference of the NAACP v. McCrory,* 831 F.3d 204 (4th Cir. 2016).

53. Ibid.; emphasis added.

54. Ibid.

55. "Super Suppressers: The 17 North Carolina Counties That Are Strangling Early Voting to Death," insightus, 26 Oct. 2016, http://www.insight-us .org/blog/super-suppressors-the-17-north-carolina-counties-that-are -strangling-early-voting-to-death/#more-570; *North Carolina State Conference of the NAACP v. State Board of Elections,* 2016 U.S. Dist. LEXIS 153249; *North Carolina v. N.C. Conference of the NAACP,* 137 S. Ct. 1399 (2017).

56. Leadership Conference Education Fund, "The Great Poll Closure," Nov. 2016, pp. 4–6, http://civilrightsdocs.info/pdf/reports/2016/poll-closure -report-web.pdf.

57. "Maricopa County Board of Supervisors Formal Meeting," 17 Feb. 2016, video, http://maricopa.siretechnologies.com/sirepubtest/mtgviewer.aspx ?meetid=2870&doctype=AGENDA; Rob O'Dell and Caitlin McGlade, "Map: Areas Hardest Hit by Slim Polling Options," *Arizona Republic,* 28 Mar. 2016, http://www.azcentral.com/story/news/politics/elections/2016/03/27/slim -polling-options-maricopa-county/82278474/.

58. "Democracy Diminished: State and Local Threats to Voting Post-*Shelby County, Alabama v. Holder,*" *Legal Defense Fund,* 31 Oct. 2016, p. 7, http://www.naacpldf.org/files/publications/Democracy%20Diminished -State%20and%20Local%20Voting%20Changes%20Post-Shelby%20v.%20 Holder_4.pdf.

59. Unless otherwise indicated, all information on Texas redistricting is from Allan J. Lichtman, "Report for the Quesada Plaintiffs," 28 Feb. 2014, *Perez v. Texas,* Case 5:11-cv-00360-OLG-JES-XR, Document 1065-5, http:// moritzlaw.osu.edu/electionlaw/litigation/documents/Perez11606.pdf.

60. *Perez v. Perry,* United States District Court, Western District of Texas, San Antonio Division, no. SA-11-cv-360, Trial Transcript, 1839:2–7, Sept. 14, 2011.

61. "Defendants' Response to Plaintiffs and the United States Regarding Section 3(C) of the Voting Rights Act," *Perez v. Texas,* 26 Aug. 2013, p. 19, https://www.scribd.com/document/160397574/Texas-Response-to -Plaintiffs-and-United-States.

62. Greg Abbott, "Obama's Scheme to Take over Texas," *Washington Times,* 30 July 2013, http://www.washingtontimes.com/news/2013/jul/30 /obamas-scheme-to-take-over-texas; "The United States versus Texas: Lone Star Republicans Continue to Hurl Rhetorical Missiles at Eric Holder," MySA, 25 July 2013, http://blog.mysanantonio.com/texas-on-the-potomac /2013/07/the-united-states-vs-texas-lone-star-republicans-continue-to -hurl-rhetorical-missiles-at-eric-holder/.

63. *State of Texas v. United States and Eric H. Holder,* 887 F. Supp. 2d 133 (D.D.C. 2012).

64. *Perez v. Abbott,* 250 F. Supp. 3d 123 (2017); emphasis added.

65. For examples of objections, see Gromer Jeffers, Jr., "Texas House Panel's Dallas Hearing on Redistricting Grows Contentious," *Dallas News,* 6 June 2013, https://www.dallasnews.com/news/local-politics/2013/06/06 /texas-house-panel-s-dallas-hearing-on-redistricting-grows-contentious.

66. *Perez v. Abbott,* 274 F. Supp. 3d 624 (2017).

67. "*NAACP v. Steen* (Consolidated with *Veasey v. Abbott)*," Brennan Center for Justice, 21 July 2017, https://www.brennancenter.org/legal-work /naacp-v-steen.

68. *Abbott v. Veasey,* 137 S. Ct. 612 (2017), Statement of Roberts, C.J.

69. *Veasey v. Abbott,* 249 F. Supp. 3d 868 (2017).

70. Jim Malewitz, "Federal Judge Tosses New Texas Voter ID Law, State Plans to Appeal," *Texas Tribune,* 23 Aug. 2017, https://www.texastribune.org /2017/08/23/federal-judge-tosses-new-texas-voter-id-law/.

71. United States District Court, Middle District of Louisiana, *Terrebonne Parish Branch, NAACP v. Jindal,* No. 14-0069-JJB-EWD, Ruling, 17 Aug. 2017.

72. *Hill v. Virginia State Board of Elections,* 137 S. Ct. 788 (2017); *Cooper v. Harris,* 137 S. Ct. 1455 (2017); *Covington v. North Carolina,* 137 S. Ct. 1624 (2017).

73. *Shaw v. Reno,* 509 U.S. 630 (1993); *Cooper v. Harris.*

74. *Common Cause v. Rucho,* 279 F. Supp. 3d 587 (2018), court quoting *Ariz. State Legislature v. Ariz. Indep. Redistricting Comm'n,* 135 S. Ct. 2652, 2658 (2015).

75. Republican State Leadership Committee, "2012 REDMAP Summary Report," 4 Jan. 2013, http://www.redistrictingmajorityproject.com/.

76. Ibid.

77. Jonathan Lai and Liz Navratil, "Pa. Congressional District Map Upheld as U.S. Supreme Court, Federal Judges Reject Republican Challenges," *Philadelphia Inquirer*, 19 Mar. 2018, http://www.philly.com/philly/news /politics/state/pennsylvania-congressional-map-federal-lawsuit-dismissed -gerrymandering-20180319.html.

78. Michael Wines, "Pennsylvania Lawsuit Says House Redistricting Is a Partisan Gerrymander," *New York Times*, 15 June 2017, https://www .nytimes.com/2017/06/15/us/gerrymander-pennsylvania-Congressional -district-lawsuit.html; Michael Wines, "Key Question before the Supreme Court: Will It Let Gerrymanders Stand," *New York Times*, 21 Apr. 2017, https://www.nytimes.com/2017/04/21/us/democrats-gerrymander -supreme-court.html; *Gill v. Whitford*, no. 15-cv-421 (W.D. Wis. 2017); Greg Stohr, "Another Gerrymandering Case Added to the Supreme Court's Docket, This Time against Democrats," Governing, 12 Dec. 2017, http://www .governing.com/topics/politics/tns-supreme-court-maryland-gerryman dering.html. See, previously, *Vieth v. Jubelirer*, 541 U.S. 267 (2004), and *LULAC v. Perry*, 548 U.S. 399 (2006).

79. *A. Phillip Randolph Institute v. Husted*, 838 F.3d 699 (2016); "Brief for American History Professors as Amicus Curiae in Support of Respondents," 22 Sept. 2017, p. 32, https://www.americanbar.org/content/dam/aba/publications /supreme_court_preview/briefs-2017-2018/16-980-amicus-resp-american -history-professors.authcheckdam.pdf.

80. National Voting Rights Act, sec. 8(b)(2); *APRI v. Husted*, 838 F.3d 699 (6th Cir. 2016); "Brief of Georgia and 16 Other States as Amici Curiae Supporting Petitioner," *SCOTUSblog*, 16 Aug. 2017, http://www.scotusblog.com /wp-content/uploads/2017/08/16-980-tsac-Georgia-and-16-other-states .pdf; "Brief of the States of New York, et al., as Amici Curiae in Support of Respondents," *SCOTUSblog*, Sept. 2017, http://www.scotusblog.com/wp -content/uploads/2017/09/16-980-bsac-states-of-NY.pdf.

81. "Joint Statement from the Department of Homeland Security and Office of the Director of National Intelligence on Election Security," 7 Oct. 2016, https://www.dhs.gov/news/2016/10/07/joint-statement-department -homeland-security-and-office-director-national; "Intelligence Community Assessment: Assessing Russian Activities and Intention in Recent US Election," 6 Jan. 2017, https://www.dni.gov/files/documents/ICA_2017_01.pdf.

82. Massimo Calabresi, "Election Hackers Altered Voter Rolls, Stole Private Data, Officials Say," *Time*, 22 June 2017, http://time.com/4828 306/russian-hacking-election-widespread-private-data/; Jessica Kwong,

"Russians Successfully Hacked U.S. Voter Systems before 2016 Election, Top Official Says," *Newsweek*, 7 Feb. 2018, http://www.newsweek.com /russians-successfully-hacked-us-voter-systems-2016-election-top -official-says-801253.

83. Eric Lipton and Scott Shane, "Democratic House Candidates Were Also Targets of Russian Hacking," *New York Times,* 13 Dec. 2017, https://www .nytimes.com/2016/12/13/us/politics/house-democrats-hacking-dccc.html ?_r=0.

84. Michael Morell and Mike Rogers, "Russia Never Stopped Its Cyber-attacks on the United States," *Washington Post,* 25 Dec. 2017, https://www .washingtonpost.com/opinions/russia-never-stopped-its-cyberattacks-on -the-united-states/2017/12/25/83076f2e-e676-11e7-a65d-1ac0fd7f097e _story.html?tid=a_inl&utm_term=.69b7d5b77b3a; Ellen Nakashima and Shane Harris, "The Nation's Top Spies Said Russia Is Continuing to Target the U.S. Political System," *Washington Post*, 13 Feb. 2018, https://www .washingtonpost.com/world/national-security/fbi-director-to-face -questions-on-security-clearances-and-agents-independence/2018/02/13 /f3e4c706-105f-11e8-9570-29c9830535e5_story.html?utm_term= .5a0eba047e1f.

85. "Hackers Easily Bust into Voting Machines in Conference Challenge," Fox News, 31 July 2017, http://www.foxnews.com/politics/2017/07/31 /hackers-easily-bust-into-voting-machines-in-conference-challenge.html.

86. Aaron Blake, "Trump and Kobach Say Illegal Votes May Have Given Clinton the Popular Vote: The Math Disagrees," *Washington Post,* 19 July 2017, https://www.washingtonpost.com/news/the-fix/wp/2017/07/19/the-white -house-still-thinks-illegal-votes-may-have-given-clinton-the-popular-vote -basic-logic-and-math-disagree/?utm_term=.a6a3933842a4; Allan Smith, "Trump Makes Outlandish Claims during Grilling by ABC News Anchor over Voter-Fraud Falsehoods," *Business Insider,* 25 Jan. 2017, http://www .businessinsider.com/trump-voter-fraud-abc-interview-2017-1; Eli Yokley, "Many Republicans Believe Trump Won Popular Vote," Morning Consult, 26 July 2017, https://morningconsult.com/2017/07/26/many-republicans -think-trump-won-2016-popular-vote-didnt/.

87. Kris W. Kobach, "Why the States Need to Assist the Presidential Commission on Election Integrity," Breitbart.com, 12 July 2017, http://www .breitbart.com/big-government/2017/07/03/kobach-why-states-need-to -assist-the-presidential-commission-on-election-integrity/; "Kobach Letter to States on Election Integrity," 28 June 2017, SCRIBD, https://www.scribd

.com/document/352553337/Kobach-Letter-To-States-On-Election-Integrity; Adam Ganucheau, "Hosemann on Trump Voter ID Request: 'Go Jump in the Gulf,'" *Mississippi Today,* 30 June 2017, https://mississippitoday.org/2017/06/30/hosemann-on-trump-voter-id-request-go-jump-in-the-gulf/.

88. Kris Kobach, "The Case for Voter ID," *Wall Street Journal,* 23 May 2011, https://www.wsj.com/articles/SB10001424052748704816604576333650886790480; Sherman Smith, "Kobach Witness Can't Support Claim That Illegal Votes Helped Hillary Clinton," *Topeka Capital-Journal,* 13 Mar. 2018, http://www.cjonline.com/news/20180313/kobach-witness-cant-support-claim-that-illegal-votes-helped-hillary-clinton.

89. *Steven Wayne Fish v. Kris Kobach,* United States District Court for the District of Kansas, Case no. 16-2105-JAR-JPO, Order, 23 June 2017, pp. 4, 8; *Fish v. Kobach,* "Memorandum and Order," 25 July 2017, p. 8.

90. Blake, "Trump and Kobach"; Manuela Tobias, "Is There Evidence of Voter Fraud in New Hampshire, as Kris Kobach Said? Not Really," Politi-Fact, 15 Sept. 2017, http://www.politifact.com/truth-o-meter/statements/2017/sep/15/kris-kobach/there-evidence-voter-fraud-new-hampshire-kris-koba/.

91. John Hanna, "Kansas Secretary of State Files 2 New Election Fraud Cases," *U.S. News and World Report,* 31 Aug. 2017, https://www.usnews.com/news/best-states/kansas/articles/2017-0-31/kansas-secretary-of-state-files-2-new-election-fraud-cases; Jonathan Shorman, "Kobach Cites Non-Citizen Voters in Kansas as Trump Election Panel Begins," *Wichita Eagle,* 19 July 2017, http://www.kansas.com/news/politics-government/article162505228.html.

92. U.S. Government Accountability Office, Report to Congressional Requesters, *Issues Related to State Voter Identification Laws,* Sept. 2014, p. 52, https://www.gao.gov/products/GAO-14-634195.

93. Zoltan L. Hajnal, Nazita Lajevardi, and Lindsay Nelson, "Voter Identification Laws and the Suppression of Minority Votes," *Journal of Politics* 79 (2017): 363, 377. Although the authors do not limit their analysis to states with photo ID as opposed to non-photo ID laws, all but one of the states analyzed have photo ID laws.

94. Sharad Goel et al., "One Person, One Vote: Estimating the Prevalence of Double Voting in U.S. Presidential Elections," 24 Oct. 2017, https://5harad.com/papers/1p1v.pdf.

95. John Wagner, "Trump Voting Fraud Panel Member Lamented Adding Democrats, 'Mainstream' Republicans," *Washington Post,* 13 Sept. 2017,

https://www.washingtonpost.com/politics/trump-voting-panel-member
-lamented-inclusion-of-democrats-mainstream-republicans/2017/09/13
/03f89a90-98bb-11e7-82e4-f1076f6d6152_story.html?utm_term=
.4bc955c7e7d7; Christopher Ingraham, "Trump's Fraud Commission Is
Hearing a Proposal to Make Every Voter Pass a Gun Background Check,"
Washington Post, 12 Sept. 2017, https://www.washingtonpost.com/news
/wonk/wp/2017/09/12/trumps-voter-fraud-commission-is-hearing-a
-proposal-to-make-every-voter-pass-a-gun-background-check/?utm
_term=.74641fb0af42; "Legal Actions Taken against Trump's 'Voter Fraud'
Commission," Brennan Center for Justice, 26 Dec. 2017, https://www
.brennancenter.org/legal-actions-taken-against-trump%E2%80%99s
-%E2%80%9Cfraud%E2%80%9D-commission.

96. Elizabeth Landers, Eli Watkins, and Kevin Liptak, "Trump Dissolves
Voter Fraud Commission; Adviser Said It Went 'Off the Rails,'" CNN, 4
Jan. 2018, http://www.cnn.com/2018/01/03/politics/presidential-election
-commission/index.html; *United States of America v. Internet Research Agency,
et al.,* Criminal No. (18 U.S.C. §§ 2, 371, 1349, 1028A); Jessica Taylor, "Fact
Check: Where Roy Moore's Voter Fraud Claims Fall Flat," NPR, 28 Dec. 2017,
https://www.npr.org/2017/12/28/574222257/fact-check-where-roy-moores
-voter-fraud-claims-fall-flat.

97. Manny Fernandez and Eric Lichtblau, "Justice Drops a Key Objection
to a Texas Voter ID Law," *New York Times,* 27 Feb. 2017, https://www.nytimes
.com/2017/02/27/us/justice-dept-will-drop-a-key-objection-to-a-texas-voter
-id-law.html?mcubz=1&_r=0; Sari Horwitz, "Justice Dept. Sides with Ohio's
Purge of Inactive Voters in Case Heading to Supreme Court," *Washington
Post,* 8 Aug. 2017, https://www.washingtonpost.com/world/national-security
/justice-department-reverses-position-to-allow-ohio-to-purge-inactive
-voters-from-rolls/2017/08/08/e93c5116-7c35-11e7-9d08-b79f191668ed_story
.html?utm_term=.9839eff39970; Amber Phillips, "The Time That the Senate
Denied Jeff Sessions a Federal Judgeship over Accusations of Racism," *Washington Post,* 10 Jan. 2017, https://www.washingtonpost.com/news/the-fix/wp
/2016/11/18/that-time-the-senate-denied-jeff-sessions-a-federal-judgeship
-over-accusations-of-racism/?utm_term=.cb97ed637a86.

98. Economist Intelligence Unit, "Democracy Rankings 2017," 2018,
http://pages.eiu.com/rs/753-RIQ-438/images/Democracy_Index_2017.pdf.

99. "Views on Perceptions of the American Political Process and Voter
Fraud," AP-NORC, Sept. 2016, http://www.apnorc.org/projects/Pages/views
-on-the-american-election-process-and-perceptions-of-voter-fraud.aspx.

100. Freedom House, "Democracy in Crisis: Freedom House Releases Freedom in the World 2018," 16 Jan. 2018, https://yubanet.com/world/democracy-in-crisis-freedom-house-releases-freedom-in-the-world-2018/.

101. "Press Briefing by Press Secretary Sarah Huckabee Sanders," White House.gov, 20 March 2018, https://www.whitehouse.gov/briefings-statements/press-briefing-press-secretary-sarah-sanders-032018/.

8. Reforming American Voting

1. Jack Raymond, "Germans Go to Polls Calmly: Take Free Elections as Duty," *New York Times,* 15 Aug. 1949, p. 1; Gert-Joachim Glaessner, *German Democracy: From Post-World War II to the Present Day* (New York: Berg, 2005), p. 91.

2. "International Covenant on Civil and Political Rights," https://treaties.un.org/doc/publication/unts/volume%20999/volume-999-i-14668-english.pdf.

3. Pamela S. Karlan, "Voting Rights and the Third Reconstruction," in *The Constitution in 2020,* ed. Jack M. Balkin and Reva B. Siegel (New York: Oxford University Press, 2009), p. 161; *Crawford v. Marion County Election Board,* 553 U.S. 181 (2008).

4. H.J. Res. 44, 14 May 2013, Congress.gov, https://www.Congress.gov/bill/113th-Congress/house-joint-resolution/44/text.

5. "International Comparison of Felon Voting Laws," ProCon.org, May 2014, http://felonvoting.procon.org/view.resource.php?resourceID=000289.

6. Christopher Uggen, Ryan Larson, and Sarah Shannon, *Six Million Lost Voters: State-Level Estimates of Felon Disenfranchisement, 2016* (Washington, DC: Sentencing Project, 2016), pp. 4–13.

7. Ibid.; Heather Monahan, "Florida Set to Decide If Felons Have the Right to Vote Again," News Channel 8, 4 Feb. 2018, http://www.wfla.com/news/florida-set-to-decide-if-felons-have-right-to-vote-again/1030530664.

8. Ibid., pp. 3, 15, 16; Bridgett A. King and Laura Erickson, "Disenfranchising the Enfranchised: Exploring the Relationship between Felony Disenfranchisement and African American Voter Turnout," *Journal of Black Studies* 47 (2016): 799–821; Ed Kilgore, "An Initiative to Give Ex-Felons Voting Rights Could Remake Florida's Politics in 2020," *New York Magazine,* 23 Jan. 2018, http://nymag.com/daily/intelligencer/2018/01/florida-ballot-initiative-could-give-ex-felons-voting-rights.html.

9. *Richardson v. Ramirez,* 418 U.S. 24 (1974).

10. *Sauvé v. Canada (Chief Electoral Officer),* [2002] 3 S.C.R. 519, 2002 SCC 68.

11. Jerrold G. Rusk, *A Statistical History of the American Electorate* (Washington, DC: CQ Press, 2001), pp. 52–53; U.S. Elections Project, "Voter Turnout 2000–2106," http://www.electproject.org/home/voter-turnout/voter-turnout-data.

12. T. M. Holbrook and Aaron Weinschenk, "Campaigns, Mobilization, and Turnout in Mayoral Elections," *Political Research Quarterly* 67 (2014): 42–55.

13. Drew DeSilver, "Turnout Was High in the 2016 Primary Season, but Just Short of a Record," Pew Research Center, 10 June 2016, http://www.pewresearch.org/fact-tank/2016/06/10/turnout-was-high-in-the-2016-primary-season-but-just-short-of-2008-record/; Jay O'Callaghan, "Republican 2014 Primary Turnout Tops Democrats for the Second Time since 1930," *Human Events,* 18 Oct. 2014, http://humanevents.com/2014/10/08/republican-2014-primary-turnout-tops-democrats-for-the-second-time-since-1930/.

14. Drew DeSilver, "U.S. Trails Most Developed Countries in Voter Turnout," Pew Research Center, 15 May 2017, http://www.pewresearch.org/fact-tank/2017/05/15/u-s-voter-turnout-trails-most-developed-countries/.

15. David A. Lieb, "Possible Effects of Gerrymandering Seen in Uncontested Races," *U.S. News,* 25 June 2017, https://www.usnews.com/news/best-states/georgia/articles/2017-06-25/democracy-with-no-choices-many-candidates-run-unopposed.

16. "Trust in Government, 1958–2017," Pew Research Center, 3 May 2017, http://www.people-press.org/2017/05/03/public-trust-in-government-1958-2017/.

17. Ellen Shearer, "Nonvoters in America 2012," Ipsos Public Affairs, 13 Dec. 2012, http://nonvotersinamerica.com/wp-content/uploads/2015/12/Summary-Report-12-13-12.pdf.

18. *Citizens United v. Federal Election Commission,* 58 U.S. 310 (2010).

19. Center for Responsive Politics, "Lobbying Database," https://www.opensecrets.org/lobby/; "How Many Lobbyists Are There in Washington?" *Reuters,* 13 Sept. 2009, https://www.reuters.com/article/us-obama-lobbying-sb/factbox-how-many-lobbyists-are-there-in-washington-idUSTRE58C1NX20090913; Megan R. Wilson, "Lobbying's Top 50: Who's Spending Big," The Hill, 17 Feb. 2017, http://thehill.com/business-a-lobbying/business-a-lobbying/318177-lobbyings-top-50-whos-spending-big; Guy Rolnik,

"How Many Newt Gingrich's Are There in Washington? Much More Than You Might Think," Pro-Market: Stigler Center at the University of Chicago Booth School of Business, 3 Apr. 2017, https://promarket.org/many-newt -gingrichs-washington-much-might-think/; John Delaney, "The Solution to Fixing Dysfunction in Congress," *Washington Post,* 2 Sept. 2014, https://www.washingtonpost.com/opinions/the-solution-to-fixing -dysfunction-in-Congress/2014/09/02/0f0d0a9a-31e6-11e4-9e92 -0899b306bbea_story.html?utm_term=.7eabaof9afd4.

20. Martin Gilens and Benjamin Page, "Testing Theories of American Politics: Elites, Interest Groups, and Average Citizens," *Perspectives on Politics* 12 (2014): 564–581.

21. Maria Gratschew, "Case Study 4: Sweden," in International Foundation for Electoral Systems, *Getting to the Core: A Global Survey on the Cost and Registration of Elections,* Center for Transitional and Post-Conflict Governance, International Foundation for Electoral Systems, and Bureau of Development Policy, United Nations Development Programme, June 2005, p. 95, http://www.ifes.org/sites/default/files/corepublcolor_2.pdf.

22. "Oregon Motor Voter Act FAQ," Oregon Secretary of State, http://sos .oregon.gov/voting/Pages/motor-voter-faq.aspx.

23. Rob Griffin et al., "Who Votes with Automatic Voter Registration?" Center for American Progress, 7 June 2017, https://www.americanprogress .org/issues/democracy/reports/2017/06/07/433677/votes-automatic-voter -registration/.

24. "Automatic Voter Registration," Brennan Center for Justice, 13 Mar. 2018, https://www.brennancenter.org/analysis/automatic-voter-registration.

25. For a listing of studies and their findings, see U.S. Government Accountability Office, "Issues Related to Registering Voters and Administering Elections," June 2016, pp. 88–92, 113–115, http://www.gao.gov/assets/680 /678131.pdf; "Election Fraud in America," News21, 12 Aug. 2012, https:// votingrights.news21.com/interactive/election-fraud-database/.

26. "Same Day Voter Registration," National Conference of State Legislatures, 12 Oct. 2017, http://www.ncsl.org/research/elections-and-campaigns /same-day-registration.aspx.

27. Art. 3, secs. 20, 21, Florida Constitution, http://www.leg.state.fl.us /statutes/index.cfm?submenu=3#A3S20.

28. "U.S. House Results," CNN, 16 Feb. 2018, http://www.cnn.com/election /results/house.

29. *Arizona State Legislature v. Arizona Independent Redistricting Commission,* 576 U.S. (2015).

30. Bruce E. Cain, "Redistricting Commissions: A Better Political Buffer," *Yale Law Journal* 121 (2012): 1808.

31. Claire Daviss and Rob Richie, "Fuzzy Math: Wrong Way Reforms for Allocating Electoral College Votes," Fairvote, Jan. 2015, https://fairvote.app .box.com/v/fuzzy-math-wrong-way-reforms.

32. Residents of the District of Columbia can vote for president (Twenty-Third Amendment) and local officials. Voting rights for the U.S. House and Senate would require either statehood or a merger with Virginia or Maryland. Neither alternative has gained traction in Congress.

33. *Voting Rights Coalition v. Wilson,* 60 F.3d 1411 (9th Cir. 1995), cert. denied, 516 U.S. 1093 (1996); *Foster v. Love,* 522 U.S. 67 (1997).

34. Zoltan L. Hajnal and Paul G. Lewis, "Municipal Institutions and Voter Turnout in Local Elections," *Urban Affairs Review* 38 (2003): 656. Also, at the state level, California has adopted a voting rights act (Election Code Section 14025-14032) that makes it easier for minorities to challenge discriminatory at-large election systems.

35. Paul Weyrich, speech, National Affairs Briefing of the Religious Roundtable, Dallas, TX, 22 Aug. 1980, https://www.youtube.com/watch ?v=QFIYS8xb-QY. On the importance of Weyrich, see American National Biography Online, s.v. Paul Weyrich, http://www.anb.org/articles/07/07 -00849.html.

36. Aaron Blake, "Republicans Keep Admitting That Voter ID Helps Their Party, for Some Reason," *Washington Post,* 7 Apr. 2016, https://www .washingtonpost.com/news/the-fix/wp/2016/04/07/republicans-should -really-stop-admitting-that-voter-id-helps-them-win/?utm_term= .c02c9ca55c08; Scott Tranter, speech, Newseum, Washington, DC, 10 Dec. 2012, https://www.youtube.com/watch?v=-4KUj_hB2lA; "Tea Party Activist: No Thanks for Black Voters Voting Democratic," Bloomberg News, 4 June 2013, http://go.bloomberg.com/political-capital/2013-06-04/tea-party -activist-no-thanks-for-black-voters-voting-democratic/.

37. Blake, "Republicans Keep Admitting"; Alice Miranda Ollstein, "The 4 Most Damning Revelations in Wisconsin's Voter ID Trial," ThinkProgress, 27 May 2016, https://thinkprogress.org/the-4-most-damning-revelations-in -wisconsins-voter-id-trial-8e71a37b0762; Dale Schultz, interview with Radio 92.1, http://www.themic921.com/onair/the-devils-advocates-47215/state -senator-dale-schultz-on-sd-12150295/.

38. "Rand Paul Warns Texas Could Turn Blue," Politico, 9 Feb. 2014, http://www.politico.com/story/2014/02/rand-paul-texas-could-turn-blue-103292.html.

39. Schultz, interview; James Sensenbrenner, "Suppress Votes? I'd Rather Lose My Job," New York Times, 31 Mar. 2016, https://www.nytimes.com/2016/03/31/opinion/suppress-votes-id-rather-lose-my-job.html?mcubz=1&_r=0.

40. Charles Stewart, "2016 Survey of the Performance of American Elections, Final Report," https://dataverse.harvard.edu/file.xhtml?fileId=3012344&version=RELEASED&version=.0; Dan Lohrmann, "What Election Technology Actions Are Needed Now," Government Technology, 15 Jan. 2017, http://www.govtech.com/blogs/lohrmann-on-cybersecurity/what-election-technology-actions-are-needed-now.html.

41. Mo Rocca hosted an award-winning 2012 PBS documentary, Electoral Dysfunction, on voting and voting rights.

42. Franklin D. Roosevelt, "Address at Marietta, Ohio," 8 July 1938, American Presidency Project, http://www.presidency.ucsb.edu/ws/?pid=15672.

Conclusion

1. Pew Research Center, "The Party of Non-Voters," 31 Oct. 2014, http://www.people-press.org/2014/10/31/the-party-of-nonvoters-2/. Pew defines nonvoters in its survey as "those who are either not registered to vote or are considered unlikely to vote in the upcoming midterms."

2. "Remarks of Senator Paul Wellstone before the Grassroots Training Seminar at Iowa State, 11 July 1998," Grassroots Heroes, http://www.geocities.ws/demcrat/newgrass.html.

ACKNOWLEDGMENTS

This book is dedicated to my extraordinary family. Karyn Strickler, my wife of twenty-seven years, is the light of my life. She is the smartest political analyst I have ever known and a continuing source of remarkable insights. My creative son, Sam Lichtman, is a master of fine arts graduate of Emerson College, and his advice keeps me from straying too far into the academic weeds. My daughter, Kara Lichtman, is a brilliant psychiatrist and a font of wisdom about human behavior. My brother, Steven Lichtman, and my sister, Ronnie Lichtman, have unwaveringly supported my career since I switched from a biology to a history major as an undergraduate at Brandeis University.

I would like to thank a number of other people who have contributed to this book, especially Dan Ballentyne, Amanda Brower, and Scott Vehstedt. Special thanks go to the extraordinary team at Harvard University Press: my astute editor Joyce Seltzer and meticulous copyeditor Margaret Hogan, along with Kathleen Drummy and Louise Robbins. Final thanks go to my Brandeis University professors David Hackett Fisher, Morton Keller, Ray Ginger, and Marvin Meyers, who inspired me to pursue a career in history, and to my Harvard University thesis advisor, Frank Friedel, who guided me into the study of political history. All errors, of course, I claim for myself.

INDEX